Historia de la donzella Teodor

Edition and Study

A Global Academic Publishing Book

Historia de la donzella Teodor
Edition and Study

Isidro J. Rivera and Donna M. Rogers

Published by

Global Publications/CEMERS
Binghamton University, State University of New York
Binghamton, NY 13902-6000

For information, contact State University of New York Press, Albany, NY
www.sunypress.edu

Library of Congress Cataloging-in-Publication Data

Rivera and Rogers, *Historia de la donzella Teodor: Edition and Study*

1. donzella Teodor 2. Abu'l Husn and His Slave Girl Tawaddud

ISBN 1-58684-001-0

International Medieval and Early Modern Studies

Medieval Studies Worldwide

Center for Medieval and Renaissance Studies
Binghamton University

Editors

For our fathers

GILBERTO RIVERA TORRES

PETER ANTHONY ROGERS

TABLE OF CONTENTS

ACKNOWLEDGEMENTS

The genesis of this book was the 1990 NEH Summer Institute on Alfonso el Sabio at the University of Kentucky, where we met and discovered a mutual interest in Teodor. For that, we have Aníbal Biglieri and John Keller to thank, and we are profoundly grateful to both for their guidance and support, then and since.

IJR and DMR, May 1999

Throughout the long gestation of this project, I was fortunate to have the support of a number of institutions and individuals, and I am pleased to recognize them here. The Research and Graduate Studies Office, College of the Liberal Arts, of the Pennsylvania State University, provided funding during the summer of 1993 for me to study and transcribe the original texts in Spain. The Biblioteca Nacional in Madrid, the library at El Escorial, the Biblioteca de Catalunya, and the University of Salamanca library all generously provided access to the texts.

For instilling in me a love for and discipline towards philology, I thank Joseph Gulsoy, who will probably never know just how much I owe him. John Dalbor was, and remains, a mentor and role model. Montserrat, Phil, August, Larry, Mark, John—la colla catalana—have, over the years, been exemplary colleagues and even better friends. The graduate students in my Old Spanish classes at Penn State contributed in tangible ways to this book, offering their comments and insights into the text as they wrestled with it in class. My friends—and model medievalists—Robert Frank, Jr., Alan Knight, and Jeanne Krochalis provided encouragement and moral support through this and much else. My husband, Michael Ramsay, shared the gifts of his intellect and understanding with me in this endeavour, and every other. And last but very definitely not least, Isidro Rivera has been my dear friend for the past decade, and a co-author *como Dios manda*. I humbly offer my deepest gratitude to them all.

DMR, Middlebury, Vermont May 1999

As this project was taking shape, I received encouragement from a number of readers, listeners, and friends who challenged me to be more attentive to my claims. Their comments gave shape to some of my thinking. I am especially indebted to Anthony Corbeill, Lisa Bitel, Laura Delbrugge, Sherry Velasco, Luis Corteguera, and Lee Skinner for the sharing of insights and suggestions. I wish to thank Roberta Johnson for her support during crucial moments in this project and to Mike Doudoroff for his encouragements. José Ballesteros and Yarlenis Coletta read early drafts of the edition and made valuable observations. Andrea Baldomir's enthusiasm and perceptive comments gave vitality to this project. I am indebted to two of my teachers, James Marchand and Spurgeon Baldwin, who long ago exposed me to the rich diversity of the medieval encyclopedia.

At several times during my research, I benefited from the help of specialists who generously gave of their time. The Interlibrary Loan Unit of the University of Kansas's Watson Library provided assistance on various arcane requests. I am most appreciative of Jana Krentz, Spanish Bibliographer at Watson Library, whose support was invaluable to this project. I also wish to thank the Curators and Staff of the Hispanic Society of America, New York, for their help. I am grateful to Doña Dolores Vives of the Biblioteca Bartolomé March Severa, Madrid, for expediting access to some materials.

To Donna Rogers, *ilustre colega*, who has collaborated in this project from its inception and whose friendship and gentle counsel have meant a great deal to me, I express my deepest gratitude for her willingness to pursue this text.

Finally, I thank Cynthia for her patience as I worked through this project. Her kind readings of portions of the edition saved me from numerous mistakes. For those errors which remain, I alone am responsible. Cynthia's love inspires me. Eleanor and Austin make it all worthwhile.

IJR, Lawrence, Kansas May 1999

INTRODUCTION

The *Historia de la donzella Teodor* (*HDT*) belongs to a select group of medieval works that emerged during the early period of printing in Spain and that continued to be printed into modern times.[1] The Castilian translation produced during the second half of the thirteenth century recounts the story of a young slave who is offered to the king in the hopes of saving her master from financial ruin. Intrigued by claims of her superior intelligence, the Caliph orders his court scholars to quiz the girl. In each of the examinations, Teodor demonstrates unparalleled skills and triumphs over the inquisitors. As a result, the Caliph decides to grant Teodor a wish; she chooses to return to her master.[2] Out of respect for her skills, the king pays off the debts of the master, thus saving him from ruin. The story derives from a ninth-century Oriental tale that eventually becomes incorporated into the collection known as the *Arabian Nights*.[3] The survival of Teodor's story into the modern period is due in large part to the activities of publishers who transformed the medieval tale of the young slave girl Teodor into a "popular text" capable of satisfying the demands of a broad and diverse readership.

---

1 Bizzarri has observed the need to differentiate between the early versions of the Teodor materials ("aquella traducci6n del cuento que se hizo en el siglo XIII") and those versions that appear in print and that contain new textual materials ("Labor crítica..." 96). Aware of the complex issues related to the text, we have opted to maintain consistency and refer to the Castilian redactions of the Tawaddud tale as *Historia de la donzella Teodor* (*HDT*). In our edition and notes, we will distinguish among the versions of the *HDT* by referencing them according to provenance and source.

2 With reference to the *HDT*, Parker (127-36) provides a useful discussion of this motif. Solterer has studied this motif in medieval French Literature.

3 The Tawaddud tale occurs in nights 436-462. See Gerresch 61-64.

Compared to similar Castilian texts from this period, the *HDT* fared quite well. The number of manuscript copies attests to the popularity of the text during the later Middle Ages. The *HDT* circulated in at least five manuscripts produced during the fifteenth century. With the advent of printing, it entered a new phase of reception. Although several textual changes were introduced during the first decades after the invention of the press, it became one of the most frequently reprinted texts in Early Modern Castile. Baranda and Infantes in their recent survey of the printed editions of the *HDT* have identified some twelve reprintings of the work between 1500 and 1554 (70-74). The number becomes more significant when we consider the fortunes of other pre-1400 texts that appeared in print during the first century of the press. According to Simón Díaz's survey (382) of Castilian texts printed between 1480-1560, only one pre-1400 work, the *Crónica troyana* with thirteen editions, surpasses the number of reprintings of the *HDT* prior to 1560. *Calila e Dimna* with twelve printings during that same timeframe matches the numbers of the *HDT.* By comparison, one of the most widely disseminated Castilian texts in the medieval period, the *Bocados de oro*, was reprinted only six times. Simón Díaz, moreover, notes that only two pre-1400 Castilian texts, the *HDT* and *Historia de los siete sabios*, have the distinction of continuous publication from the incunabular period to the present era (374). The *Bocados de oro*, for example, saw its last printed edition in 1527. Similar dates exist for the *Crónica troyana* with a last printing in 1587 and for *Calila* with a date of 1547.

THE ORIENTAL CONTEXT

Beginning in the eleventh century, Western Europe entered a phase of intense intellectual and literary activity.[4] Contacts with Ara-

[4] Said's study remains an essential guide to the European-Oriental encounter — "the Orient's special place in European Western experience" (Said 1). Southern (34-41); Daniel; and Menocal provide excellent overviews of this European-Oriental encounter as it relates to the Iberian Peninsula.

bic culture introduced the intellectual and literary heritage of the Middle East into Latinized Europe and provided a foundation for the development of the disciplines of the sciences, mathematics, and philosophy.[5] This Oriental material entered the Latin West primarily from the south, with Sicily, Southern France, and Spain forming the geographical points of contact with Arabic culture. Throughout Europe, scholars such as Adelard of Bath (fl. 1116-42), Gerard of Cremona (ca. 1114-87), Hermann the Dalmatian (fl. 1138-43), and Robert of Chester (fl. 1141-50) became instrumental in the spread of Oriental materials into the rest of Europe. Márquez Villanueva has pointed out that many of these translators visited the Peninsula and occupied important positions within clerical and religious institutions of Castile (*Concepto cultural* 78-79). Archbishop Raimundo of Toledo (1125-1151), who had established a vigorous center of translation in Toledo, supported a number of these translations of Arabic treatises. Similarly, Peter the Venerable, Abbot of Cluny, who was responsible for the activities and projects associated with some of these men, played a crucial role in the dissemination of Arabic materials as well as in the development of European attitudes toward Arabic culture and religion[6].

The political situation of Spain, especially, permitted the evolution of close contacts with Arabic culture and the fostering of cultural exchanges. These links resulted in a stream of Oriental materials from the Iberian Peninsula, usually in the form of scholarly translations first into Latin and then into the vernacular.[7] The desire

---

[5] The transmission of Arabic culture and its intellectual heritage to the rest of Europe during the Middle Ages is the subject of numerous studies. With reference to the transmission of this cultural material, see the studies by Walzer; Lindberg; Gabrieli; Rodinson.

[6] For information concerning Peter the Venerable, see Kritzech. Metlitzki provides an important discussion of the dissemination of these Arabic works in England during this period in Chapter Two of her study (13-46).

[7] For the situation in Iberia during this Middle Ages, especially see O'Callaghan, 89-190; Gabrieli2; MacKay 79-94; Chejne; Hourani; and Haskins, 3-19 and

to appropriate Arabic culture reached its zenith in the thirteenth century with Alfonso X, el Sabio, who encouraged an active program of translating Arabic materials into the vernacular. The period associated with the Alfonsine court is a defining moment for the Peninsula and marks a point of confluence of two cultures (*Concepto cultural* 14-15). Alfonso's commissions made accessible scientific texts, philosophical tracts, and literary works. The translation of the *donzella Teodor* materials belongs to this period of cultural florescence and marks an intersection of Arabic literary culture with the emerging culture of Christian Iberia.

The tale of the *donzella Teodor* derives from an Arabic story entitled "Abu'l-Husn and his Slave-Girl Tawaddud." The tale dates from the late ninth century or early tenth century (Gerresch 61), and recounts how financial woes force a merchant's son to offer Tawaddud, a young slave woman, for sale to the caliph Harun. Before paying the price demanded, the caliph learns of Tawaddud's unsurpassed knowledge and asks her to submit to examination by a number of learned men from the court. Tawaddud must submit to questioning from seven experts in the areas of Koranic law, theology, astronomy, medicine, philosophy, poetry, and logic.[8] Much to the dismay of the assembled scholars, Tawaddud achieves victory in each of these areas. The achievement is made more impressive by the fact that she is allowed to challenge each of the scholars with a riddle or question. The scholars, unable to respond correctly, are discredited and forced to

113-120. Menocal's comments (27-70) are quite instructive. For a discussion of the various centers of translation in the Iberian Peninsula, see Gil.

[8] This type of situation was not unusual in medieval Andalusian society. There are several examples of learned, Andalusian "female slaves" who were educated for the purpose of providing this type of entertainment. Valero Cuadra especially points to one "esclava" from the eleventh century with accomplishments similar to those of Teodor: "incluso sabía de medicina, historia natural y anatomía y otras ciencias en las que los sabios de la época se hubieran revelado inferiores" (from Ibn Bassam in *Dajira*, cited by Valero Cuadra [1994] 151). Valero Cuadra [1996] (39-53) includes an extensive treatment of this topic.

accept defeat. Tawaddud must then prove herself an expert in chess, backgammon, and card games. Finally, she is asked to perform on the lute and sing. She successfully demonstrates her skills to all in the court. As a result of her victories, the caliph grants Tawaddud a wish. She in turn requests that she be allowed to return to her master. The two are reunited, and with assistance from the caliph the financial difficulties are resolved.

The distinctive feature of the Arabic tale is its exchange of questions accompanied by answers in order to instruct and entertain. This literary form was quite common in Medieval Culture. Versions of question and answer lists exist in Latin, Arabic, and the European vernacular languages. Valero Cuadra [1996] also reminds us that the tale shares formal affinities with the *adab*, a didactic genre that flourished in Arabic intellectual communities during the Middle Ages. These questions, intended to impart knowledge and provide amusement, also offered an introduction to the concepts and attitudes that shaped medieval Islamic culture. Haddawy (xi) has noted that many of the stories comprising the *Arabian Nights* provide a distinctive synthesis of the cultural and artistic history of Islam. With the Tawaddud tale, the reader is able to glimpse the vibrancy and diversity of Oriental Culture.

The form and structure of the tale in particular reflect a genre of writings known as didactic *quaestiones*. This category of texts typically embraced a variety of topics, often without a distinguishable logical sequence. Brian Lawn has observed that *quaestiones* played an important role in the teaching of theology, philosophy, medicine, and other disciplines (Lawn 1). Examples of the *quaestiones* genre can be found in a variety of forms from the ninth century onward (Cross; Suchier; Valero Cuadra [1996] 22-27; Haro Cortés, *Los compendios*). This method of instruction especially influenced the pedagogy of medicine and the physical sciences until the sixteenth century (Cadden 88-104). In Spain, the didactic *quaestio* genre survives in the Castilian redactions of the dialogues of Secundus and the Emperor Hadrian (Bizzarri; Severin; Morrás). A version of these dialogues circulated in manuscript form in Castile during the late medieval period

(Bizzarri 17-18). The *princeps* of the Teodor utilizes this late fifteenth-century Castilian *quaestio* literature as a source for its elaboration of the material. These *quaestio* texts, enormously popular throughout the Late Middle Ages, offered concrete advice concerning human knowledge and experience through a series of concise exchanges. The format made learning more palatable and transformed instruction into a game (Bizzarri 22-25).

The earliest Castilian version produced during the thirteenth century remains faithful to the framework of the original Arabic tale. Tawaddud, called Teodor in the Castilian version, responds to a wide variety of questions from the scholars at the court. While the original Arabic tale focuses on topics derived from the Koran, from Arabic medical and scientific knowledge, and from Islamic cultural customs, the Castilian version of the Tawaddud tale eliminates all references to Islamic practices and religious tenets. In the Castilian translation, the number of examiners also decreases from seven to three with the result that the examinations only cover the areas of cosmogony, natural science, and philosophy. The Castilian version also omits episodes related to Teodor's skills at games as well as her musical talents. The scientific and medical information found in the Arabic version in some cases undergoes a recasting, in order to accord with a Christian perspective. The Castilian tale borrows extensively from didactic compendia, *regimina*, and wisdom literature collections that had already exerted a profound impact on the culture of Latinized Europe. The translation thus filters elements that are ideologically problematic. The tale of Tawaddud loses its Islamic identity and becomes aligned with the Christian West through the skillful manipulation of the original source.[9]

The translator's activities are in keeping with Alfonso's cultural and literary projects. Alfonso's court undertook a program of Christianization of the Orient, which resulted in the production and dissemination of numerous translations into Latin and Castilian. The

[9] For a discussion of this process of alignment, see comments by Bremond (267-271) and Dabord (17-22).

HDT reflects this process of appropriation and transference during the reign of Alfonso X. The Oriental material so dominant in the original source is recast so as to privilege certain concepts, thus effecting a *translatio* of material without compromising Christian ideological concerns.

Despite its popularity in the literature of the late Middle Ages, the *HDT* has remained outside the recognized canon of medieval European literature. The Tawaddud tale circulated independently in North Africa and other Arabic-speaking regions before entering the *corpus* of tales known collectively as the *Arabian Nights*, which does not reach its definitive form until the 14th or 15th centuries.[10] With reference to the Iberian Peninsula, an Arabic version of the Tawaddud tale most likely circulated independently. A manuscript of Andalusian provenance containing an Arabic version attests to the circulation of the tale in Medieval Spain.[11] The translation of the *Tawaddud* material during the second half of the thirteenth century marks a crucial moment in the text's evolution (Haro Cortés, *Los compendios* 44). The tale appears under the title of "Capítulo que fabla de los enxenplos de Teodor donzella." Within the literary culture of late medieval Iberia, the story of Teodor becomes associated with collections of sapiential literature and didactic writings (Deyermond 183; Haro Cortés, *Los compendios* 41-45). Parker has recently noted that the survival of the *Teodor* text was due in part to its affiliation with "the wisdom literature category" (120). The text is sometimes found as one of the appendices to the *Bocados de oro*, a Castilian translation of *Mukhtâr al hikam* produced in the court of Alfonso

---

[10] See Grotzfeld 86-91 and Irwin 42-62.

[11] Vázquez Ruiz's description of an Arabic manuscript of Andalusian provenance containing the Tawaddud tale confirms the presence of this story in Southern Spain during the Middle Ages. The Manuscrito Gayangos, Academia de Historia, also contains an Andalusian version of the *HDT*. For a discussion of the content of the content of the Manuscrito Gayangos, see the studies by Menéndez Pelayo and Valero Cuadra [1996] (69-89).

X.[12] The manuscript tradition of the *donzella Teodor* attests to only one witness from the fifteenth century (Biblioteca Nacional, Madrid, Ms. 9055) in which the material is not coupled with the *Bocados.*

Although the spread of the *HDT* during the Middle Ages appears to be limited to the Iberian Peninsula, there is evidence that the *Teodor* material may have circulated outside of Castile. Metlitzki points to similarities between the *Teodor* material and Chaucer's *Squire Tale* (159). The popularity and circulation of the story is also attested by the numerous reprintings and translations of the text during the sixteenth and seventeenth centuries (Mettmann 91-93). It is important to note that the Teodor material became the basis for Lope de Vega's minor play *La doncella Teodor* (Menéndez Pelayo 503-11). The *Teodor* materials were subsequently translated into Tagalog (Eugenio 301-312) and into Maya (Brotherston 320).

DISPUTING WOMAN

In the *HDT*, the sequencing of question and response reviews a broad array of topics related to the physical sciences, folk traditions, medicine, and social practices. In this questioning, the court scholars demand from Teodor proof of her mastery of a wide range of knowledge:

> E dixo el fisico quales son las frutas & dixo la donzella para los dolientes las mançanas & las almendra[s] & otorgo conella el fisyco & pregunto dela sangrya & dyxo la donzella la sangria es buena martes & luna menguante & el çielo esconbrado de nubes & sera el

---

[12] Version C of the *Bocados de oro* contains the *HDT*. Witnesses to this tradition exist in Escorial Ms. h.III.6, BNM Ms. 17822, BNM Ms. 17853, and Salamanca Universitaria Ms. 1866 (*Bocados de oro* xxiii-xxxviii). Excellent overviews of the relations of these versions can be found in Taylor and in Haro Cortés (*Los compendios* 50-54).

> cuerpo espaçioso & alegre el figado... (Escorial, Ms. h-III-6, folio 120r)
>
> E rrespondio & dixole lo que es mas pesado que los montes es el agua & mas apresurado que la saeta el ojo & mas aguda que la espada la lengua & mas ardiente que el fuego es coraçon & mas dulçe que la miel el buen fijo & dolençia syn melezina es la locura.... (Escorial, Ms. h-III-6, folios. 122v-123r)

The question-answer structure becomes a useful vehicle for assessing expertise in a given topic. In the Middle Ages, this type of intellectual engagement formed an essential part of the instructional environment of the University. Learning entailed a process of disputation and verbal conflict, which in turn established a student's mastery of a particular body of knowledge. The teacher or master (*magister*) traditionally engaged students in a series of verbal confrontations that sought to validate the disciple's ability to assume the role of master.[13] The process distinguished those who met the requirements from those who failed to achieve the expected level of expertise. This process of education transformed intellectual endeavors into a mode of exercising power over others. The question-answer mode trained students to achieve superiority over their teachers or masters and was constituted along male lines. Attainment of mastery resulted in a certain amount of authority and control over others. In the *HDT*, it is possible to plot a series of moves intended to affirm the *sabios'* power and mastery. Each question-answer episode creates a disputational dynamic in which Teodor assumes the role of student subjected to interrogations. Within this learned culture, Teodor must adopt a masculine posture and speak/respond like a man. Underlying much of the disputations is a reluctance to accept Teodor's suitability because of the figuration of woman within medieval culture.

---

[13] See Solterer's comments, 23-30.

In a culture in which women were subordinated to male power, Teodor's expertise represents a threat to this masculine order. Through the repetition of disputation, the *HDT* sets in motion a formal structure of verbal engagements that construct the feminine as its target. In the course of the tale, Teodor's responses contend with the masters' efforts to assert their dominance. In each contest, Teodor is able to counteract this force by affirming her own control of knowledge and thus destabilizing the master's own control over the feminine. Her command of scientific and practical information is impressive to each of the *sabios* who seek to prove her unsuited to become a master (*magistra*). It is important to stress that Teodor achieves mastery through intellectual means. Solterer has pointed out that in the medieval period this type of intellectual contention produced a struggle that "leads some to dominate and others to submit" (24). Teodor's disputations constitute an affirmation of her ability to control others and to resist their efforts to discredit her.

Teodor's responses bring into relief the tension associated with the relationships of power and knowledge between master and disciple. Within this adversarial framework, the student must attain the master's respect through disputation, which seeks to topple the teacher's mastery over the student. This process is presented quite clearly in the *HDT*. Teodor submits to a series of interrogations with the purpose of proving her control of knowledge. In each episode, she maneuvers her interrogators/opponents into positions of submission through the skillful exercise of her intellectual powers. Given the disputational dynamics of each episode, Teodor is able to validate her learning and affirm her position of mastery (*magistra*). The last disputation with Abrahán, "sabidor de gramática e de lógica," especially exemplifies this struggle to validate her command of knowledge and her mastery. Unlike the previous disputations, this episode includes an agreement in which the loser must strip and suffer public humiliation. As in the other episodes, Teodor is subjected to an examination, proves her command of the requested body of knowledge, and achieves victory. At the end of the episode, she demands that Abrahán strip completely: "Abraán, dadme vuestros paños menores, commo fue puesto que me diésedes todos vuestros paños." In the manuscript version, Abrahán negotiates a face-saving solution to this contest. Instead of clothing, he offers her money ("diez mill doblas de buen oro") in order to avoid humiliation. The capitulation by Abrahán erases any doubts with reference to Teodor's abilities. In the printed redactions, the issue of clothing becomes elaborated to the extent that Abrahán is unable to avoid the humiliation of disrobing: "que el que perdiesse que hauia de quedar desnudo como la hora en que nacio....E el rey mando luego al sabio que se descalc'asse & gelos diese ala donzella so pena dela su merc'ed porque otro dia se auisasse & mirase como apostaua" (Appendix I, 71). Teodor emerges victorious and asserts her own mastery over the scholars who had attempted to discipline her. This final episode thus constitutes an affirmation of Teodor's own position of superiority. More importantly, it sets a standard by which a community measures the value of women.[14]

In the *HDT*, the triumph over the court scholars provides Teodor with a new freedom and control. After defeating Abrahán, the King gives Teodor the opportunity to choose her future. Rejecting an offer of marriage from the King, Teodor decides to return to the merchant and thus to reincorporate herself into the paradigm of mastery that had originally shaped her identity. Given the dynamics of this text, it is surprising that Teodor should pick this option. By returning to the merchant, the story brings to the surface the fact that women could not escape the legacy of subordination. While knowledge may in fact have offered freedom, it was unable to erase the system of gendered relationships enacted by Western Society.

The image of a learned woman who engages in debate with men is not unique to this tale. Solterer (29) reminds us that the Western tradition often represents knowledge as a woman (*scientia*) and that scholastic activity of disputation frequently comes to be figured through women. Within the literature of the Middle Ages, one of the models for this type is found in the life of Saint Catherine, a

[14] With reference to the significance of the disrobing, see the useful comments by Valero Cuadra [1994] (149).

woman of great intelligence and conviction, who reputedly was martyred in Alexandria during the fourth century. In his study of analogues to the Tawaddud tale, Wesselski (370-78) has pointed to links with the Catherine legend. Margaret Parker (127) has in fact called the *vita* of Catherine a "principal analogue" to the story of Teodor. Similarly, Goldberg (64-68) links the riddling nature of the Catherine story to various medieval Hispanic narratives, including the *HDT.* The central episode of Catherine's *vita* depicts her struggles to defeat a pagan Emperor who persecutes her for her faith. Catherine takes the initiative in this struggle, debates the Emperor, and wins the disputation. As a response to his defeat, the Emperor orders fifty of his best scholars to engage Catherine in debate. Catherine draws on her faith and intellect to contend with these opponents and achieves an impressive victory over the group. In addition, her persuasiveness convinces the fifty scholars to convert to Catholicism. This action angers the Emperor who has Catherine imprisoned, tortured, and beheaded.

The *Vita* of Catherine at one level projects the image of an exceptional woman who is able to defend her faith against overwhelming odds. At the same time, Catherine suggests another image, that of *magistra* whose learning and intelligence allows her to resist the power of those who seek to control her. Joan Ferrante has characterized Catherine as a "figure of great knowledge and skill in debate, who does not hesitate to teach men in public, whether emperors or scholars or the people" (Ferrante 183-84). In the Middle Ages, this story provided an exemplary model to offer to women and men who wished to use their intelligence in the service of God. The legend of Catherine circulated widely throughout Christian Europe. The earliest manifestations of her cult occur in Greece and Egypt during the eight and ninth centuries. Veneration of the saint reached France during the eleventh century and subsequently spread to other parts of Europe (Nevanlinna 4-6). The *Legenda aurea*, a popular collection of saints' legends and stories drawn from the Bible, includes a version of her martyrdom. Vernacular translations of Catherine's *Vita* circulated in English, French, German, Provençal, Catalan, and Spanish.

Solterer (23-60) and Ferrante (188-89), in their respective studies, have pointed to the ubiquity of the learned-woman figure during the medieval period. While the story of Catherine provides an important source for this type of woman, it is not the only manifestation of this figure in the literature of the Middle Ages. With reference to medieval Castilian literature, an example of the learned-woman can be found in the *Libro de Apolonio*, a thirteenth-century translation of the *Historia Apollonii*, a prose narrative from late antiquity that circulated widely in the Middle Ages. The *Libro de Apolonio* thematizes the importance of learning through a series of micro-narratives in which various characters employ their intellectual skills to survive the challenges of their world. In particular, the tale focuses on Tarsiana, the daughter of Apolonio, and the extent to which she employs her learning and skills in order to survive. Like Teodor, Tarsiana is able to utilize these skills to counteract the mechanisms of control imposed by men. The *Libro de Apolonio* with its emphasis on the value of learning offers an analogue that attests to circulation of the figure of the learned woman in medieval Castilian literature.[15]

The influence of other literary texts on the *HDT* is difficult to pinpoint since the original material went through a series of evolutions that transformed its Arabic context into a Christianized version of the text. The translation of the original Arabic tale, moreover, attests to a series of negotiations by an adaptor/translator who actively draws from the Arabic source in order to create a text that conforms to the traditions and values of its intended Christian audience. Given the efforts of the Castilian court to translate the Oriental, the adaptor of the tale was most likely reshaping the *Teodor* material with the intent of promoting the values of learning and education, an ideology strongly supported by Alfonso's court. The learned woman who does not hesitate to engage in this intellectual activity coincides with other literary traditions that circulated in the

---

[15] Goldberg (63-75) provides a useful overview of this motif in medieval Hispanic texts.

Christianized West. This figure ultimately would crystallize some of the ideological prerogatives of thirteenth-century Castile.

DATING THE TEXT: LINGUISTIC EVIDENCE

The earliest Castilian manifestation of the *HDT* is the set of versions of the text in manuscript form. As has been noted, this work fits generally within the tradition of wisdom literature; indeed, the bound volumes in which this version of the tale of Teodor is found are entitled *Bocados de oro*, *Colección de sentencias*, and *Dichos de los filósofos*.

There are substantive differences between the earlier and later versions of *Teodor*. There are four complete manuscript versions known and extant of the *HDT*. Two of these are in the Biblioteca Nacional in Madrid, one in the University of Salamanca library, and one in the library at the Escorial. There is also a fragment, consisting of five folios within a *Libro del conoscimiento de todos los rregnos*; this book is also in the collection of the Biblioteca Nacional.

These documents comprise the entire known manuscript tradition for the medieval *HDT*. This edition contains new transcriptions and a textual and linguistic study of them, as well as a complete list of variants among them.

After noting every variant form or spelling among all the texts, it was determined that certain distinctions—for instance, substitution of *u* for *v* or vice-versa, both vocalic and consonantal—were essentially irrelevant. All other, meaningful variants were compiled and compared to establish possible or probable relationships among the manuscripts.

Biblioteca Nacional MS 17822 is a fifteenth-century manuscript entitled *Bocados de oro*. It contains 123 folios, and the story of Teodor is found at the end of the compendium, on folios 116-122. It begins with a chapter title in rubric: "Capitulo que fabla de los enxemplos de teodor donzella." It appears to be a reasonably careful and complete version of the story, with few errors and omissions. The manuscript is in good condition.

Universidad de Salamanca Library MS 1866 is entitled *Colección de sentencias.* It is dated February 1433. This volume was originally in the library of the Palacio Real in Madrid. It contains 112 folios; the Teodor chapter is found toward the end, on folios 91-96. There is no chapter title, but space was left for the rubricator to insert one; there is also a small blank space left for an illuminated capital. The Salamanca *Colección de sentencias* and the BN *Bocados de oro* just described present very similar versions of the text, with only slight variants throughout. The Salamanca manuscript is also in good condition.

Biblioteca Nacional MS 17853 also looks to be a fifteenth century manuscript; its spine title is *Dichos de los filósofos.* It contains 117 folios, and the Teodor material is found once again at the end, on folios 112-117. It begins with a chapter title in rubric: "Capitulo que fabla delas preguntas que fizieron alą donzella teodor." This manuscript is clearly of the same family as the two already described, with miscellaneous minor variants, but no important deviance from the text of the story presented in BN 17822 and Salamanca 1866. It is also in good condition.

Escorial MS h-III-6 is a fifteenth century manuscript entitled *Bocados de oro.* It contains 124 folios, and the story of Teodor is found at the end, on folios 119-124. The rubricated title "Capitulo que fabla de los enxemplos & castigos de teodor la donzella" precedes the tale. The manuscript is of generally the same tradition as the three just described, but presents a number of variants not found in any of them, and so is quite probably from another subfamily, on which more below.

Finally, Biblioteca Nacional MS 9055 is a later manuscript, entitled *Libro del conoscimiento de todos los rregnos.* It is a compendium of miscellaneous materials, beginning with an illustrated list of arms suggested to be from 1305, and ending with an account of the death of King John on 22 July 1454. It contains 78 folios, and includes only fragments of the Teodor story. What there is of it is found on folios 69-74; folio 70 is completely blank, and there also seems to be material missing between the folios numbered 71 and 72.

The elements of the story that are present occur in different order and with markedly different details in this manuscript. There is no doubt that it is the story of Teodor—it includes the unmistakable list of questions and answers between Abrahen el trobador and the donzella Teodor—but it is obviously from a different manuscript family.

None of the manuscripts can be dated before the fifteenth century—and two of them are explicitly dated by the scribes to the early-to-mid fifteenth century—yet the literary, cultural and linguistic contents and contexts point farther back, to the "cultural awakening," as Deyermond calls it, of the prose tradition of Alfonsine Spain.

In this regard, the book and chapter titles themselves (in the manuscripts that have them) point to a close connection with the traditions of the *Flores de filosofía, Poridat de las poridades, Castigos y documentos para bien vivir ordenados por el rey don Sancho IV*, collections of *exempla*, etc. Nevertheless, the Teodor titles are somewhat misleading. There is not an *exemplum* to be found anywhere in the story, nor a *sentencia*, nor really even a *castigo*. Once the pretext is established for the interrogation of Teodor by three *sabios* of the royal court (a *físico*, an *alfaquí*, and a *trobador*), the text consists entirely of a series of questions posed by a learned man and answers provided by the young woman. This is interrupted only briefly by a wager made between Abrahen *el trobador* and Teodor over the series of questions he will ask her. It leads to the delightful moment when he pays her off in order to avoid removing his undergarments in the presence of Teodor, the king and all the other *sabios*.

The chapter and book titles, then, point us towards the mid-to-late thirteenth century for the genesis of the Castilian version of the Teodor story. There is additional evidence from within the texts themselves.

THE LANGUAGE OF THE MANUSCRIPTS

A number of phonetic features represented in this text are clues to its dating. One of the most obvious of these is apocope of final /-e/ and the subsequent devoicing of sonorants in word-final position. According to Paul Lloyd, "a feature of medieval Castilian that came to characterize much of the literature written in the twelfth and thirteenth centuries was the widespread loss of word-final /-e/ (207). ... in literary works [...] the apocopating custom predominated and seemed destined to triumph as the wave of the future. In the early thirteenth century in all Castile, forms with loss of/-e/ far outweigh those preserving it (212). ...Although examples of extreme apocope are very common in writing throughout the thirteenth century, toward the middle of the century there is a perceptible decrease in the number of apocopated forms as compared with non-apocopated ones" (321). Indeed, Rafael Lapesa traces the abrupt decline in apocopated forms in written Castilian to Alfonso X himself, demonstrating that texts known to have been written by the king show markedly less apocopation than those written by others at his court (Lloyd 321).

A search of the Teodor texts shows essentially standard post-Alfonsine apocopation; that is, /-e/ remained apocopated after the apical consonants, but is present to support consonant clusters (*noche*, *parte*, etc.). The exceptions to this are the special case of *grande*, some forms of the second-person plural imperatives, and a few nouns ending in *-dad*.

The preposed adjective *grande* is regularly apocopated: in BN 17822 it is generally *grand* and occasionally *gran*. In the other manuscripts it is *grand* or *grant*; this latter form shows devoicing of now-final /-d/ to /-t/. But the form *gran*, with no final dental at all, shows the extent to which the original apocope had proceeded.

The second set of forms that show this phenomenon are the second-person plural imperatives. Predominant are forms ending in /-t/: *dat*, *yt*, *pedit*, *glosat*, *dezit*, *mundat*, *perdonat*, etc. All texts show some vacillation here, and there are several instances of preservation of sonorant /-d/ and metathesis with the /l/ of a clitic: *dezilde*, *pedilde*, etc.

The third group that shows apocope plus devoicing is a group of nouns in *-dad*. Examples are *poridat*, *verdat*, *unidat*, etc.

All of these phenomena are consistent with a dating of the text to the mid-to-late thirteenth century or later.

There are also several lexical clues to the dating of the text to the Alfonsine period or shortly thereafter. *Mercader* appears in all texts, with variants *mercador* in BN 17822 , BN 17853 and the Salamanca and Escorial manuscripts. BN 17822 also has one occurrence of *mercadero*. *Mercader* is a Catalan borrowing that appears in Castilian around the mid-thirteenth century. The etymological Castilian term derived from MERCATORE, *mercador*, is older. *Mercadero* is an attempt to Castilianize *mercader* with the addition of final /-o/ or by analogy to the many agent nouns ending in *-ero*, derived from -ARIU. The extent of the vacillation here suggests that the foreign-sounding *mercader* (*-er* is very rare as an agent suffix in Castilian) was not entirely comfortable yet, supporting a textual dating within the second half of the thirteenth century.

Other lexical clues include the musical instruments that Teodor has learned to play, and which she describes to the king as she documents her worth to him. Both *cañon* and *laúd* enter Castilian around this time, and Corominas dates the latter's earliest documentation to the *Cantigas de Santa Maria* (not Castilian, of course, but nevertheless Alfonsine).

The term *axedrez* (variants *axedres*, *axedes*) was documented in Castilian around the time of the earliest Alfonsine texts. Its standard form *axedrez* began to be normalized during the Alfonsine period (though the Libro de ajedrez has both *acedrex* and *axedrez*; here we still see vacillation among the texts. Again, this points to the mid-thirteenth century.

There are no discernible dialectal traits in any of these texts, which yet again points to the influence of the Alfonsine period in spreading normative standards for Castilian. This observation can also be made about the orthography of the manuscripts. Representations are quite regular for /ts/ - *ç*, /dz/ - *z*, /s/ - *ss*, /z/ - *s*, /s/ - *x*, /z/ - *j*, *g*, /l/ - *l*, palatal /l/ - *ll*. There are remarkably few exceptions, and they may in fact be attributable to scribal error.

All of the internal evidence, then, serves to place the four complete manuscript versions of the story of the *donzella Teodor* squarely in the middle of the thirteenth century. There is strong Alfonsine linguistic influence on the forms, their spelling, and their standardization. While the documents themselves are all later copies, the text they transmit can be dated with certainty to that time.

The fragment (BN 9055) is different from the other texts, as we mentioned above. In this manuscript, the elements of the story occur in different order and with different details (for example of vocabulary: *biuora* vs. *sierpe*, *enseñó* instead of *demostró/mostró*, etc.), and with additional content in some places. The document itself must be later than 1454. Nevertheless, many of the same observations made above apply to it. It is harder to be certain, however, due to the brevity of the fragment.

After its genesis in Castilian during the latter part of the thirteenth century, the text clearly continued to be read. The only manuscript witnesses we have date from the fourteenth and the fifteenth centuries. There is a small number of them but, in fact, a good, fairly uncomplicated line of transmission. Indeed, the fragment in BN 9055 shows that there were at least two quite distinct families.

So the first printers to pick up this story and rework it were not reaching back over two centuries to ferret out an obscure, unknown text. They had only to cast back a few decades, at the most, for an interesting subject to feed the burgeoning demand for books in the wake of the invention of the printing press.

THE RECEPTION OF THE HDT IN PRINTED EDITIONS

Although the five extant manuscript versions of the *HDT* form the core of the present critical edition, it is important to acknowledge the impact of print culture on the reception and dissemination of this medieval text. Baranda and Infantes have identified fifty-two printed editions of the *HDT* since the incunabular period (Baranda and Infantes 70-84). The vigorous printing history of the Teodor material testifies to its popularity in Early Modern Iberia.

Print also introduced a number of additions and innovations that affected the textuality of the *HDT*. Its survival during the first century of printing is due to a variety of factors, some literary and others related to the demands of book production.

Most research on the *HDT* has overlooked the publisher's role in bringing a text into production during the early years of printing. Publishers during the incunabular period participated in the selection and adaptation of works for consumption by an imagined public (Eamon 112). Cynthia Brown, in a study of early printed texts, has suggested that a text acquires identity through the involvement of a publisher who, recognizing the market potential of the work, decides to oversee the production of a book (Brown 61-62). Roger Chartier has observed that publishers created books as a response to what they perceived as the wishes of their readership: "Thus, the very structure of their books was governed by the way that book publishers thought that their target clientele read" (*The Order of Books* 13). In some instances, publishers created new identities for texts by altering or refashioning the original work in order to suit individual needs (Brown 61-62). In the case of the *HDT*, publishers exerted a strong influence on the creation and production of the text. It is not within the scope of this introduction to describe the entire printing history of the *HDT*; of particular interest, however, is the evolution of the Teodor materials during the formative period between 1500 and 1540. The *HDT* went through a total of seven reprintings (Baranda and Infantes 70-72). The four surviving editions from this period offer crucial insight into the strategies of production utilized by publishers to transform the text into a marketable commodity suitable for early modern readers.

The earliest extant printed edition of the *HDT*, published at Toledo by Pedro Hagenbach around 1500-03, survives in an imperfect copy now housed in the Biblioteca de Catalunya, Barcelona with the shelfmark Inc. 7. Only 14 of the original 16 folios remain of this imprint. A semi-paleographic transcription with annotations is found in Appendix I of the present edition. Hagenbach was active in Toledo from 1498 until 1503, when his press passed to an anonymous successor (Norton 366). Hagenbach plays a crucial role in the diffusion of the *HDT* since his decision to print this work creates a distinctive textual identity for the Teodor materials. Hagenbach's version expands the contents by inserting a popular hygienic calendar with recommendations for each of the months of the year, a series of recommendations concerning human sexology, and excerpts from the *Preguntas que el emperador Adriano hizo al infante Epitus*, a widely-known collection of *quaestiones*. The calendar materials and the hygienic recommendations derive from Andrés de Li's *Reportorio de los tiempos*, a miscellaneous compilation of useful astrological information and knowledge concerning a variety of natural phenomena (López Piñero 194-96). Although a Zaragoza 1492 imprint is known to have existed, the earliest extant witness of the *Reportorio de los tiempos* is the edition published in 1493 at Burgos by Fadrique de Basilea.[16] Because of its appropriation of Li's text, the Sevilla imprint of the *HDT* attests to the importance of this genre of scientific writing and to its dissemination in late fifteenth-century and early sixteenth-century Iberia. In addition to this scientific information, Hagenbach includes selections from the *Preguntas*, a text based on the medieval didactic *quaestiones*. This textual material reaffirms the *HDT*'s filiation with the teaching of religion, philosophy, and other disciplines. These textual additions by Hagenbach reflect the emergence in late medieval Castile of a readership that preferred utilitarian works (Nalle 92). In this case, the *HDT* provided the readers with "down-to-earth" information that might be exploited for profit or "used for the betterment of humanity" (Eamon 4). Although devotional, moralizing, and historical works accounted for most of the book production in early modern Castile (Whinnom 168), the utilitarian preferences of the readership also exerted a profound influence on the production of texts such as the *HDT*. It is clear that Hagenbach adapted the medieval version of the *HDT* in order to produce a text better suited to the needs of his contemporary readers. As we shall see, other publishers followed Hagenbach's text of this work.

---

[16] For information concerning Li, see Delbrugge's study.

A second edition of the *HDT*, published at Sevilla by Juan Varela de Salamanca in 1516-1520, reproduces the text of Hagenbach's edition without changes to the content or form (Baranda and Infantes 61). The only extant witness of the Sevilla 1516-20 survives in a complete copy housed in the Biblioteca de Don Bartolomé March, Madrid, with the shelfmark A/7/5/23. Juan Varela de Salamanca, the publisher of this edition, had established his first press in Granada in 1504. After some years in Granada, Varela moved his workshop to Toledo where he produced from 1509-1514 some twenty works. Although Varela had transferred some of his operations to Sevilla in 1509, he did not complete his move there until 1514. His workshop remained active in Sevilla until 1539. Varela's press specialized in "reprints of stock Seville titles, literary or devotional" (Norton 17). Given the dynamics of early print culture, it is likely that Varela would have had contact with other printers in the region or with the books produced by their workshop. The sharing of materials and texts among publishers was a common practice in the early years of printing. The title page of Varela's edition, for instance, reflects his own ties within the Sevilla publishing community. The image of Venus derives from a woodcut originally published by Cromberger in the 1510 imprint of the *Reportorio* (Griffin number WC 847).[17] Varela's reprinting of the *HDT* was in turn responding to the market forces of the early sixteenth century, especially in the area of scientific books for the "common man." Hagenbach's publication of the *HDT* had already carved a niche in that market by aligning this text with the scientific writings of the period and by making accessible this type of information to a broad, non-specialist readership. The years in Toledo most likely brought Varela in contact with Hagenbach's edition. The realities of early modern publishing forced vernacular publishers to keep in mind the marketability of their products. Without a doubt the popularity of the *HDT* played an important role in the decision to reprint this text. Varela was working within a climate in which book production was viewed as a

[17] For a reproduction of this title page, see *Narrativa popular* (14).

commercial venture. Since the original text had already achieved a level of popularity among readers, Varela was in essence ensuring the success of his own printing venture by appropriating a text with an established record of marketability.

With the appearance in Sevilla of a third edition published ca. 1526 by Juan Cromberger, the *HDT* enters another phase in its evolution as a printed text. The sole witness of this edition, found in the British Library, shelfmark C.63.B.15, contains several innovations not found in earlier printed editions. Cromberger most likely knew of the Teodor material through Varela's Sevilla imprint. Varela and Cromberger had participated in a series of joint business transactions and purchases of supplies (Norton 15). Several of Varela's type styles are similar to those employed by the Cromberger and Polono presses (Norton 15-16). As noted earlier, the title page of Varela's edition of the *HDT* attests to an association between these two publishers. Varela utilizes a woodcut of Venus that appears in Cromberger's 1510 edition of Li's *Reportorio* (Griffin number WC 847). These relations would logically suggest that Cromberger, the most prominent printer in sixteenth-century Sevilla, had access to a book with such a proven record of popularity. Cromberger, however, employs a different tactic for bringing this text to press. Mindful of the marketplace, he repackages the *HDT*, inserting a rich complement of illustrations and woodcuts. Cromberger, like Hagenbach before him, conceived of the Teodor text as a compendium of utilitarian information for use by a wide readership. During this period, printers, translators, and artists would play key roles in disclosing to laymen the complexities of medieval science. The visual program incorporated into the Cromberger edition makes more accessible the calendar and medical materials of the *HDT*. The Cromberger imprint includes illustrations of zodiac and astrological phenomena, a version of the "homo signorum" (zodiac man), and factotum blocks illustrating the questioning of Teodor. The illustrations of the zodiac signs and the "homo signorum" come from an edition of Li's *Reportorio de los tiempos* produced by the Cromberger workshop in 1510 and reinforce the ties to scientific texts produced during the early years of print. Although Cromberger borrows heavily from these previously published scientific materials, he does not lose track of the strong didactic focus in the work. In compiling his edition, Cromberger reworks some of the calendar selections from Li in order to provide more utilitarian details. His edition incorporates textual and paratextual elements that transform the text to suit the needs of ordinary people.

Cromberger's interests in popular scientific writings reflect a larger cultural current in Early Modern Iberia. The production of scientific books destined for a broad readership experienced a phenomenal rise during this period in Europe as well as Spain. Sevilla, with nearly 20% of its output dedicated to scientific writings, had become an important center for this type of publishing in the early sixteenth century (López Piñero 128). With the *HDT*, it is possible to see the accommodation of scientific discourse to the needs of the ordinary person.

The visual materials added by Cromberger in his printing of the *HDT* establish a distinctive paratext, which becomes the basis for subsequent reprintings of the text. The impact of the visual is evident in the edition published at Zaragoza in 1540 by Juana Milián. The Zaragoza imprint, which is transcribed in Appendix VI, follows the text of Cromberger's Sevilla, ca.1526. The edition survives in a unique exemplar located in the Biblioteca Nacional, Madrid, shelfmark R/10688. The imprint incorporates numerous pictorial elements based on the Cromberger edition of the *HDT*. The Zaragoza edition includes pictorial representations of the signs of the zodiac, a version of the "homo signorum," and a number of factotum blocks illustrating the questioning of Teodor. In addition to the visual materials, the Zaragoza imprint incorporates new textual materials in the form of an interrogation episode conducted by the King. The episode, missing from the manuscript witnesses of the text and from the Toledo 1500, Sevilla 1516-20, and Sevilla 1526-28, occurs after the questioning by Abraham. The king probes Teodor's knowledge of beliefs related to sin, religious practices, and marriage. This emphasis on religious dogma seems curious given the nature of the Teodor materials and may very well reflect a desire on the part of the publisher to give the text a more Christian feel. These particular questions derive from a sixteenth-century Castilian version of *Las preguntas que el emperador Adriano hizo al infante Epitus* published at Burgos by Juan de Junta in 1540[18] and continue the practice of incorporating materials from other sources into the *HDT*. With the addition of these questions, the compiler of the Zaragoza edition enhances the story's didactic context. This scene with the king brings closure to the story by emphasizing Teodor's mastery of religious doctrine. The addition of the new *quaestiones* constitutes a third significant phase in the early modern redactions of the Teodor material and attests to the continuing accretion of didactic materials to the text of the *HDT*.

By focusing on the early printed texts of the Teodor materials, it becomes clear that publishers were integral to the continued success of the *HDT*. At each stage of its evolution in print, the publishers were able to fashion a distinctive textual identity that made the work more appealing to its readership. These strategies transformed it into a text that provided a broad spectrum of utilitarian information. The popularity of the Teodor material is evidenced by the number of reprintings and translations since 1540. Baranda and Infantes, for instance, have catalogued some forty-five Castilian editions (Baranda and Infantes 73-84). Mettmann has identified 14 Portuguese editions, including one from Brazil (Mettmann 91-93). In addition to these translations, there exist several Tagalog versions of the story (Eugenio 301-312). The *HDT* also migrated to the Americas, where it was translated into Maya and became part of the corpus of *Books of Chilam Balam*. Brotherston has located versions of the *HDT* in community books from Kaua, Chan Kan, Mani, and Ixil (320). According to Mignolo, the appropriation of this type of text by Amer-

[18] An edition of this text is available in Suchier, 1910 (364-405).

indians is consistent with their own indigenous traditions of compiling miscellaneous, encyclopedic knowledge into a single unit. In the case of the Maya, the translation of the *HDT* represents a way for indigenous people to preserve their own cultural heritage and to accomodate the Christianization of their native culture to their own needs (Mignolo 206-07).

THE TEXT

The most widely used edition of the *HDT* is that produced by Mettmann in 1962. Mettmann based his text on the early imprints of the book and supplied in his appendices transcriptions of the five manuscripts. A recent edition produced by Baranda and Infantes essentially follows Mettmann's approach to the Teodor materials and gives priority to the Sevilla: Jacobo Cromberger 1526-28 (designated *P*) (*Narrativa popular* 47). In the present edition, we recognize the value of the early imprints of the *HDT*. Since the manuscript versions have received limited attention, we also perceived a need to edit this important group of texts so that specialists and students could have access to a critical edition of the early redactions of the tale. While we have opted to give priority to the manuscripts containing the Teodor materials, this edition has tried to balance the demands of accurate transcription of these manuscript texts with the need to clarify the problems associated with the circulation of the medieval version of the text. The manuscripts under consideration date from the fifteenth century and provide insights into the evolution of the thirteenth-century redaction of the text. Because of the lexical richness of the manuscripts, we have also provided semi-paleographic transcriptions of all extant manuscript witnesses in the appendices for reference purposes. The exclusion of the printed witnesses from our critical edition affirms the need to clarify the manuscript tradition that gave rise to a rich printed tradition of the *HDT*. In addition to the transcriptions of these manuscript versions, we found it helpful to transcribe two important early imprints of the text: Toledo: Pedro Hagenbach, ca. 1500 (designated *B*) and Zaragoza: Juana Milián, 15 May 1540 (*M*). The transcriptions of these two printed editions document the changes experienced by the *HDT* during the first four decades of its printing and provide a context for understanding the complex relationships of the manuscript redactions and the early imprints. Since Baranda and Infantes have recently edited *P* (Sevilla: Cromberger 1526-28), we have not found it necessary to provide a transcription of the Cromberger edition. Specialists and students will, it is hoped, use the critical edition, the semi-paleographic transcriptions, the appendices, and the annotations to supplement their investigation of the *HDT.*

Since the goal of our editing project is to produce a critical edition of the extant manuscript versions of the *HDT,* we have selected Ms. 17822, Biblioteca Nacional, Madrid, as the base text for our edition. Ms. 17822, designated *p* by Mettmann, provides the most complete version of the tale within the manuscript group. It is a fifteenth-century codex containing *Bocados de oro.* The *HDT,* the final piece of the book, begins at folio 117vb18 and ends at 123vb29. A semi-paleographic transcription can be found in Appendix IV.

The variants recorded in the critical edition are from the following manuscript witnesses (sigla in italics follow Mettmann):

m Biblioteca de la Universidad de Salamanca, MS 1866, spine title "Colección de sentencias." The Teodor section begins at 91vb19 and ends at 96va4. The first 91 folios contain "Bocados de oro," while from 91v to 112r there is additional material in the form of a chronological compendium. The last folio of the codex bears the date, 4 February 1433. A semi-paleographic transcription appears in Appendix II.

g Biblioteca Nacional (Madrid) MS17853, entitled "Dichos de los filósofos." The Teodor chapter begins at 112ra5 and ends at 117ra24. The manuscript was copied in the fifteenth century. A semi-paleographic transcription appears in Appendix V.

h El Escorial MS h-III-6, entitled "Bocados de oro." The Teodor chapter begins at 118v15 and ends at 123v13. The manuscript was copied in the fifteenth century. A semi-paleographic transcription appears in Appendix VI.

There is another extant fragment of the thirteenth-century story of Teodor: Biblioteca Nacional (Madrid) MS 9055, folios 69r-74r (folio 70 is blank; there is text missing between folios 71 and 72). This manuscript, designated *a* by Mettmann, belongs to a volume entitled "Libro del conoscimiento de todos los rregnos," and its final text refers to the death of King John in Valladolid in 1454. The Teodor material in *a* clearly belongs to a different family from that of *m*, *g* and *h*. The text is different enough that it would be unreadable if confined to a list of variants; for that reason, and due to its brevity and fragmentary nature, it does not form part of this list of variants. In Appendix III, however, it is transcribed in its entirety, and the important differences between it and the other family of manuscripts are noted.

The appendix also contains semi-paleographic transcriptions of two important early printed editions. Appendix I offers a transcription of *B*, the *editio princeps* attributed to the Toledo press of Hagenbach, circa 1500. The sole witness for this imprint is housed in the Biblioteca de Catalunya, Barcelona, with the shelfmark Inc. 7 and lacks the first and last folio. A transcription of *M*, an edition published at Zaragoza by Juana Milián on 15 May 1540, can be found in Appendix VII. The sole witness for the Zaragoza (1540) imprint is housed in the Biblioteca Nacional, Madrid, shelfmark R/10688.

CRITICAL EDITION

Base MS is *p* (see *apparatus criticus* following this text for explanation of sigla): BN Madrid manuscript 17822 entitled "Bocados de oro"

(*Teodor* section begins at 117vb 18)

Capítulo que fabla de los enxenplos de Teodor, donzella.

Auía en Bauilonia vn mercader muy rrico, e muy linpio, e oraçionero en las çinco oraçiones, e fazedor de bondades a los menesterosos e a las biu*[fol. 118r]*das, e auía muchos algos, e tenía muchos hermanos e muchos parientes, e non tenía fijo nin fija. E acaeçió vn día que mercó vna donzella, e dio por ella muchas doblas e muchos aueres, e leuóla a su casa e mostróle todas las artes e sabidurías quantas pudo saber[1].

E dende a tienpo, allegó el mercador a gra[n]d menester, e dixo a la donzella: "Sabed que me a traydo a gran menester, que non e algo nin consejo e non se me escusa que vos non aya de vender. Pues dadme consejo por onde aya mejoría e bien." E abaxó la donzella los ojos e la cabeça contra tierra, comidiendo. E después alçó los ojos arriba e dixo: "Non auedes que rreçelar, con la merced de Dios." E dixo: "Ydvos agora al alcaçería de los boticarios, e traedme afeitamientos para muger e nobles vestiduras, e lleuadme al alcaçar del rrey Abomelique Almançor. E quando vos preguntare por vuestra venida, dezilde: 'Quiero vos vender esta donzella'; e peditle por mí diez mill doblas de buen oro fino. E si dixere que es mucho, dezilde: 'Señor, si conoçiésedes la donzella, non lo terníades por mucho.'"

---

[1] With reference to the education of women in Late Medieval Castile, the *Jardín de nobles donzellas* observes: "Otras henbras ouo de grand industria, las quales aquí dexo por que paso a otros loores dellas, pero aquí ay vna quistón marauillosa; pues que enel antiguo siglo mugeres fallaron tantas industrias & artes, especialmente las letras; ¿por qué agora, eneste nuestro siglo, las henbras no se dan al estudio de artes liberales & de otras ciencias, antes paresce como le sea deuedado?" [*Jardín* 243].

E fuése el mercador al alcaçería de los boticarios, e fue a vno que dezían Mahomad e saluólo. E el boticario le dixo: "Mercador, ¿qué auedes menester?" E el mercador le contó la rrazón por qué venía, e dixo: "Quiero que me dedes fermosas vestiduras *[fol. 118v]* e fermosos afeitamientos para mi donzella." E el tendero ouo dél grand piadad, e de lo que dixo de la donzella, que la quería vender, e dixo: "Amigo, mucho me amjnazillastes mi coraçón, e fezistes llorar mis ojos por la vuestra pobreza, e porque queredes vender la vuestra donzella; e la vuestra demanda presta es." E leuantóse el boticario e dióle las nobles vestiduras e nobles afeitamientos para muger, e el mercadero tomólo todo e lleuólo a la donzella. E ella pagóse dello e dixo: "Esto vos será buen comienço, con la ayuda de Dios."

E leuantóse la donzella, e vistióse e afeytóse muy bien. E dixo a su señor: "Leuantadvos e sobid comigo al alcaçar del rrey." E leuantóse su señor e fuéronse para el alcaçar del rrey, e pidieron liçençia que entrasen al rrey. E el rrey mandó que entrasen, e entraron e pararonse amos antel rrey. E quando el rrey los vido, començó de fablar con el mercador, e preguntóle por su venida e qué era lo que quería. E el mercador le dixo: "Señor, quiero vos vender esta donzella." E el rrey le dixo: "¿Quánto es su preçio?" E el mercador le dixo: "Señor, quiero por ella diez mill doblas de buen oro finísymo bermejo." E el rrey lo tomó por estranno, el preçio de la donzella, e dixo al mercadero: "Mucho vos estendistes en su preçio: o ssallistes de vuestro acuerdo, o la donzella se alaba de cosas que no pueden ser." E rrespondio *[fol. 119r]* el mercadero e dixo al rrey: "Señor, non tengas por mucho el precio de la donzella, ca poco es; que yo la crié de pequenna, e es moça, e costóme muchos aueres fasta que aprendió e entendió todas las artes e los nobles menesteres, e esto non será çelado a vos."[2]

---

[2] The description of Teodor's education is striking. The various skills she has attained reflect a social and cultural environment which recognized the need to educate and train women in a variety of arts. For a discussion of some of these impulses, see Herlihy, *Opera* 49-74. In Islamic society, female slaves often received an education in a wide ranges of arts and sciences in order to make them more marketable. Valero Cuadra [1994] (150-51) provides several examples of these "esclavas" within Andalusian society. The education of women is often a topic in medieval

E començó el rrey a fablar con la donzella, e ella abaxó el velo de vergüença. E el rrey alçó los ojos e vido su fermosura, que semejaua al sol quando salía, que non auía en ese tienpo más fermosa quella. Díxole el rrey: "Donzella, ¿qué auedes nonbre?" E rrespondió la donzella e dixo: "Señor, a mí dizen Teodor." E díxole el rrey: "Donzella, ¿qué aprendistes de las artes?"[3] E dixo la donzella: "Señor, yo aprendí la ley[4] e el libro; e aprendí los quatro libros e las siete planetas e las

---

literature. In Castilian literature, the clearest example occurs in the *Libro de Apolonio* where Luciana and Tarsiana are both given instruction in the liberal arts. French literature of the central Middle Ages also offers parallels. Jean Renart's *Galeran de Bretagne* (ca. 1225) describes how Fresne is taught to read, to play the harp, to sing, to make fabric, to play chess, and to embroider cloth:

> Le jour fors lire mon saultier
> Et faire euvre d'or ou de soie,
> Oÿr de Thebes ou de Troye,
> Et en ma herpe lays noter,
> Et uux eschez autruy mater... (*Galeran*, lines 3880-84).

In the *Jardín de las donzellas*, a guidebook designed to educate women in the court of the Catholic Monarchs, Fray Martín de Córdoba encouraged Queen Isabel of Castile to engage in a defined course of study: "...deue captar algunas oras del día en que estudie & oya tales cosas que sean propias al regimiento del reyno" [*Jardín* 244]. The description of the various disciplines is common in the wisdom literature tradition. *El libro de los buenos proverbios*, for example, lists the following: "Esta es la manera del ensennamiento que fizo el philosopho a sus discipulos en la letra griega. [Y des]pues de aquesto muestra la gramatica e versificar, despues el aresmetica, despues la geometria, despues [la] estrologia, despues fisica, despues musica, despues dialetica, despues la filosofia e saber. . . e la materia de todas las cosas que son deyuso del cielo. E estas diez artes aprendio el discipulo en diez annos" (Knust 13).

[3] The *Glosa castellana al regimiento de príncipes* (Seville, Meynardo Ungut and Stanislano Polono, 1494), based on the *De regime principium* of Giles of Rome, explains the rationale for the Liberal Arts: "...e llámanlas artes liberales, porque los fijos de los libres e de los nobles las deven aprender, porque sean por ellas ennoblescidos" (*Glosa castellana* II: 153).

[4] The reference to the law is curious since the legal system of medieval Europe generally barred women from the study and practice of law. The Theodosian Code,

estrellas e las leyes e los mandamientos e el traslado e los prometimientos e las cosas que crió en los cielos[5]; e aprendí las fablas de las aues e de las animalias,[6] e la físyca e filosofía e la lógica[7] e las cosas prouadas e el juego del axedrez; e aprendí tañer laúd[8] e cañon e las

---

for example, contains an imperial edict from 393 which forbids women from appearing in court as lawyers or advocates, except in their own cases. Various Church councils upheld this exclusion (see Herlihy 115). In the Iberian peninsula, Alfonso X codified this prohibition in *Partida* III.6.3 "Quien non puede abogar et puédelo facer por sí": "Ninguna muger quanto quier que sea sabidor non puede seer abogada en juicio por otri". Carmen Millán de Benavides has brought to our attention that in the *Espéculo* I.XII reference is made to the fact that women are barred from the study of the law: "...las mugieres sse pueden escussar por rrazon que sson de fflaca et de liujana natura, et aun porque les non cae de aprender leys en escuelas njn de usar pleitos a menudo entre los varones."

[5] The Old Norse *Dínus saga drambláta* (14th century) offers an interesting analogue to Teodor's skills. The *saga* describes Philotemia, daugther of King Maximilianus, in terms of her education and learning: "She studied the seven liberal arts with their branches so well as though each of the arts flowed and derived from her, so that she had no equal in the entire kingdom. She had learned the art of magic and the runic alphabet so well that in these matters she considered no one her equal in the entire world, so she was acquainted with all the powers of the earth as well as the course of the moon and all the science of the stars; the characteristics of all herbs, stones, trees, branches, and springs, which were in the entire world; and because of all of this she practiced great sorcery and many things..." [Kalinke 91].

[6] The number of languages spoken by mankind is a common topic. Isidore observes: "Et quoniam septuaginta duae linguae in hoc mundo erant diffusae"[*De ecclesiasticis*, 1. xi.7, PL 83, col. 746]. Similar comments can be found in medieval *altercatio* texts: "Quante lingue hominum? --.lxxii" [Suchier 1955, C, #24]; "Quot linguae? Septuaginta duae" [*Collectanea*, col 544c].

[7] The Arabic tale relates the following information: "...and I have studied the exact sciences, geometry and philosophy, and medicine and logic, and rhetoric and composition; and I have learned by rote and am passionately fond of poetry" [*Arabian Nights*, IV:148-49].

[8] This aspect of Teodor's education resembles that of Tarsiana in the *Libro de Apolonio*:

treynta e tres trobas; e aprendí las buenas costumbres de leyes; e aprendí baylar e cantar e sotar[9]; e aprendí texer paños de peso; e aprendí labrar paños de seda; e aprendí labrar de oro e de plata e de todas las otras artes e cosas nobles."

E en que oyó el rrey estas palabras de la donzella, *[fol. 119v]* fízose marauillado e mandó llamar los mayores sabios de sus artes,[10] e díxo-

---

> Criaron a gran viçio los amos la moçuela.
> Quando fue de siete anyos diéronla al escuela;
> apriso bien gramátiga et bien tocar viuela,
> aguzó bien, como fierro que aguzan a la muela.
> *LA* copla 350

[9] The musical skills mentioned by Teodor reflect several aspects of Medieval Culture. According to Valero Cuadra [1994] (150), Teodor is representative of the "esclavas cantoras" which flourished within Islamic society during the Middle Ages. From a literary perspective, the *Libro de Apolonio* makes specific reference to Tarsiana's musical abilities:

> Luego el otro día, de buena madrug(a)da,
> levantóse la duenya ricamiente adobada;
> priso huna viola buena et bien tenprada
> e sallió al mercado violar por soldada.
>
> Començó hunos viesos et hunos sones tales
> que trayén grant dulçor et eran naturales.
> Finchiénse de omnes apriesa los portales,
> non les cabi(e)én las plaças, subiénse a los poyales.
> *LA* 426-27

The Late Medieval romance, *La historia del noble caballero París y de la muy hermosa donzella Viana*, offers another literary parallel. Viana attained various skills including the ability to recite poetry and song: "Leer romances y canciones de tañer instrumentos y dançar y todas cosas en que tomassen plazer le eran enseñadas en tal manera que crescía..." (*Narrativa popular* 130).

[10] The liberal arts are constituted by the *trivium*, grammar, logic, and rhetoric, and the *quadrivium*, music, geometry, astronomy, arithmetic. Alfonso X characterizes the *trivium* and the *quadrivium* as "ca por las tres del triuio se dizen los nom-

les que prouasen esta donzella. E salleron luego a ella tres omnes letrados, e todos le preguntaron, espeçialmente vn físico que le preguntó e dixo: "Donzella, ¿las flores son sanas?" E dixo la donzella: "Son sanas en su tienpo e dolientes en su tienpo." E dixo el físico: "¿Quáles son las frutas?" E dixo la donzella: "Las granadas para los dolientes, e las almendras, e las mançanas."[11] E otorgó con ella el físico.

E preguntó de la sangría, e dixo la donzella: "La sangría es buena en martes, e la luna menguante, e el çielo ascondido de nuues; e será el cuerpo espaçioso, e alegre el fígado; e el sangrador, avn que sea sabidor de las conplisiones de los omnes." E otorgó con ella el físico.[12]

---

bres alas cosas, e estas fazen al omne bien razonado, e por las quatro del quadriuio se muestran las naturas de las cosas" [Alfonso X. *General Estoria.* Ed. A.G. Solalinde. Madrid: Junta para Ampliación de Estudios e Investigaciones Científicas, 1930. I: 94].

[11] Several variant answers exist for this question. The Arabic version makes the following recommendation: "What are the most excellent fruits? -- Pomegranate and citron" [*Arabian Nights*, IV:178]. The Andalusian text reflects the version from the *Arabian Nights*: "¿Cuáles son las mejores frutas? -- La granada y la toronja" ["Una versión del cuento" 354]. The medicinal values of these fruits are described in the *Compendio de medicina (Mujtasar fi l-tibb)* of Ibn Habib: "El membrillo dulce es ligero, excelente para el estómago y abre el apetito; es menos astringente que el ácido y más alimenticio y contiene algo de calor....La granada es suave, húmeda y fría. Es astringente, debido a su humedad, a sus granos y a su acidez...Es excelente para el pecho, para la tos como alimento. Su corteza y su flor son astringentes si se cuecen con agua y se deja reposar. Resulta beneficiosa contra la debilidad de estómago y contra la humedad que afecta a los testículos" [Ibn Habib 93].

[12] In the Middle Ages, the theory and practice of therapeutic blood-letting or phlebotomy derived from the humoralism of Galen. The treatises on blood-letting frequently incorporated information on diagnosis of illness and their treatment by means of letting blood. In some case, these writings included indications of the astrological aspects of blood-letting as well as calendars for determining the most propitious days for evacuation of the humors. The studies by P. Gil-Sotres. J. Martínez Gázquez, and L. García Ballester describe the influence of these theories on the practice of phlebotomy in medieval Aragon.

E dixo a la donzella: "¿Quál cosa es la que encaneçe al omne ante de su tienpo?" E dixo la donzella: "La debda descubierta, e la poridad, e yazer con muger vieja, que es pecado mortal."[13] E otorgó con ella el físico.

E preguntó de la entrada del baño, e dixo la donzella: "Bueno es baño, saluo que a menester condiçiones." E dixo el físico: "¿Quáles son?" E dixo la donzella: "La vergüença, e cobrir lo que es de cobrir, e que sea el baño con agua fría e dulce, e sallirá luego el cuerpo del omne alegre."[14] E otorgó con ella el físico.

E preguntóle de la carne, quál era las más sana, e dixo la donzella: "El *[fol. 120r]* carnero es melezina e su carne es vianda; e otrosí la

---

[13] In a commentary to the Pseudo-Albertus Magnus's *De secretis mulierum*, the following observation appears: "Thus women who have much sexual intercourse do not have their lives shortened as men do..." and "The more women have sexual intercourse, the stronger they become, because they are made hot by the motion that the man makes during coitus....On the other hand, men who have sex frequently are weakened by this act because they become exceedingly dried out" (Pseudo-Albertus 71; 127). Along similar lines, the *Poridat* suggests abstinence from carnal relations with women: "Alexandre, non querades fornicio seguyr, que es de natura de los puercos. Et qual bien a en la cosa que las bestias an mayor poder que los mones? Et demas es cosa que enueieçe el cuerpo et enflaquece el coraçon, et mingua la uida et metesse omne en poder de mugeres" (*Poridat* 38).

[14] Bathing was assigned an important role in the hygienic regimen of the Middle Ages. Constantinus explicity links bathing with sexual health: "Antiqui dixerunt in libris suis: res que conservant sanitatem sunt exercicium, balneum, cibus, potus; sompnus et coitus" [*De coitu* 112]. Other medical writings make similar recommendations. The *Compendio* prescribes: "Porque no es bueno el ayuntamiento luego en saliendo del baño. Responde porque entonces estan todos los poros abiertos: e el calor derramado por todo el cuerpo, el qual conel tal acto se enfriaria por forma que seria muy dañoso" [fol. 20r]. Juan de Aviñón in his medical treatise observes: "...que non se bañe despues q[ue] durmiere con la muger" [fol. 98r]. A similar recommendation can be found in the Prose Salernitan Questions: "Duplex igitur est mulieris in coitu delectatio, videlicet in emissione propii seminis et in receptione alterius. Viri autem simplex est, est enim in sola emissione. Hac ergo ratione mulieres viris ferventiores sunt in libidine" [*Prose* 4].

carne es manteca e es sanidad."[15] E otorgó con ella el físico, e dixo a la donzella: "¿Qué dezides de la carne gorda?"[16] E dixo la donzella: "Es pensamiento del alma." E "¿Qué dezides de la carne magra?" E dixo la donzella: "Es vianda caliente." E otorgo con ella el fisyco.

E dixo: "¿Qué dezides del yazer con las mugeres?" E la donzella, con gran vergüença que ouo, abaxó sus ojos con su rrostro contra tierra; e leuantóse el físico en pie e dixo al rrey: "Sabed, señor, que es vençida la donzella, pues que non rresponde a esta demanda." E dixo la donzella: "Señor, non lo mande Dios, ca yo oue vergüença de vos porque so yo niña pequeña e so virgen." E el rrey ouo muy gran amor della e mandóle que le rrespondiese, e dixo la donzella: "Físico, todo yazer con muger es dolencia; e quando ouieres de yazer con ella, podrá ser que sea preñada, o que críe fijo macho a sus tetas, o otra muger que guarde, e es menester que sea el varón sabidor desto." E díxole el físico: "¿En qué a menester que sea el varón sabidor?" Dixo la donzella: "Si fuere tal que viniere a la muger su talente tarde, e la del varon ayna, tollerse a el talente della ante que del varón, e podrá ser que sane la muger dello; e a menester que sea el yazer con la muger en el terçio postrimero *[fol. 120v]* de la noche, porque sea el coraçón caliente e el cuerpo e el estómago destrauado de la vianda."[17]. E otorgó con ella el físico.

---

[15] A similar prescription is found in the *Libro del cuidado*: "La carne de vacuno es de substancia pesada y de bilis negra. Resulta fría y seca para la complexión del hombre y además, difícil y lenta de digerir" *[Libro del cuidado* 117].

[16] The *Libro del cuidado* provides a dietetic regimen which bears on the *HDT*: "Son preferibles las carnes grasas a las magras, bien cocinadas y preparadas con ólea; y la humedad de la carne procedente de las crías, puede contarrestarse con los alimentos mencionados" [*Libro del cuidado* 118].

[17] In *Bocados de oro*, similar advice is given: "E preguntaron a Aristotiles: ¿Quándo es bueno yazer con la muger? E dixo: Quando quisieres enflaquescer tu cuerpo" [*Bocados* 168]. Contemporary medical treatises offer the similar recommendation. Juan de Avión suggests: "El tiempo convenible para usar co[n] la muger: y es conestas condiciones. La primera que la materia lo requiere por si. La segunda que sea sano de su cuerpo et de sus miembros / sin dole[n]cias y su flaqueza. La tercera que non venga por acarreo de ver muger. o de ymagen en ella...la

"E ¿qué dezides de la hedad de las mugeres?" E dixo la donzella: "Que la muger de veynte años es commo nobleza; e la muge[r] de treynta años es commo carne con limón; e la muger de quarenta años es de seso; e la muger de cinquenta es para el cuchillo; e la muger de sesenta años es para el otro mundo; e la muger de setenta años es vieja tierra; la muger de nouenta años—non me preguntedes del ynfierno, que es la cosa más esquiua de todo el mundo."[18] E el físico preguntó por las fermosuras de las mugeres, quáles eran, e dixo la donzella: "Acuçioso sodes de preguntar."

E el vno dellos era alfaquí, sabidor de justiçias e de leyes; e el otro era físico, de las cosas que perteneçen a la física; e el otro era sabidor

---

quinta que lo faga despues que sea decendida la vianda del estomago: et dirigida en el figado: y començado la digestion...La sexta q[ue] non use con la muger empos de vaziamiento / assi como desque toma purga / o fiziere vomito: o sangria o saliendo del baño" [fols. 109v-110r]. In the Arabic tale, the following variant is attested: "What is the best copulation? --If the woman be tender of years, comely of shape, fair of face, swelling of breast and of noble race, she will add thee strength and health of body" [*Arabian Nights*, IV:178]. The Andalusian version offers the following: "¿Cuál es el mejor coito? --El que se hace con una joven que tenga buen cuerpo, de mejillas hermosas, que sea fuerte y de senos exuberantes. Una mujer que reúna estos atractivos aumenta la fuerza de tu cuerpo" ["Una versión del cuento" 354].

[18] Compare with the following observations from *Speculum al foder*: "Las edades de las mujeres son cinco; la niñnez, hasta que tiene ocho años; la segunda, hasta que tiene los veinte; la tercera, hasta que ha cumplido los treinta; la cuarta, hasta que ha cumplido los cuarenta; la quinta hasta que la falla el período. La característica de la primera edad es que contesta la verdad a cualquier cosa que se le pregunte y no esconde todo lo que conoce; además no tiene vergüenza ni del hombre ni de la mujer. En la segunda edad es más vergonzosa y guarda mejor lo que sabe. En la tercera edad está formada de todo lo que necesita; ésta es ya una mujer hecha. En la cuarta edad le gustan más los hombres y suaviza sus andares, su hablary sus obras y le gusta observar. Con la quinta edad disminuye su vista y su calor, se le relajan las carnes y sirve mucho al hombre. La que pasa de esta edad ya es vieja y nadie debe desearla" [*Speculum al foder* 43-44].

de la gramática e de la lógica e de la buena fabla.[19] E el alfaquí sabidor de las leyes e del libro de Dios dixo a la donzella: "Rrespondedme a lo que vos preguntaré." E dixo la donzella: "Rresponderé con la merçed de Dios e de nuestro señor el rrey Abomelique Almançor, que Dios mantenga." E dixo el alfaquí: "Donzella, ¿qué ordenó Dios sobre nos en nuestro día e sobre su syeruo en su día?" E dixo la donzella: "A las gentes e a las animalias dixo 'Seruidme e non me menospreçiedes, *[fol. 121r]* e yo non menospreçiaré a vos.'" E dixo el alfaquí: "Donzella, muy bien rrespondistes. E pregúntovos quáles son los juizios e los mandamientos de Dios." E dixo la donzella: "Son tres e çinco." E dixo el alfaquí: "Glosadme quáles son." E dixo la donzella: "Perdonar quando ouieres poder e quando fuéredes poderoso e grande el día alto delante vuestros ojos." E dixo el alfaquí: "Muy bien dexistes. ¿E los tres que son çinco?" E dixo la donzella: "Los tres que son cinco es el Criador, e el testimonio que non ha otro criador sy non Dios, e mundad el cuerpo e alinpiadlo." E otorgó con ella el alfaquí en quanto dixo la donzella.

E estonçe dixo la donzella: "Alfaquí, el Señor alto e bendito sea con syete çielos, e puso en ellos las estrellas, vna partida dellas para ennobleçer los çielos e otra para los moros e otra para las gentes e otra para el poder del diablo maldito." E dixo el alfaquí: "Muy bien dexistes." E dixo estonçes la donzella: "Alfaquí, el nuestro Señor alto e

---

[19] Isidore defined grammar as "scientia recte loquendi et origo et fundamentum liberallium litterarum" [*ETY* I,v,1]. Alfonso X defines the *artes* as "...gramática, que es arte para aprender el lenguaje del latín; y otrosí de lógica, que es para saber y conocer distinguir la verdad de la mentira; y aun de retórica, que es ciencia que muestra ordenar las palabras apuestamente y como conviene...la aritmética, es arte que muestra las maneras de las cuentas; y el otro, geometría, que es para saber cómo se pueden medir y estimar las cosas por estimación o por vista; y el tercero, la música, que es saber de acordanza de los sones y de las otras cosas; y el cuarto, astronomía, que es para saber el movimiento de los cielos y el curso de los planetas y de las estrellas..." [*Siete Partidas*, Primera Partida, Ley 37.1]. In the Middle Ages, the following distich was often used to describe the relations of the Seven Arts:

Gram loquitur; Dia vera docet; Rhet verba colorat;
Mus canit; Ar numerat; Ge ponderat; As colit astra.

bendito sea con siete çielos, e con doze signos." E dixo el alfaquí: "Glosadme quáles son." E dixo la donzella: "Acarius, Geminis, Aries, Taurus, Geminis, Pisçis, Cançer, Leo, Virgo, Libra, Escorpius, Sagitarius, Capicornius."[20]

E dixo la donzella: "Alfaquí, el que fiziere oraçión, e non fuere quito de pecado, non será oyda su oraçión; *[fol. 121v]* e el que es quito de pecado, si non fiziere oraçión, non será oyda su castidad; e el que es casto e fiziere oraçión entrará en la gloria de Paraíso." E dixo el alfaquí: "Donzella, bien dexistes, más ¿en qué deue omne de ser casto?" E dixo la donzella: "En la plata, e en el trigo, e en la ceuada, e en el çenteno, e en las frutas, e en las azeytunas, e en el ganado ouejuno e vacuno, e de todas las otras cosas que Dios les diere." E leuantóse el alfaquí e dixo al rrey: "Señor, por uerdad más sabe esta donzella que non yo, e yo le do mejoría en el saber." E el rrey ouo desto grand plazer, e mandó al otro que fablase con ella.

E leuantóse el físico e dixo a la donzella: "Rrespondedme a lo que vos preguntaré." E dixo la donzella: "Sí rresponderé con la merçet del Criador e de nuestro señor el rrey Abomelique, que Dios mantenga." E dixo el físico: "Donzella, dezitme de la confaçión del cuerpo o del omne." E dixo la donzella: "Así es, que nuestro Señor Dios tenpró la

---

[20] Medieval writers did not distinguish between astrology and astronomy. Isidore of Seville, for example, associated astronomy with "astrorum lex, quae cursus siderum et figuras et habitudines stellarum circa se et circa terram indagabili rationes percurrit" (*ETY* III.24). For an overview of the problems associated with this term, see studies by Lemay and by Vescovini. The writer of *HDT* juxtaposes cosmological aspects with the predicative or judicial quality of astronomy. The mention of "casas" is significant since astrologers utilized a system of Houses of the heavens to predict favorable or unfavorable events. This system of prognostication was subsequently utilized by physicians in order to determine the best treatment for a particular illness. The study by Roger French on the use of astrology in the medical arts is quite helpful. These concepts persist in the fifteenth century. The *Glosa castellana al regimiento de príncipes* (Seville, Meynardo Ungut and Stanislano Polono, 1494), based on the *De regime principium* by Giles of Rome, defines Astrology: "...es ciencia de los cuerpos del cielo e de los movimientos e de las distancias de las estrellas e de las virtudes que han sobre los cuerpos de la tierra, ca esta sciencia vale mucho para las obras de los omnes" (*Glosa castellana* II:158).

humidad con la secura, e Él fizo dende la tierra; e tenpró la secura e la humidad, e fizo dende el ayre, e abafó la tierra; e si non fuese por los bafos de la tierra, federían nuestros fuelgos contra el çielo e la tierra. E el omne es de quatro elementos."[21] E dixo el físico: "¿Quáles son?" E dixo la donzella: "Tierra e fuego e agua e ayre. E en el año son quatro temporales: ynuierno e verano *[fol. 122r]* e estío e otoño[22]; e en estos quatro tienpos rremaneçe la colora e la maletía e la sangre e la flema. E a menester que sea el físico sabidor de las conplisiones e de las melezinas que perteneçen al cuerpo, e según fueren menester al cuerpo." E otorgó con ella el físico.

E dixo: "Donzella, dezidme, ¿quáles son las señales para la muger ser fermosa?" E dixo la donzella: "Aquella muger es fermosa que es señora de diez e ocho señales." E dixo el físico: "Dezidme quáles son estas diez e ocho señales." E dixo la donzella: "La que es luenga en tres, e pequeña en tres, e ancha en tres, e blanca en tres, e bermeja en tres, e prieta en tres." E dixo el físyco: "Dezidme commo es esto." E dixo la donzella: "Luenga en tres: que sea luenga de estado, e que aya el cuello largo, e los dedos luengos; blanca en tres: el cuerpo blanco, e los dientes blancos, e lo blanco de los ojos blanco; prieta en tres: cabellos prietos, e lo pri[e]to de los ojos prieto, e las cejas prietas; e bermeja en tres: mexillas bermejas, e beços bermejos, e ensías ber-

---

[21] Ibn Habib's *Compendio de la medicina* provides insight into this *quaestio*: "Cuando creó Dios a Adán mezcló en su cuerpo cuatro cosas: la sequedad, la humedad, el calor y el frío. Ello se debe a que lo creó de polvo y agua y luego puso en él el aliento vital y el espíritu. La sequedad procede del polvo, la humedad del agua, el calor del aliento vital y el frío del espíritu. Más trade, y relacionado con ello, le puso Dios cuatro humores, que son el soporte del cuerpo y su fundamento, sin que el cuerpo pueda subsistir más que con ellos y sin que ninguno de ellos pueda ser ayudado más que iguales. Estos humores son la sangre, la flema, la bilis roja y la bilis negra" [Ibn Habib 104].

[22] This answer reflects the humoral theories of this period. Ibn Habib's *Compendio de la medicina* comments: "El año está dividido en cuatro estaciones a las que corresponden cuatro humores: verano, otoño, invierno y primavera" [Ibn Habib 105].

mejas; e pequeña en tres: boca pequeña, e nariz pequeña, e los pies pequeños; e ancha en tres: ancha de caderas, e ancha de espaldas e ancha la fruente; e que sea muy placentera a su marido e muy ayudadora, e que sea pequeña de hedad."[23] E leuantóse el físico e dixo a la donzella: "Dios vos faga bien, que en todo fablastes bien." E dixo al rrey: "Por verdat, señor, yo vos digo que esta *[fol. 122v]* donzella que sabe más que non yo, e yo la do por verdadera." E el rrey preçiólo mucho e mandó luego al otro sabidor que se leuantase a fablar con la donzella.

E leuantóse luego Abrahán el trobador e sabidor de gramática e de lógica, e dixo: "Donzella, aparejaduos, que non so yo de aquellos que auedes ençerrado e vencido." E preguntóle la donzella que quién era e cómo auía nonbre, e dixo él: "Yo so Abrahán el trobador." E dixo la donzella: "Abrahán, yo nunca vos conocí, pero asentadvos e preguntadme, que yo vos rresponderé, con la merced de Dios e de nuestro señor el rrey, que Dios mantenga." E luego dixo Abrahán a la donzella: "Sy vos me rrespondierdes çiertamente a todo lo que vos preguntaré, que yo que vos dé todos los mis paños; e sy vos non me rrespondierdes çiertamente, que vos que me dedes los vuestros paños." E dixo la donzella: "E yo así lo pido por merçed a nuestro señor el rrey, que nos lo mande a vos e a mí." E el rrey mandólo luego e otorgógelo asy a amos a dos.

E Abrahán el trobador dixo[24]: "Donzella, ¿quál es la cosa más pesada que ay en los montes?; ¿e más apresurada que la saeta?; ¿e más

---

[23] Compare with the suggestions found in *Speculum al foder*: "En cuanto a la nobleza y a la belleza de las mujeres, se trata que tengan cuatro cosas muy negras; el pelo, las cejas, las pestañas y los ojos; cuatro cosas muy negras; las mejillas, la lengua, las encías y los labios; cuatro muy blancas; el rostro, los dientes, el blanco de los ojos y las piernas; cuatro muy estrechas; los orificios de la nariz y de los oídos, la boca, los pechos y los pies; cuatro muy delgadas; las cejas, la nariz, los labios y las costillas; cuatro muy grandes; la frente, los ojos, los pechos y las nalgas; cuatro muy redondas; la cabeza, el cuello, los brazos y las piernas; y cuatro muy perfumadas; la boca, la nariz, las axilas y el coño" [*Speculum al foder* 47].

[24] The following section of the *HDT* is a version of the didactic *quaestiones*. Examples of these dialogues or *altercatio* exist in a variety of languages and formats

aguda que espada?; ¿e más ardiente quel fuego?; ¿e más dulce que la miel?; ¿e lagrimas de ojos?; ¿e dolençia syn melezina?; ¿e más rrezio quel hueso?; ¿e talante de vna ora?; ¿e plazer *[fol. 123r]* de tres días?; ¿e plazer de un mes?; ¿e plazer de cinco días?; ¿e vna aue que se cría en los montes que ay en ella ocho señales de grandes animalias?[25]" E rrespondió la donzella: "Aparejad vuestras rropas, que yo vos rresponderé, con la merçed de Dios." E rrespondióle e díxole: "Lo que es más pesado que los montes es el agua; e más apresurado que la saeta es el ojo; e más aguda que la espada es la lengua;[26] e más ardiente quel

---

from the ninth century onward (see the studies by Suchier, Daly, Valero Cuadra [1996] and Cross and Hill). Brian Lawn (1) has observed that *quaestiones* played an important role in the teaching of theology and other disciplines throughout the medieval period. While the *quaestio* format provided a didactic tool, it eventually became a form of entertainment which tested the knowledge of the participants. The extant *quaestiones* or dialogues embrace a number of subjects: history, theology, scriptural information, medieval scientific information, and proverbial lore. In the *HDT*, the obsession with factual knowledge is supplemented by a desire to outwit the questioner/opponent. Teodor proves herself capable and ultimately triumphant because she has mastered that knowledge and the techniques of the *quaestio*. In the *HDT*, this section comprises a variety questions from the *Secundus* Dialogue tradition, from the *Joca monachorum* tradition, and from medieval sapiential literature. Barry Taylor makes note that the Version B of the *Bocados de Oro* contains a version of the *Dialogue of Secundus* and that Version C of *Bocados de Oro* (Escorial h.III.6, BNM 17822 and 17853, Salamanca University 1866) replaces the *Secundus* with the *HDT*.

[25] This riddle circulated widely in the Middle Ages. Darbord (24-25) links this particular riddle to concepts prevalent in the Middle Ages of man as "microcosmo de todo lo creado." Mettmann (166-67) has inventoried the variants in the extant Teodor materials. The sequencing in the *HDT* follows the version found in the *Arabian Nights*: "...last, the beast that woneth not in the cultivated fields, but lodgeth in waste places and hateth the sons of Adam and hath in him somewhat of the make of seven strong beast, is the locust, whose head is as the head of a horse, its neck as the neck of the bull, its wings as the wings of the vulture, its feet as the feet of the camel, its tail as the tail of the serpent, its belly as the belly of the scorpion, and its horns as the horns of the gazelle" [*Arabian Nights*, IV:194].

[26] Various analogues exists for this *quaestio*. In *Bocados*, the following appears: "¿Quál es la cosa que es más aguda que espada? E dixo: La lengua del mal ome"

fuego es el coraçón[27]; e más dulce que la miel es el buen fijo [28]; e dolençia syn melezina es la locura; e el más çierto es el llamamiento del señor del mundo; e lo que es más rrezio quel hueso es la verdad[29]; e talante de vna ora es yazer con la muger; e solaz de vn día es ganancia; e plazer de tres días son obras de baño; e plazer de siete días es el nouio los primeros syete días[30]; e plazer de vn mes es el que viene de su camino; e el aue que se cría en los montes que a en ella ocho señales de grandes animales es la çigarra, quel su pescueço es de vaca,

---

[*Bocados* 24]. A similar *quaestio* exchange occurs in the 15th-century Castilian redaction of the *Ynfante Epitus* in Ms Egerton 939: "La lengua del onbre es mas aguda que la navaja" [Bizzari 114:94] In *De vita*, two examples of this *quaestio* appear: "'¿Que cosa es mas aguda que el cuchillo?' dixo 'La lengua del mal onbre'" [*De vita* 21]; see also "'¿Que cosa es buena y mala en los onbres?' rrespondio 'La lengua'" [*De vita*, 51]. The Arabic versions also attest to this *quaestio*: "...that which is sharper than the sword is the tongue" [*Arabian Nights*, IV:193] and "...más cortante que la espada es la lengua" ["Una versión del cuento" 362].

27 The 15th-century Castilian redaction of *Yfante Epitus* contains: "El coraçon del onbre es mas ardiente que el fuego, quando esta ayrado y enbuelto en saña" [Suchier 1910, Spanish N # 105]. A variant version of this *quaestio* topic appears in the Alfonsine version of the *Secundus* Dialogue: "¿que es el coraçon? Recebimiento de uida" [PCG 147].

28 This *quaestio* seems to derive from an Arabic source: "Now that which is sweeter than honey is the love of pious children to their two parents" [*Arabian Nights*, IV:193] and "¿Qué es más dulce que la miel...? --Más dulce que la miel es el amor que tienen los padres a los hijos..." ["Una versión del cuento" 362]. In Knust's edition, we find: "e mas dulce que la miel [es] el buen fijo" [Knust 515].

29 "La verdat es mas fuerte que el asero" [Suchier 1910, Spanish N #109].

30 The original tale of Teodor (Tawaddud) displayed a keen interest in reviewing aspects of Koranic law and doctrines associated with Islam. In an Arabic analogue of this exchange, the following variant is found: "'And for a year?' 'Marriage with a virgin.' 'And for ever?' 'To talk with friends in this world and the pleasures of Paradise in the next'" [*The Glory* 175]. And in the redaction from Granada, the following occurs: "...el gozo de una semana es la desposada..." ["Una versión del cuento" 362].

el su pecho es de cauallo, e sus rrostros de león, e sus alas de águila, e su çinta de alacrán, e la cola de sierpe, e los pies de avestruz, e el vientre de buey."

E Abraán el trobador se leuantó en pie e dixo al rrey: "Señor, sed çierto que sabe esta donzella más que non yo e avn nin quantos sabios vos tenedes, *[fol. 123v]* e todos le deuen dar la mejoría en el saber." E luego el rrey Abomelique dixo a la donzella: "Dios vos guarde de mal e vos dé su gracia, porque tan bien vos rrespondistes a todas aquellas cosas a estos sabios, quellos e yo vos preguntamos, e tan çiertamente vos rrespondistes a ellas." E luego que esto ouo dicho, Abrahán despojó sus paños e diólos a la donzella. E luego la donzella se leuantó en pie e dixo: "Abraán, dadme vuestros paños menores, commo fue puesto que me diésedes todos vuestros paños." E Abraám dio a la donzella diez mill doblas de buen oro por non pasar tal uergüença, commo le fuera sy los paños menores le ouiera de dar allí delante del rrey.

E luego el rrey le dixo: "Donzella, pedidme merçed e dezidme en qué manera la queredes, si la queredes en mi casa en buen casamiento; ca sed çierta que vos lo daré qual vos demandardes." E luego rrespondió la donzella al rrey e dixo: "Señor, ¡manténgavos Dios! E si merçed me auedes de fazer, enbiadme con mi señor el mercador, ca yo non conosco otro padre saluo a él, que me crió e fizo mucho por me allegar en este estado, e me mostró lo que sé." E el rrey mandóle luego dar diez mill doblas de buen oro e de preçio. E la donzella tomólas e besó al rrey las manos, e la tierra antel rrey, e fuése con su señor el mercador, e casóse con el, e fueron muy rricos dende en adelante.

Deo gracias.

Apparatus criticus

The base text chosen was Biblioteca Nacional (Madrid) manuscript 17822, entitled "Bocados de oro" (designated *p* by Mettmann). In it, the *Teodor* section begins at folio 117vb18 and ends at 123vb29. It is the final chapter of the book. A paleographic transcription can be found in Appendix IV.

The variants recorded here are from the following manuscripts (sigla in italics follow Mettmann):

m Biblioteca de la Universidad de Salamanca, manuscript 1866, spine title "Colección de sentencias." The Teodor section begins at 91vb19 and ends at 96va4. The first 91 folios contain "Bocados de oro," while from 91v to 112r there is additional material (a chronological compendium). The last folio of the manuscript is dated 4 February 1433. For transcription, see Appendix II.

g Biblioteca Nacional (Madrid) manuscript 17853, entitled "Dichos de los filósofos." The Teodor chapter begins at 112ra5 and ends at 117ra24. For transcription, see Appendix V.

h El Escorial manuscript h-III-6, entitled "Bocados de oro." The Teodor chapter begins at 118v15 and ends at 123v13. For transcription, see Appendix VI.

There is another extant fragment of the thirteenth-century story of Teodor: Biblioteca Nacional (Madrid) manuscript 9055, folios 69r-74r (folio 70 is blank; there is text missing between folios 71 and 72). The title of the volume is "Libro del conoscimiento de todos los rregnos," and its final text refers to the death of King John in Valladolid in 1454. The Teodor material here clearly belongs to a different family from that of *m*, *g* and *h*. The text is different enough that it would be unreadable if confined to a list of variants; for that reason, and due to its brevity and fragmentary nature, it does not form part of this list of variants. In Appendix III it is transcribed in its entirety.

The appendices also provide transcriptions of two important early printed editions. Appendix I offers a transcription of *B* (sigla in italics follow Mettmann), the *editio princeps* attributed to the Toledo press of Hagenbach, circa 1500. The sole witness is housed in the Biblioteca de Catalunya, Barcelona, with the shelfmark Inc, 7 and lacks the first and last folios. A transcription of *M*, an imprint published at Zaragoza by Juana Milián on 15 May 1540, can be found in Appendix VII. The sole witness for the Zaragoza: 1540 imprint is housed in the Biblioteca Nacional, Madrid, shelfmark R 10688.

The following apparatus does not note regular orthographic variation between **v/u**, or between **y/i**. The underlying criterion for judgment was that of phonetic equivalence: if a variant represented a mere spelling difference, it does not appear here. All instances of initial **R** for the multiple vibrant have been regularized as **rr**.

The following abbreviations are used:

ed. = editorial emendation om. = omitted rep. = repeated

Variants and emendations (line numbering is continuous)

1 Capítulo que fabla de los enxemplos de Teodor donzella: *m* om. (two lines of blank space left for rubric); *g* capitulo que fabla de las preguntas que fizieron ala donzella teodor; *h* capitulo que fabla delos enxemplos & castigos de teodor la donzella
2 auía: m uia (blank space left for initial)
2 Bauilonia: *g*; *p* vauilonia; *mh* babilonia
2 mercader: *mg* mercador
2 rrico: *mgh* rrico e bueno
2 e: *g* om.
3 biudas: *h* bybdas
3 tenía: *h* om.
4 tenía: *g* auia
5 muchos: *h* om.
5 aueres: *mgh* florines
5 mostróle: *mg* demostro le; *h* enseñole
7 tienpo: *h* poco
7 allegó: *mgh* llego
7 mercador: *h* mercader
7 grand: *mg* grant
7 dixo: *h* dix
7 sabed: *m* sabet
8 a: *mgh* ha dios

8 gran: *m* grant; *gh* grand
8 non: *h* nin
8 non (2nd): *g* om.
8 aya: *h* aya menester e
9 pues: *m* e pues
9 dadme: *m* datme
9 onde: *g* donde; *h* do
9 aya: *m* aure; *g* avre
9 mejoría e bien: *m* bien e mejoria
10 tierra: *h* la tierra
10 comidiendo: *h* om.
10 ojos (2nd): *h* om.
10 que: *h* de
11 dixo: *m* dixole
11 ydvos: *mg* ytvos
11 al: *h* ala
11 boticarios: *m* buticarios
11 traed: *g* traet
12 lleuad: *mg* leuad
12 Abomelique: *h* abomely que es
12 Almançor: *g* almançor que dios mantenga
13 por: *h* que es
13 dezilde: *h* dezidle
13 peditle: *m* pedilde; *gh* pedidle
14 dixere: *m* dixiere
14 que es: *h* ques
14 dezilde: *h* dezidle
15 terníades: *h* avryades
16 mercador: *h* mercader
16 al: *h* ala
16 de los: *mgh* alos
16 boticarios: *m* buticarios
16 Mahomad: *g* mahmad; *h* mahomada
17 el: *g* om.
17 boticario: *m* buticario
17 mercador: *h* mercader
19 e: *h* om.

19 dél: *mgh* del mercador
19 grand: *m* grant
19 piadad: *mh* piedad
19 e (2nd): *h* om.
19 dixo de: *m* dixo e de
20 amjvazillastes: *m* amanzillastes; *g* mauzillastes; *h* manzillastes
20 fezistes: *g* feziste
21 la vuestra (2nd): *m* vuestra; *g* la
21 e: *h* que
22 boticario: *m* buticario
22 las: *gh* om.
22 nobles afeitamientos para: *h* afeytamiento de
23 mercadero: *mgh* mercador
23 lleuo: *mgh* leuo
23 ella: *h* om.
23 dello: *g* della
23 esto vos sera: *h* estos vos seran
25 vistióse: *h* leuantose e adobose
25 a su señor: *h* om.
25 sobid: *g* subit
26 alcaçar: *g* alcaçeria
26 fuéronse para el: *h* fueron al
26 alcaçar (2nd): *m* alçar
26 pidieron: *h* pedieron
27 mando: *h* mandoles
27 paráronse: *h* apartaronse
27 amos: *mg* entramos; *h* anbos
27 antel: *m* ante el; *h* con el
28 de: *h* a
28 preguntóle: *mgh* pregunto
29 el rrey le dixo: *m* el rrey dixo; *h* dixo el rrey
30 el mercador le dixo: *m* rrespondiole el mercador e; *g* el mercador rrespondio e; *h* dixo el mercador
30 quiero por ella: *h* om.
31 finísymo bermejo: *g* bermejo finsymo [sic]; *h* fino bermejo
31 lo: *g* om.
31 tomó: *m* touo

32 mercadero: *mgh* mercador
32 vos: *mg* bos
32 estendistes: *m* estendiestes
32 o: *mh* e
33 no: *mg* non
33 de cosas que no pueden ser: *h* mas de lo que sabe
33 e rrespondió: *mh* e rrespondiole; *g* rrespondiole
33 mercadero: *mgh* mercador
33 rrey: *gh* om.
34 tengas: *m* tengades
34 mucho: *h* grande
34 ca poco es: *h* om.
34 que: *g* ca
34 moça: *g* maça
35 e entendió: *g* los nobles menesteres; *h* om.
35 nobles: *h* nobres
35 e los nobles menesteres: *g* om.
36 çelado: *h* negado
37 e (2nd): *h* y
37 e ella abaxó el velo de vergüença: *p* rep.
38 semejaua: *h* rrelunbraua
38 al: *m* el; *gh* commo el
38 quando salia: *m* que rrelozia; *g* que rreluzia; *h* om.
38 ese: *h* este
38 más: *g* otra mas
39 quella: *mg* que ella
39 díxole: *mg* e dixole; *h* e dixo
39 señor: *g* sabed señor que; *h* om.
40 a mí dizen: *h* om.
40 díxole: *mgh* dixo
40 aprendistes: *m* aprendiestes
40 e (2nd): *m* om.
41 libro: *m* libro de dios
41 aprendí los quatro libros: *mgh* aprendi mas los quatro vientos
41-42 e las estrellas: *h* las estrellas
42 prometimientos: *mgh* prometimientos de dios
43 fablas de las: *mgh* (added above the line in *p*)

43 filosofía: *mgh* la filosofia
43 e la lógica: *h* om.
44 e el: *mg* e aprendi mas el: *h* e aprendy mas el
44 axedrez: *gh* axedres
44 tañer: *mgh*; *p* taner
44 laúd e; *g* laud
45 baylar e cantar e sotar: *h* vaylar e sotar e cantar
45-46 texer paños de peso: *h* labrar panos de seda
46 e aprendí labrar paños de seda: *mg*; *p* om.; *h* e aprendy texer panos de oro e de peso
46 de todas: *h* aprendy todas
46 otras artes: *g* artes; *h* om.
48 en que oyó: *h* quando
48 palabras: *g* palabras e cosas nobles
49 sus artes: *m* sus cortes; *h* su corte
49 esta: *h* aquella
49 salleron: *m* sallieron; *gh* salieron
50 omnes: *h* onbres
50 todos: *h* todos tres
50 espeçialmente: *h* speçialmente
50 que: *h* om.
50 preguntó: *mgh*; *p* preguntaron
50 e (2nd): *h* om.
51 e dixo la donzella: *h* la donzella le respondio
52-53 la donzella las granadas para los dolientes e: *mg*; *p* el fisico (scribe expunged "fisico"); *h* la donzella para los dolientes
53 almendras: *h* mançanas
53 e (2nd): *g* om.
53 mançanas: *h* almendra
54 e dixo la donzella: *mh*; *p* e dixo; *g* dixo la donzella
54 la (3rd): *m* om.
54 en: *g* om.
54 e la: *m* la; *h* e
55 ascondido: *mgh* esconbrado
55 nuues: *h* nubes
55 alegre: *mg* alegre e
56 sangrador: *h* sabidor

56 omnes: *h* onbres
56 e: *h* e
57 cosa es la: *h* es la cosa
57 encaneçe: *g* caneçe
57 omne: *h* onbre
57-58 quál cosa es … donzella: *g* rep.
58 la: *mgh*; *p* a la (in MS *g* "a" was added above the line, apparently by a later hand)
58 poridad: *m* poridat; *h* porydat descobierta
58 yazer: *h* dormir
58 e (3rd): *h* que
60 pregunto: *m* preguntole
60 baño: *mg*; *ph* vaño
60 e dixo la donzella: *mg*; *p* e dix; *h* dixo la donzella es
60 es: *h* el
60 baño (2nd): *g*; *p* vaño; *m* el baño
62 que sea el baño: ed.; *p* que sea el vaño; *m* que el baño sea; *g* quel baño sea; *h* que el vaño sea
62 sallirá: *m*; *p* saliria; *gh* salira ("saliria" emended to "sallira" based on syntactic requirement for future, supported by readings of other MSS, and the "ll" spelling found elsewhere in MS *p*, for instance at 118vb25)
62 omne: *h* onbre
64 preguntó: *mh*; *pg* preguntaron
64 dixo: *h* rrespondio
65 e (2nd): *mgh* om.
65 manteca e es: *h* om.
65 sanidad: *m* sanidat
66 a: *h* om.
66 dezides: *h* dizes
66 gorda: *mgh*; *p* om.
66 dixo (2nd): *g* dixo a
67 del: *h* de la
67 dezides: *h* dizes
69 gran: *m* grant; *gh* grand
70 sus: *g* los
70 con su rrostro contra: *h* a
70 al rrey: *h* om.

70 sabed: *m* sabet
72 ca: *mgh* que
72 de vos: *g* deso
72 so yo niña pequeña: *m* so moça e niña; *g* soy moça e niña; *h* so niña
72 e so: *h* om.
72 virgen: *g* vergen
72 e (2nd): *h* om.
73 muy gran: *mg* grant; *h* gran
73 que le: *mh* que
74 dolencia e: *h* dolença
74 ouieres: *h* ayas
75 macho: *h* om.
75 que guarde e: *h* om.
75 sabidor: *h* guarde e sea sabidor
75 desto: *m* de esto; *h* om.
76 díxole: *mgh* dixo
76 en qué a ... donzella: *h* om.
76 el varón: *mg* om.
76 dixo: *mg* e dixo
76 la donzella: *g* om.
76-77 tal que viniere a la muger: *m* la muger tal que viniente; *g* la muger tal viniere a; *h* tal la muger dixo la donzella sy la muger fuere tal que sepa o vyniere el
77 talente: *g* talante
78 podrá ser que sane la muger: *m* acaesçe que non podra sanar la muger; *g* acaesçe que no podra sañar la muger; *h* podra la muger sanar
78 yazer: *h* tienpo de yazer
78 en el terçio: *h* el
81 hedad: *mh* hedat
81 dixo: *mg*; *p* dize; *h* rrespondio
81 que: *mg* om.
82 e: *mgh* om.
82 limón: *g* lino (?)
82 e: *g* om.
83 e: *g* om.
83 cinquenta: *m* çinquanta; *g* cinquenta años; *h* quarenta años
83 sesenta: *mh*; *p* setenta; *h* los sesenta

84 e: *gh* om.
84 muger (2nd): *h* om.
84 setenta: *m* los setenta
84 la (2nd): *m* e la
84 de nouenta: *h* ochenta
85 preguntedes: *g* preguntedes de las cosas; *h* preguntes
85 que: *h* es que
85 de todo el mundo: *m* que ay enel mundo todo
85 e: *h* om.
86 sodes: *h* soys
87 e: *g* om.
87 alfaquí: *g* el alfaqui
88 perteneçen: *mh* pertenesçian
88 e: *h* om.
88 la: *h* om.
88 de la lógica: *g* de logica; *h* logica
88 la buena: *g* buena; (the fragment contained in BN Madrid 9055 begins here, at the word "buena")
89 del libro: *h* de los libros
89 de Dios: *g* om.
89 rrespondedme: *m* rrespondet
90 rresponderé: *h* om.
90 e de: *h* om.
90 el: *h* e del
91 Abomelique: *h* abomenalique
92 sobre nos: *g* om.
92 e: *g* om.
92 e dixo la donzella: *g* om.
93 dixo: *h* e dixo
93 seruidme: *mg* seruitme; *h* seruid
93 me (2nd): *h* om.
93 menospreçiedes: *mgh*; *p* menospreçides
93 menospreçiaré: *h* menospresçiaredes e yo no menospresçiare
94 rrespondistes: *m* rrespondiestes
94 quáles son: *mgh*; *p* om.
94-95 juizios e los mandamientos: *g* juizios e los mandimientos; *h* mandamientos e juyzio des

95 de Dios e: *h* om.
95 la donzella: *g* om.
95 son: *mgh* om.
96 glosad: *m* glosat
96 perdonar: *m* perdonat; *h* perdonad
96 ouieres: *m* ouieredes; *h* ouierdes
96 fuéredes: *h* fuerdes
96-97 poderoso e grande: *h* poderosos e grandes
97 alto delante: *h* ante
97 alfaquí: *mg* alfaqui donzella
97 dexistes: *m* dixiestes
97 e (2nd): *g* om.
98 e: *g* om.
98 el Criador e: *mgh* om.
98 non ha: *m* ha; *h* non ho
99 mundad: *mh* mundat; *g* unidat (?)
99 alfaquí: *mh*; *pg* fisico
101 e: *h* om.
101 estonçe: *g* entonçe; *h* estonçes
101 e (2nd): *h* om.
101-102 e puso en … çielos: *g* om.
102 ellos: *h* ellas
102 vna: *h* et una
102 otra: *h* otro
103 gentes: *h* otras gentes
103 alfaquí: *m* alfaqui donzella
103 dexistes: *m* dixiestes
103 e (3rd): *h* om.
105 glosad: *m* glosat
105 Geminis: *g* gemis
106 Taurus: *g* tauros
106 Geminis: *m* om.; *g* gemines
106 Escorpius: *h* scorpius
106 Capicornius: *h* caprycornius
107 fuere quito de pecado: *h* confesare sus pecados
107 e (2nd): *h* om.
107-108 non será oyda … pecado: *g* om.

108 castidad: *mh* castidat
109 e: *h* om.
109 de: *h* del
110 dexistes: *m* dixiestes
110 omne: *h* onbre
110 de: *mg* om.
111 las: *m* la
111 azeytunas: *h* azetunas
112 las otras: *h* om.
112 que Dios les diere: *mh* que dios le diere; *g* vedadas
112 leuantóse el: *g* om.
112 e (2nd): *g* om.
112-113 señor por uerdad: *m* señor por verdat; *h* por verdat señor
113 más sabe esta donzella: *mg* esta donzella mas sabe; *h* esta donzella sabe mas
113 mejoría: *m* la mejoria
114 grand: *m* grant; *h* muy gran
114 al otro que fablase: *h* el rrey que fablase el otro
115 a la: *h* om.
115 rresponded: *m* rrespondet
115 la: *mgh*; *p* a la
116 merçet: *mgh* merçed
116 del Criador: *h* de dios
116 Abomelique: *h* abomenelique
117 físico: *g* alfaqui
117 donzella dezitme: *g* donzella dezidme; *h* dezidme donzella
117 confaçión: *g* confuçion
117 cuerpo o del: *g* om.; *h* cuerpo del
117 omne: *h* onbre
118 donzella: *mg* donzella al fisico
118 Dios: *gh* om.
118 tenpró: *mgh*; *p* tenplo
118 humidad: *h*; *p* humanidad; *m* humidat
119 humidad: *gh*; *p* hunidad; *m* humidat
119 abafó: *g* abaho (?)
119 fuese: *mgh*; *p* om.
120 bafos: *m*; *p* bafas (scribe added "ba" above the line); *g* bahos; *h* vafos

120 federían: *g* fedrian; *h* federan
120 nuestros fuelgos: *g* los huelgos
120 el çielo: *h* tierra
120 e la: *mg* e en la; *h* e contra el çielo
120 el omne: *h* lonbre
120 es: *m* commo es
121 e fuego: *m*; *pgh* om.
121 ayre: *h* ayre e fuego
121 e (6th): *m* om.; *h* e dixo la donzella
122 año: *mgh*; *p* ayre
122 ynuierno e: *h* yuyerno
122 e estío e otoño e: *h* estio otoño
123 a: *h* es
124 conplisiones: *h* cosas
124 según: *m* segunt; *h* segunde
124 fueren menester: *h* que pertenesçen
126 dezidme: *h*; *p* om.; *mg* dezitme
127 aquella: *mg*; *p* a aquella; *h* la
127 diez e ocho señales: *h* deziseys señales o deziocho
127-128 e dixo el físico ... señales: ed.; *mg* e dixo el fisico dezitme quales son estas diez e ocho señales
128 la donzella: *h* om.
129 e blanca en tres: *mg*; *p* om.; *h* e angosta en tres e blanca en tres e negra en tres
129 bermeja: *mg* prieta; *h* vermeja
129 e prieta en tres: *h* om.
129 prieta: *mg* bermeja
130 dezid: *mg* dezit
130 dixo la donzella: *h* digo que
130 de estado: *h* destado
131 blanca: *m* e blanca
132 prieta: *mh* e prieta
132 cabellos: *h* a cauellos
132 e (2nd): *m* e pestañas prietas e; *h* e las cejas pryetas e
132 prieto: *h* om.
132 prieto (2nd): *h* negro que sea prieto
132-133 e las cejas prietas: *g*; *pmh* om.

133 e: *h* om.
133 mexillas bermejas e beços bermejos e ensías bermejas: *h* labros maxillas enzias
133 ensías: *mg* enzias
134 nariz pequeña: *g* naris pequeña; *h* narizes pequenas
134-135 ancha de espaldas e ancha: *mg*; *p* ancha de caderas ("caderas" expunged); *h* espaldas e ancha a
135 fruente: *m* frente
135 placentera: *mgh* plazentera
135 ayudadora: *m* ayudadora a su marido; *gh* ayudadera
136 hedad: *mh* hedat
136 leuantóse: *h* leuantos
137 verdat: *g* verdad
137 yo vos digo que: *g* om.
137 que esta: *p* rep.
137-138 que sabe más: *g* mas sabe
138 luego: *h* om.
140 Abrahán: *mgh* abrahen
140 e (2nd): *g* om.
140 de (2nd): *h* om.
141 aquellos: *mgh* los
141 auedes ençerrado e vencido: *h* vencidos o enterrados auedes
142 que (2nd): *m* om.
142 Abrahán: *mgh* abrahen
142 trobador: *mg*; *p* trobadodor; *h* trouador
142 la donzella: *gh* ella
143 Abrahán: *mgh* abrahen
143 vos: *h* os
143 asentad: *m* asentat
143 preguntadme que: *mg*; *p* om.; *h* preguntad que
144 nuestro señor el rrey: *h* el rrey nuestro señor
144 Abrahán: *mgh* abrahen
145 sy: *h* que sy
145 rrespondierdes: *mg* rrespondedes; *h* respondierdes
145 çiertamente: *h* om.
145 que: *mh* que yo
145 que vos: *h* os

146 sy: *h* que sy
146 rrespondierdes: *m* rrespondedes
146 que: *p* que yo que ("yo" expunged)
146 que me dedes: *mh*; *p* de; *g* me dedes
146 los (2nd): *h* om.
147 nos: *h* om.
148 a vos e: *h* de vos
148 otorgógelo: *mg*; *p* otorgolo; *h* otorgojelo
148 amos: *h* anbs
149 e: *g* om.
149 Abrahán el: ed.; *p* abrahan; *mg*; abrahen el; *h* abrahun
149 cosa: *mgh*; *p* cossa
149 que: *mh* que la
150 quel: *mgh* que el
151 quel: *mh* que el
151 talante: *m* talente
153 ay en ella: *mg* en ella ay
154 Dios: *h* dio
155 rrespondiόle: *mg* e rrespondiole; *h* e rrespondio
155 díxole: *m* om.
155 es: *h* om.
156 quel: *mg* que el
156 es (2nd): *h* om.
157 el (2nd): *g* om.
158 e: *h* om.
158 quel: *mh* que el
158 verdad: *m* verdat
158 talante: *mh* talente
159 solaz: *g* solas
159 baño: *mg*; *ph* vaño
160 siete: *mgh*; *p* tres
160 e: *h* om.
160 es (2nd): *h* om.
160 su: *h* om.
161 a: *h* ay
161 señales: *m* maneras
161 animales: *mg* animalias; *h* alymañas

161 es: *h* el
162 çigarra: *g* çigara
162 quel: *mh* que el
163 avestruz: *g* abestruz
164 Abráan: *m* abrahen; *g* abrahem; *h* brahen
164 el: *h* om.
164 sed çierto que sabe esta donzella: *h* sabed que esta donzella sabe
165 e avn: *mgh* om.
165 vos: *h* om.
165 tenedes: *m* tenes
165 le: *mgh*; *p* les
165 mejoría: *h* mejoria e yo gela do
166 Abomelique: *m* abemelique
166 vos (2nd): *mh* om.
167 rrespondistes: *m* rrespondiestes
167 a todas: *h* om.
167 aquellas cosas: *m* estas cosas; *h* om.
167 a estos sabios quellos: *m* que aquellos sabios; *g* que; *h* a estos sabios
167 e: *gh* om.
167 yo: *g* yo e todos estos sabios; *h* om.
167-168 vos preguntamos: *h* om.
168 vos rrespondistes: *m* rrespondiestes; *h* rrespondiste
168 ellas: *h* todas las preguntas
168 dicho: *mg* el rrey; *h* el rrey abomenique
168 Abrahán: *mh* abrahen
169 despojó: *h* desnudo
169-170 e diólos a ... paños: *h* om.
169 Abraán: *m* abrahen; *g* brahen
170 dad: *m* dat
171 Abraám: *mgh* abrahen
171 buen: *mgh* om.
171 non pasar: *h* que non pasase
171-172 le fuera: *h* om.
172 menores: *m* om. ("me" added above the line in *p*)
172 le: *g* om.
172 le ouiera de ... rrey: *h* ally delante el rrey le ouieran de quitar
172 del: *g* el

173 luego: *g* luengo
173 pedid: *mg* pedit
173 dezidme: *m* dezit; *g* dezitme
173 queredes: *h* querres
174 la: *h* om.
174 casa: *m* casa o
174 ca: *mgh* que
174 çierta: *h* çierto
174 daré: *mg* de
174 demandardes: *m* demandares; *h* quesyerdes
175 dixo: *mh* dixole
175 e (3rd): *m* om.
176 enbiad: *mg* enbiat
176 ca: *mgh* que
176 otro: *h* a otro
176 saluo: *gh* sy non
176 que me crió: *g* om.
177 e: *mgh* quanto mas que
177 allegar en: *mgh* llegar a
177 mostró: *h* enseño
177 luego dar: *g*; *p* luego dar luego; *m* dar; *h* luego
179 antel: *h* ante el
179 rrey: *m* om.
179-180 en adelante: *m* adelante para sienpre jamas
181 Deo gracias: *m* om.

APPENDICES

Norms for the paleographic transcriptions provided in these appendices are based generally on the Madison, Wisconsin Seminary of Hispanic Studies transcription norms (see *Hispanic Seminary* for details). Some obvious differences include the use of "ñ" rather than "n~" and of "ç" rather than "c'".

Paragraph markers (also known as *calderones*) are given as %. A % symbol followed by the number 2 denotes text continued from the previous line. The "et" sign is represented by &. The expansion of abbreviations is marked with braces, i.e. q<ue>. The symbol "\" denotes a letter written above the line. Square brackets mark an addition, either by the scribe [^] or by the editors [ ]. Round brackets indicate a suppression, again either by the scribe (^) or by the editors ( ).

The column boundaries are indicated by {CB. at the beginning and } at the end. Rubrics {RUB.} and initials {IN.} are indicated where they occur.

Biblioteca de Catalunya, Barcelona, Inc. 7 (incomplete)

This book is missing its first and last folios. It has no illustrations.

[fol. 1r; sig. aII recto]
{CB1.
cho ruego fija mia señora q<ue> vos me q<ue>rays co<n>sejar d<e> lo
q<ue> a vuesdtro entendimie<n>to mas le parescera q<ue> yo deue
hazer: que segun la mucha sciencia v<uest>ra yo te<n>go gra<n> co<n>-
fia<n>ça: que co<n> vuestro co<n>sejo yo sere remediado & haure
manera co<n> que me pueda ma<n>tener & salir de mis trabajos. E la donzella teodor: como esto oyo hablar a su señor: vuo d<e>llo muy gra<n> tristeza & pesar: & abaxo sus ojos
a tierra: & començo de llorar: & estuuo asi vna gra<n> pieça que no fablo pensa<n>do en su coraço<n>. E desque vuo bi-
en pensado & mirado ensu entendimie<n>to el cobro q<ue> podia dar a su señor el qual la hauia criado: & gastado co<n>
ella d<e> sus thesoros enla mostrar todo lo que sabia. Alço la cabeça & dixo le: esforçad señor mio: & no tomeys
cuytado d<e> cosa alguna: & tened buena espera<n>ça en nuestro señor dios que el vos ayudara: & os dara bue<n> consejo co<n> que salgays deste trabajo & d<e>la gra<n> pobreza en
q<ue> agora estays & no cureys d<e> mas pe<n>sar sobre esto. que
dios os porna cobro. Pore<n>de leua<n>tad vos luego & yd
vos para los joyeros & trahed me co<m>posturas: & afeytes co<n> q<ue> se afeyta<n> las mugeres & trahed me paños de
fina color p<ar>a q<ue> me vista: & vestir los he & co<m>poner me
he co<n> ellos. & despues q<ue> you sea afeytada & co<m>puesta leuar me heys al rey admiramamolin alma<n>çor & d<e>zid le
que me quereys vender. & qua<n>do el os preguntare que
es lo que por mi querys / respondelde enesta manera.
Señor yo vengo a vuestra alteza co<n> gra<n> menester q<ue> te<n>-
go con esta donzella / si os plaze de me la comprar / yo
gela ve<n>dere por lo que iusto sea. & si el rey os preguntare: por quanto precio me dareys: dezid que querys
por mi diez mill doblas d<e> bue<n> oro vermejo. E si el rey
se marauillare del precio que por mi dema<n>days / dezilde assi. Señor no se marauille vuestra alteza: porque}
[fol. 1v, sig. aII verso]
{CB1.
yo os dema<n>do este precio por esta do<n>zella / que verda-

deramente mucho mas vale de lo que yo os demando por ella. E desque el mercadero houo oydo el consejo quye la donzella le dio / conoscio que era muy bien
camino para su remedio: & fue se luego para los mer-
caderos que venden joyas: & hablo con hun moro que
llamauan mahuma / que era grandissimo amigo suyo
El qual moro vendia de todas maneras de mercaderias / asi de trapo: oro / & seda / como de joyeria & espe-
cieria. E entrando el mercader enla tienda / conto al
moro todos sus trabajos & miseria en que era venido
por sus grandes peccados. E el moro doliendo se del
le respondio assi. Verdaderamente mi gran amigo:
quebrantado has mi coraçon: & los mis ojos has fe-
cho llorar por la gran cuyta & trabajo que tienes. Empero demanda agora delo que yo tengo que sepas por
cierto que no te sera negado: que yo telo dare de muy
buena voluntad: & co<n> lo q<ue> yo te diere: plega a nuestro
señor que tu & tu do<n>zella ayas buen p<ro>uecho & ventura
E dixo le el mercader. amigo sepas q<ue> yo he menester
vnos paños d<e> muy fina color: & afeytes muy escogidos para el rostro. & esto quiero para mi do<n>zella para
la atauiar. & d<e>spues sepas amigo mio que la quiero leuar a vender al rey: porque yo pueda salir de trabajo.
E despues que el mercader huuo acabada su razon el
joyero le dio los paños & afeytes tales & ta<n> buenos como gelos hauia dema<n>dado. E el mercader desque lo
tomo: dio muchas gracias a dios por ello: porque hauia fallado ta<n> buen recaudo en aquel su amigo d<e> todo
lo que hauia menester para su do<n>zella: E dixo en su coraçon. Si al señor dios pluguiere esto sera buen comienço: & vino se luego para su casa co<n> sus paños & afey-}
[fol. 2r; sig. b[sic]III recto]
{CB1.
tes: & dio lo todo ala do<n>zella. E ella se alegro mucho
con ello: por qua<n>to ella era mucho hermosa & los paños & afeytes era<n> buenos / por lo qual ella fue muy co<n>-
te<n>ta & dixo al mercadero su señor. Alegrad vos señor
haued plazer que esto sera comienço d<e> vuesto bien si
al señor dios pluguiere. E la do<n>zella tomo los paños
& vestio se los. Los quales le venia<n> ta<n> bien como si fueran cortados a su medida: & tomo los afeytes & afey-
to se con ellos lo mejor que pudo. E quando la donze-

lla teodor fue vestida & afeytada parescia la mas hermosa & mas gentil & bella q<ue> se pudiesse fallar enel mu<n>-
do. E entonçe leuo la el mercader ante el rey admiramamolin almançor. El qual se contentaua mucho de
ver gentiles mugeres & hermosas donzellas.
{RUB. % Titulo segu<n>do que fabla como leuo
el mercadero a su donzella ante el rey a su alcaçar. & dize lo que dixo el rey ala donzella & la respuesta que dio
la do<n>zella al rey.}
{IN3.} Dize el cuento que aquel merca-
der leuo su do<n>zella teodor a<n>te el rey miramamolin almançor al su alcaçar do<n>de el estaua. &
fablo con el portero rogando le mucho que le abriesse:
& le dexasse entrar: porque que queria fablar con el rey
& el portero le abrio luego la puerta dezie<n>do le q<ue> entrasse en bue<n> hora. E el mercader entro luego: & fue se co<n>
su do<n>zella para la camara donde estaua el rey. & saluo
al rey & a todos los que ay estauan. E humillando se a
el hizo le gran reuerencia: & beso la tierra ante el rey: &
allegaro<n> se mas & besaro<n> le las manos. & el rey p<re>gu<n>to
al mercader: & dixo le. di amigo q<ue> te plaze: o q<ue> es lo q<ue>}
[fol. 2v; sig. b[sic]III verso]
{CB1.
q<ui>eres. E luego el mercader le respo<n>dio & dixo le. Señor traygo a v<uest>ra alteza esta do<n>zella si le plaze de me la
co<m>prar. E el rey le dixo q<ue> si co<m>praria & q<ue> dixiesse qua<n>to
q<ue>ria por ella. E el mercader le dixo q<ue> q<ue>ria diez mill do-
blad d<e> bue<n> oro vermejo. E el rey marauillo se mucho
d<e>l mercader por q<ue> tal p<re>cio demandaua & dixo le. Amigo mucho dema<n>das por ella / o tu eres fuera de seso / o
la donzella se alaba de tan grandes cosas que por ventura no sabe hazer. & el mercader respondio al rey de-
ziendo. Señor no lo tengays a marauilla: porq<ue> yo os
dema<n>do ta<n> gra<n> precio por esta do<n>zella: ca haueis de saber que sabe tantas maneras d<e. sciencias / que yo creo
que no ay sabio que la pueda vençer: ho<m>bre ni muger.
porq<ue> yo señor despe<n>di co<n> ella gra<n> tesoro por la fazer enseñar. lo q<ua>l ella depre<n>dio & tiene muy bie<n> estudiado de
todas maneras d<e> scie<n>çias q<ue> puede<n> ser escritas & sabios
letrados pueda<n> saber por todo el mu<n>do: asi ho<m>bres como mugeres. & el rey qua<n>do esto oyo / miro mucho a-
la donzella: & mando que se tirasse el manto que traya

puesto sobre los ojos: & que alçasse el velo / & lo pusiesse sobre la cabeça. E la donzella tiro lo luego. E fizo
quanto el rey le man do. E alli vido el rey la gran fermosura & beldad que la donzella tenia. E le precio la
mas hermosa que visto hauia en toda su vida & plugo le mucho co<n> su vista & pregunto le q<ue> le dixiesse como hauia no<m>bre. & la do<n>zella le respo<n>dio co<n> muy gran
vergue<n>ça & humilmente dizie<n>do le assi muy esclaresci-
do señor rey vuestra alteza sabra q<ue> ami llama<n> teodor
E el rey le dixo. Theodor plego te de me dezir que
es la sciencia que deprendiste de todos los saberes deste mundo. E la do<n>zella le respo<n>dio & dixo le. Señor}
[fol. 3r; sig. aIII recto]
{CB1.
rey vos d<e>ueys saber q<ue> el primer saber q<ue> yo depre<n>di es
la ley d<e> dios. & sus ma<n>damie<n>tos & d<e>pre<n>di mas todos
los sermones suyos los quales el ma<n>do alos sus san-
tos p<ro>fetas q<ue> fiziesen & d<e>prendi mas todas las co<m>pli-
siones d<e>los q<ua>tro elime<n>tos. & d<e>prendi mas el arte d<e>la
estrelleria / & las planetas & los cursos & mouimientos
d<e>llas & las casas en q<ue> mora cada vna dellas & conosco
los no<m>bres d<e>las estrellas las q<ua>les crio dios nuestro se
ñor e<n>los sus altos cielos. & d<e>pre<n>di mas la habla delas
animalias. E deprendi mas la ynnoce<n>çia & el arte de
la nigromançia & las hablas d<e> todas las otras cosas
E deprendi mas los setenta & dos lenguajes / que son
por todo el mundo:> asi de cristianos como de iudios &
moros. & de todas las leyes & cerimonias. E deprendi mas de medicina & çurugia. & todo lo tengo bie<n> estudiado & probado. E deprendi mas la sotil geometria
& Gra<m>mattica & Logica / & la natura della. E deprendi mas el arte de la Poesia / & Musica / & se tanger todos estormentos de pluma & de mano & todas quantas maneras tangen por todo el mundo: & deprendi
mas las treynta & tres maneras & artes que son fonda-
das en el arte de trobar: & toda la manera dello & se los
nombres de cadauna. & por ser mas cierta enesta arte
deprendi el motejar / & cantar / & baylar & dançar: &
los passos que se requiere<n> & pertenescen para cada vna
dança: & se tangeres viejos & nueuos: & ala llana: &
canto: & tenor: & contras: & otros ca<n>tares: & muchos
romançes cantados: & se fazer muchas canticas vie-

jas & nueuas: & se asonar las muy bien & se tañer laud
& viuela acordanças muy marauillosas: E aprendi
mas coser: assi de lienço como de paño para honbres}
[fol. 3v; sig. aIII verso]
{CB1.
& para mugeres: & se fazer q<ual>quier ropa: & labrar de seda / de oro / & de rodilla: & de bastidor: assi de vna faz como de dos: & se debuxar ymagines para fazer çanefas
para las yglesias / & broslar las: & se fazer las inuencio-
nes: asi para los caualleros como para las damas para bruslar en sus ropas. asi como seda & oro & aljofar:
& se deuisar toda manera d<e> arge<n>teria: & se ylluminar libros & asentar oro con sisa / & todas las otras colores
de matizes pertenescie<n>tes. E otrosi se conoscer todas
maneras d<e> piedras preciosas / asi las que son finas como las que no lo son: & se las muy bien sericar & cortar
& polir: & dar les colores segun pertenescen a cada pie-
dra: & se bie<n> engasonar las en oro / o en plata. & se mas
la valor d<e> cadauna segun que es: & conosco las que son
orientales / o bla<n>cas. E se conoscer aljofar granado &
menudo & su valor de cada vno dello. & se amasar lo co<n>
çumo d<e> limones en tabla de vidrio. & se mas texer paños de brocado / o d<e> seda: & poner enellos todas labo-
res gra<n>des como pequeñas: asi ralas como espessas.
E se texer paños de oro & de seda bellutados & rasos
paños de damasco & baldoquin & zarrahanas & otros
paños moriscos.
{RUB. % Titulo tercero como se marauillo el
rey delas cosas que dixo la do<n>zella teodor que sabia fazer por la q<ua>l razon ma<n>do luego que llamassen a todos
sus sabios para disputar con ella}
{IN3.} Uenidos q<ue> fuero<n> los sabios ma<n>-
do el rey que disputassen con la donzella pues
que tanto se loaua que sabia por ver si era assi
verdad todo aquello q<ue> dezia. E de todos aquellos sa-}
[fol. 4r; sig. b (sic) V recto]
bios que alli fueron ayuntados mando el rey que fuessen escogidos tres: los quales sabian mas q<ue> todos los
otros sabios. Los quales hablaron luego con la donzella en razon de disputa. E muy gran sabidor en todas las leyes: & en todos los ma<n>damie<n >tos de dios: &
el otro era sabidor & gran letrado enla sciencia dela lo-

gica / & dela çurugia: & era muy gran astrologo & filo-
sopho: & en todas las artes era muy ente<n>dido: & conoscia bien todas naturalezas & cosas deste mundo: & sabia obrar todas cosas. El tercero era sabidor enla in-
nocencia; & en gram<m>atica & logica. & era maestro en todas siete artes liberales. E estonces el primero d<e>los
tres sabios hablo primero con la donzella: & dixo le asi
Por manera de desden: teniendo la por simple & nescia
Tu donzella responder me has a todas las cosas q<ue> yo
te preguntare. E la donzella le respondio luego segun
adela<n>te oyreys. Señor & discreto sabio: yo vos respo<n>-
dere co<n> la ayuda d<e> dios padre: plaziendo a mi señor el
rey admiramamolin almançor que dios mantega su alteza: el qual esta presente co<n> toda su caualleria & nobles
ho<m>bres d<e>la su real corte: y co<n> su lice<n>cia & mandado yo
vos respondere. Estonçes dixo le el sabio que le respo<n>-
diesse a todo lo q<ue> el le p<re>guntase apriessa & sin detardar:
& la donzella dixo que le plazia: & comiençо por la manera que se sigue.
{RUB. % Titulo quarto dela primera disputa
que houo el primero sabio con la donzella.}
{IN3.} El sabio le dicho do<n>zella plega
te d<e> no te enojar: pues q<ue> aq<u>i` estamos delante
d<e>l rey: co<n>uiene q<ue> cadauno sea desaminado co<n>}
[fol. 4v; sig. b (sic) V verso]
{CB1.
gran diligençia: y que seamos bien determinados por
sabios: & por letrados qual de nosotros ha de ser vençido: o leuar la mejoria tu: o yo E la donzella dixo que
de aquello que el dizia / le plazia a ella mucho. E pregunto le entonçes el sabio & dixo le. Donzella responde me a esto que te dire agora. Di me quales son las
cosas que crio el muy alto & muy poderoso nuestro dios en los secretos & muy altos cielos. A esta p<re>gunta
le respondio la sabia discreta do<n>zella e dixo le assi Señor maestro deueys saber que nuestro señor dios crio
en los altos cielos siete planetas: las quales son estos
q<ue> yo agora os dire. El sol / la luna / las estrellas: saturno / iupit<er> / mars / ven <us> / & mercurio E otrosi co<m>puso doze signos: los q<ua>les son . aries. taur<us>. geminis. ca<n>cer.
leo. v<ir>go. libra. scorpi<us>. capricorn<us>. aq<ua>ri<us>. & piscis. E
mas crio nuestro señor dios en sus altos cielos los si-
ete cielos. & co<m>puso las quatuor partes del mu<n>do. La

primera parte es la nobleza de todas las mares: & la
segunda es la nobleza de la tierra: & la tercera es la nobleza d<e> todas las criaturas: & la quarta es los diablos
por que las gentes los aborrezcan. E dixo le el sabio
bien has dicho donzella: & pregu<n>to le mas: qual es la
cosa mejor que los ho<m>bres deuen fazer para que gane<n>
la gloria de parayso: que es aq<ue>lla gloria de dios. La
donzella le respondio & dixo assi. Señor maestro sabed
que dios querria que el ho<m>bre de cada dia hezisse oracion sin pensar en las cosas del mundo & que fexiesse li-
mosna a p<er>sonas enuergo<n>çadas & aq<ue>llos q<ue> lo ha<n> menester: & este tal ho<m>bre puede yr a parayso: E aq<ue>l q<ue> no faze limosnas no puede yr a parayso ni es reçebida sua
oracion: teniendo los bienes temporales para los po-}
[fol. 5r]
{CB1.
der dar. E el sabio le dixo: bien has dicho. E p<re>gunto
le mas. Di me donzella quales son las propiedades q<ue>
tiene cadauno de los meses para mantenimie<n>to deste
mundo.[31] La donzella le respondio. Enel mes de enero

---

[31] The text at this point digresses from its debate structure and offers a detailed calendar containing information concerning the labors of the months, useful astrological data, medical advice, and hygienic recommendations for each month. This kind of calendar circulated widely throughout the Middle Ages. The earliest known calendar of this type is the tenth-century *Calendario de Córdoba*. Similar expositions of information appeared throughout the Middle Ages. Books of Hours often dedicated a section of the text to the various activities of the year (Harthan 23-26). The *LAlex*, for example, has a similar digression (stanzas 2555-66) in which the labors of months of the year are discussed. The calendar of the *HDT* resembles the medical and hygienic calendars associated with the *regimen duodecim mensium* tradition. As the studies of Keil, Riha, and García-Ballester have shown, during the Middle Ages medical practitioners frequently relied on these hygienic *regimina* for diagnosing and preventing illnesses. The *regimina* typically contained *Lunaria*, calendars describing the most favorable periods for blood-letting, descriptions of the relationships between the signs of the zodiac and the parts of the body (*melosthesia*), and other factors which might influence the health of a patient. A third element of the calendar in the *HDT* is its preoccupation with agricultural information. Much of this information is borrowed from agricultural treatises based the *Opus agriculurae* of Palladius. A translation of Palladius into Aragonese was made in the mid-fourteenth century. The main source for the calendar in the *HDT* is Andrés de Li's

siendo vieja la luna deues alimpiar las arboles q<ue> per-
den la foja & es tie<m>po despuesto para traspla<n>tar: enxerir: cauar las viñas los rosales: & los gezmines: & raer & e<n>trecauar el alfalfa: & boluer los barbechos: & pla<n>-
tar q<ua>lquier generaci<n> de ligumes. Deues vsar en este
mes los baños & sa<n>grias: & los manjares & potages
claros. & calie<n>tes de su natura: & no deues suffrir que
se leua<n>te el estomago dela mesa con sed.[32]
% Enel mes de febrero es muy bueno podar las viñas
e se<m>brar algunos legumes / melones / & pepinos. E en
la luna nueva es muy propia cosa traspla<n>tar narange-
ros / limonares / & arrayanes / & enxerir los arboles
con agua / & sembrar lino. Es tie<m>po despuesto para conoscer las colmenas por si se pone<n> arnas en ellas / o si
quieren enxambrar. E para sangrar q<ua>lquier membro
de la persona. E en este mes es peligroso el mal en los
pies[33] % Enel mes de março es bueno alimpiar los sembrados delas yeruas dañosas & en la luna nueua plan-

---

Repertorio de los tiempos, Burgos, Fadrique de Basilea, May 21st, 1493. Li's richly illustrated text contains extensive information on the months of the year, the phases of the moon, a calendar of festive days, extensive exposition of astrological information, a guide to blood-letting, and woodcuts depicting the labors of the year.

[32] The *Compendio* makes the following observations: "En enero se deuen continuar los mañares calientes et claros et por no venir en dolencias se deuen tomar algunos liquores. No se deue pensar en sangria si necessidad no la forçare deuen se esquivar las viandas crudas et dañosas...es prouechoso entrar en baños" [*Compendio* fol. 15v]. The *Reportorio de los tiempos* observes: "En aqueste mes siendo vieja la luna deues alimpiar los arboles que pierden la foja. y es tiempo dispuesto para trasplantar e enxerir para cauar las viñas los rozales e los gezmines: e para raer e entrecavar el alfalfa: e bouer los barbechos: e para plantar qualquiere generacion de legumes. Deues vsar en aqueste mes los baños y las sangrias e los manjares e potajes claros: e calientes de su natura. e no deues suffrir que se leuante el estomago dela mesa con sed" [Li2 sig. D1 verso].

[33] The *Compendio* observes that in January: "Es malo tener mal enlas camas et avn enlos pies" (fol.15r). Andrés Li prescribes: "En aqueste mes es muy bueno podar las viñas et sembrar algunos legumes: melones y pepinos. e en la luna cosa trasplantar naranjeros: limon con ajuja" (Li2 sig. D2 verso).

tar rasgalios d<e> arboles. Es tie<m>po enel qual enge<n>dran
muchos males humores & dolores grandes en cuerpos humanos. Son peligrosas las dole<n>çias de la cabeça: & de los oydos mas que de ninguna otra parte
del cuerpo delas personas.[34]
% % Enel mes de abril deues sembrar el alfalfa: & el cañamo: & cortar les colmenas por sacar dellas la miel
& la cera. E si touieres polomar deues dexar los polu<m>-
minos que nascen enel para criar: por que salen mejo-}
[fol. 5v]
{CB1.
res q<ue> de ningu<n> otro tie<m>po del año. En este mes cresce
mucho la sangre: & purgar se es muy salutifero. & q<ua>lq<u>i`-
er mal e<n>la garga<n>ta es muy peligroso: especialme<n>te pa- [35]

---

[34] This observation is a commonplace in the *regimina* of the Middle Ages. In the *Regimen sanitatis* there appears the following:

> Nil capitis facies, *Aries* cum luna refulget;
> In manu minuas et balnea tutius intres;
> Non tanges nares, nec barbam radere debes. [*Collectio*, I:486]

The *Compendio* reflects the same concerns: "Son muy peligrosas las dolencias dela cabeça et delos oydos" [*Compendio* fol. 13v]. The Spanish translation of Johannes de Ketham links this recommendation to construction: "No es bueno començar de obrar torre o castillo o casi ni es provechoso ponerse ventosas en los braços e manos. Son muy peligrosas las dolencias de la cabeça e de los oydos" [Johannes 39]. Andrés de Li makes the following observations: "En aqueste mes es bueno alimpiar los sembrados de las yervas dañosas y en la nueva plantar rasgalios de arboles. Es tiempo en el qual se engendran muchos malos humores: y dolores grandes en los cuerpos humanos. Son peligrosos las dolencias de la cabeça y los hoydos mas que ninguna otra parte del cuerpo" [Li sig. D3 verso].

[35] The *Regimen sanitatis* from Salerno offers the following advice concerning activities under the sign of Taurus:

> Aedificari potes, et spergas semina terrae
> Et medicum timeat cum ferro tangere collum. [*Collectio*, I:486]

The observations are also present in other medical writings. For example, Johannes de Ketham states: "Es signo del mes de Abril e tiene dominio sobre la garganta,

% % Enel mes d<e> mayo deues ra- %2 ra labrar lo co<n> fierro
her los açafranales: porq<ue> no se faga<n> ratones en ellos/
& es tie<m>po dispuesto para esq<u>i`lar el ganado. & ansi mes-
mo para cortar las colmenas. Las dole<n>cias e<n>los braços en aq<ue>ste mes son peligrosas. & si touieres mal en
las manos o vñas no co<n>sientas q<ue> te sea<n> labradas co<n> fi-[36]
En<el mes d<e> junio es bueno enxerir a escudere %2 erro.
qua<n>do es vieja la luna. & deues sembrar el panizo & daça: & el mijo: & arra<n>car los ajos: & sembrar las berças
pla<n>tar los rasgalios delas figueras. E como escriue
Palladio: si en aqueste mes siegas tu trigo en luna vi-

---

hombros e las espaldas del cuerpo humano. E estando la luna en este signo es mala la sangría de los ojos, pescueço e garganta. Es bueno fazer huertos, plantas viñas e árbores porque crecen muy presto e turan mucho. Es bueno edificar casas e tomar mujer y començar todas las obras de madera, comprar heredades y començar de arar. Es malo e peligroso la dolencia en la garganta, en el pescueço, en los ojos e en las uñas" [Johannes 39; also *Compendio* fol. 13v]. Li observes: "En aqueste mes deves sembrar el alfalfa y el cañamo: y cortar las colmenas por sacar dellas la miel et la cera. E si tuvieres palomar deves dexar los palominos que nascen enel para criar: porque salen mejores que de ningun otro tiempo del año. En aqueste mes cresce mucho la sangre: et purgarse es muy salutifero. E qualquiere mal en la garganta es muy peligroso: mayormente para labrarlo con hierro" [Li sig. D4 verso].

[36] The *Regimen sanitatis* from Salerno offers the following advice concerning activities ruled by the sign of Gemini:

> Brachia non minuas cum lustrat luna *Gemillo*;
> Unguibus et manibus cum ferro curam neges,
> Numquam praestabis a promissione petitum. [*Collectio*, I:486]

A similar prescription is given by Johannes de Ketham: "Es malo tomar purga, todas las dolencias de los braços, hombros, spaldas e manos son peligrosas e cortarse la uñas. Es bueno tratar matrimonio, amistades e compañas e yr delante qualquiere juez. Assi mismo de plantar qualquiere cosa" [Johannes 40; see also *Compendio* fol. 13v]. Andrés de Li observes: "En aqueste mes deves raher los açafranales: porque no se fagran ratones en ellos, y es tiempo dispuesto para esquilar el ganado: et ansi mesmo para cortar las colmenas las dolencias en los braços en aqueste mes son peligrosas. E si tuvieres mal en las manos: o uñas no consientas que te sean labradas con fierro" [Li sig. D5 verso].

eja se coseruara mas tiempo que no si se siega enla nueua. La dolencia enlos pechos & en<e>l pulmo<n> & enel higado son peligrosas.[37]

% % En el mes de iulio se acostumbran de sembrar los grumos & luchugas. Es tie<m>po peligroso para sangria & p<ar>a purgar se. Es muy dañoso el sueño de medio dia & no deues entrar en baños. El ajo & la saluia son medicinales. E las dolencias del coraçon & d<e>l stomago son muy peligrosas.[38]

---

[37] The *Regimen sanitatis* offers the following advice under the sign of Cancer:

> Pectus, pulmo, jecur in *Cancro* non minuatur. [*Collectio*, I:486]

Other medical writers make similar recommendations for this month: "Son malas e peligrosas todas las dolencias de los pechos, pulmones e baço e començar de edificar nueua casa" [Johannes 40; *Compendio* fol. 13v]. Along similar lines, Li combines hygienic prescription with agricultural advice: "En aqueste mes es bueno enxerir escudete quando es vieja la luna. E deues sembrar el panizo et la daça. y el mijo et arrancar los ajos: y sembrar las verças: et plantar los rasgalios delas higueras. E como escriue Paladio si en aqueste mes siegas tu trigo en la luna vieja: se conservara mas tiempo: que no si se siega en la nueva. la dolencia en los pechos: y enel pulmon: y enel higado son peligrosas" [Li sig. D6 verso].

[38] The *Regimen sanitatis* from Salerno offers the following advice concerning activities under the sign of Leo:

> Cor gravat stomachum cum cernit luna *Leonum*. [*Collectio*, I:486]

The astrological link appears in other *regimina*: "Es signo del mes de Julio e tiene dominio sobre el coraçon e estómago del cuerpo humano e estando la luna en este signo es mala la sangría / especialmente del coraçon, de los neruios, lombos e esquiuazo. Es bueno començar qualquiere cosa que se ha de hazer con fuego, fundar castillos, entrar en nueva casa, hablar con juezes e principes, firmar matrimonios. Es malo e peligroso tener mal en el estómago y en el coraçón, en los pechos y en los costados e tomar medicinas para el fígado ni avn para otro qualquiere mienbro inferior, emprender luego camino e vestir nueuos vestidos" [Johannes 40-41; *Compendio* fol. 13v-14v]. Kiel edits a poem which matches many of the recommendations in the *HDT* for the month of July:

> Qui wlt solamen julio, probat hoc medicamen:

% Enel mes de agosto deues sembrar berçças: q<ue> suele<n>
enla quaresma hazer los bretones: & los nabos & hauas & arra<n>car las cebollas para que se puedan saluar.
E es muy prouechoso el sembrar ordio & trigos En
este mes la compañia d<e>las mugeres es peligrosa Y ta<m>-
bie<n> el sueño de medio dia. el bañar se es dañoso & el mucho comer; & no se deue nadi sangrar sin necessidad: ni
tomar medicina alguna.[39]}

> Venam non cedat, nec ventrem potio ledat;
> sompnum compescat ac balnea cuncta pauescat,
> nec vinum curet, nec multa commestio duret. lines 25-28 [Kiel 1982, 254]

Webster cites similar prescriptions from a twelfth-century manuscript: "Mense Julio sanguinem non minue, solutionem non accipe, erucam comede, a balneis abstine, potiones diurecticas, salviam et rutam, absinthium, flores apii, et uvae bibe" [Webster 115]. Li provides the textual source for the information printed in the *HDT*: "En aqueste mes se acotumbran de sembrar los grumos y las lechugas. es tiempo peligroso para sangrias: y para purgarse. Et muy dañoso el sueño del medio dia: et no deves entrar en los baños. E en aqueste mes el ajo y la salvia son medicinales. E las dolencias del coraçon y del estomago son muy peligrosas" [Li sig. D7 verso].

[39] The *Regimen sanitatis* from Salerno offers the following advice concerning activities under the sign of Virgo which would include August:

> Lunam *Virgo* tenet, uxorem ducere noli;
> Datur agro semen, dubitat intrare cubilem [*Collectio*, I:486]

Johannes links his recommendation to astrological knowledge: "Es malo de sangrarse en este signo especialmente de los dichos miembros. Es bueno sembrar, culturar la tierra, plantar las viñas e arbores, fazer huertos, començar de scriuir nuevas obras, tratar de paz, vestir nuevos vestidos. Es mala e peligrosa qualquiere dolencia en el vientre e en los otros miembros interiores e tomar mujer ca sera estéril o concebirá muy poco. E tomar medicina es muy provechoso" [Johannes, 41.]. The prohibition of bloodletting occurs in several texts. In the *Poridat* the following advice appears in a section concerning activities for the summertime: "et guardarse de sangrar et de fazer uentosa si non fuere con grant cueyta; nin se trabage mucho, nin siga banno nin mugeres" [*Poridat* 70]. A *regimina* of the Late Middle Ages edited by Riha also recommend avoidance of blood-letting: "In illo mense sanguinem nullus debet minuere, si uitam suam cupit diligere" [Riha 112]. The *Compendio* also provides an analogue to the recommendations for this month: "En el mes de

[fol. 6r]
{CB1.
% % Enel mes de setiembre se acostumbra<n> d<e> vendemiar
las viñas & deues coger las huuas q<ue> quieres para alçar qua<n>do la luna es vieja & enla hora mas caliente d<e>l
dia. En este mes el sembrar los panes es marauillo-
so: la leche es muy prouechosa. Puedes te sangrar sin
peligro. mas las dolencias d<e>los riñones / & d<e>las nalgas son muy dañosas.[40]
% % Enel mes d<e> octubre se deuen coger las granadas /
membrillos / & ma<n>çanas & qualquier fruta sazonada /
para saluar qua<n>do fuere vieja la luna. qualesquier aues
son ento<n>ces plazientes & p<ro>uechosas: qualq<u>i`er llaga es
dificultosa de curar: & las dolençias enlos miembros
ocultos son muy dañosas.[41]

---

agosto deue el hombre dormir poco guardarse de lugares frios et de llegar a mujeres no se deue sangrar mas guardarse de todos los mañares dañosos ni se deue tomar beuenda ni melezina ni entrar en baños." [*Compendio* fol. 15v]. Finally, Andrés de Li observes: "En aqueste mes deues sembrar berças: que fue len enla quaresma hazer los bretones: y los nabos e hauas: e arrancar las cebollas: paraque mucho se puedan saluar. E es muy provechoso el sembrar ordios e trigos. En aqueste mes la compañia de-las mugeres es peligrosa. e tan bien el sueño de medio dia. E es dañoso entrar enlos baños: e el mucho comer. e enel no se deue nadi sangrar ni purgar sin estrema necessidad: ni tomar medicina alguna" (Li2 sig. D8 verso).

[40] The "dolencias" described by the *HDT* calendar for September were commonly associated with the sign of Libra. The *Regimen sanitatis* from Salerno offers the following advice with reference to Libra:

> *Libra* tenet lunam, nemo tangat genitalis,
> Et renes, nates; nec iter capere tentes...[*Collectio*, I:486]

The *Compendio* reflects similar concerns: "el mal del vientre et delos miembros interiores de aquel es peligroso et tan bien en los rinñones..." [*Compendio*, fol. 14v]. Li is the textual source for this section: "En aqueste mes se acostumbran de vendimiar las viñas et deues coger las huvas que quieres parar alçar quando la luna es vieja y en la hora mas caliente del dia. En aqueste mes el sembrar los panes es maravilloso la leche es muy provechosa. Puedes te sangrar sin peligro. Mas las dolencias de los riñones y de las nalgas son muy dañosas" [Li sig. E1 verso].

% % Enel mes de nouie<m>bre enla luna vieja puedes tra-
spla<n>tar q<ua>lquier arbol q<ue> pierde la foja & pla<n>tar & morgonar las vides. & en luna nueua traspla<n>tar cidros & arrayanes. Es tie<m>po dispuesto para curar q<ua>lquier dole><n>-
cia d<e> reuma. & si touieres mal e<n>las piernas es peligroso. Es muy seguro el sangrar & entrar enlos baños.[42]
% % Enel mes d<e> dezie<m>bre puedes tan bien como enel d<e>
arriba pla<n>tar & morgonar las vides: & cortar cañas &
vimbres qua<n>do fuere la luna vieja. Todas las cosas
que son calientes son buenas en este mes. E es segura
la sangria d<e>la vena d<e>la cabeça. La dolençia enlas rodillas es peligrosa.[43]

---

[41] With reference to the "dolencias" associated with October, the *Regimen sanitatis* from Salerno offers the following advice for the sign of Scorpio:

Scorpius autmentat morbos in parte pudenda;
Vulnera ne cures; timeas ascendere naves...[*Collectio*, I:486]

Li once more provides an important hygenic prescription: "En aqueste mes se deuen cojer las granadas: membrillos: y mançanas: y qualquier fruta sazonada para salvar quando fuere vieja la luna. Qualesquiere aves y carnes salvajes son entonces plazientes y provechosas. Qualquier llaga es dificultosa de curar. y las dolencias en los miembros ocultos son muy dañosas" (Li sig. E2 verso).

[42] The prescription of bathing is often present in the recommendations for November:

balnia cum venere tunc nullum constat habere,
hys langwescit, mulieris ydrops quoque crescit.
lines 43-44 [Keil 1982, 254]

Li provides the following advice: "En aqueste mes en la luna vieja puedes trasplantar qualquier arbol que pierda la foja y plantar y morgonar las vides: y en la luna nueva trasplantar cidros y arrayanes. Es tiempo dispuesto para curar qualquier dolencia de reuma. E si tuviere mal en las piernas es peligroso. es muy seguro el sangrar: y entrar en los baños" [Li E3 verso].

[43] The *Regimen sanitatis* from Salerno offers the following observations concerning the sign of Capricorn:

% % E desque esto oyo el sabio: leua<n>to se luego y dixo le
assi a muy altas bozes al rey & alos caualleros. O
muy alto señor rey por verdad vos digo que esto ge-
til donzella q<ue> ante vuestra alteza esta ciertame<n>te ella
sabe mas que yo: & de aqui adela<n>te yo me doy por vencido. & digo q<ue> es la mas sabia d<e> todo el mundo.}
[fol. 6v]
{CB1.
{RUB. % Titulo dela disputa del segu<n>do sabio
que era maestro enlas siete artes liberales}
{IN3.} Despues q<ue> el primero sabio fue
vençido leua<n>to se el segu<ndo>: & dixo le assi. Di me
do<n>zella respo<n>der me has a lo que yo te pregu<n>-
tare. E ella le respondio humildosamente & dixo le.
Maestro señor yo os respondere co<n> la ayuda de dios
& luego el sabio le dixo. Donzella di me quales cosas
son las que crio nuestro señor dios enel cuerpo d<e>l hombre. Respo<n>dio la donzella co<n> humildad. Nuestro señor dios crio enel cuerpo del hombre quatro humores Dixo le el sabio: quales son. Respondio la do<n>zella
Quando te dixe quatro lo deuieras entender. Empero son aquestos. El primero es flema. el segundo me-
la<n>conia. el tercero colera. el quarto sangre. E otrosi dixo la do<n>zella. nuestro señor dios crios quatro tie<m>pos segun los quatro humores suso dichos: los quales son.
inuierno. verano.estio. & otoño. E en cada tiempo destos reyna su humor. Para lo q<ua>l los fisicos han menester hauer conoscimie,n>to destos tiempos: humores: &
las medicinas q<ue> co<n>uienen alas enfermedades segu<n> cada vn tiempo. E dixo le el sabio: bien has respo<n>dido.
E pregunto le mas d<e> todas las frutas q<ua>l es la mas s-

Caper nocet genibus, ipsa cum luna tenebit...[*Collectio*, I:486]

The *Compendio* is equally useful: "Es mala qualquiere sangria especialmente delas rodillas et neruios dellas ni tomar beuendas et es peligrosa qualquiere dolencia enlas rodillas..." [*Compendio* fol. 15r]. Li states: "En aqueste mes puedes tambien como en el de arriba plantar et morgonar vides cañas: y vimbres quando fuere la luna vieja. Todas las cosa calientes son buenas en aqueste mes: y es segura la sangria de la vena de la cabeça. la dolencia en las rodillas es peligrosa" [Li sig. E4 verso].

na. ella respo<n>dio q<ue> era<n> las granadas & los me<m>brillos.
Pregunto le mas el sabio. Que me dizes d<e>las ventosas. Ella respo<n>dio: son muy prouechosas: especialme<n>-
te las que son fechas en martes: porq<ue> esta la luna men-
gua<n>te & en aquel dia el cuerpo del hombre esta desem-
bargado d<e>los malos humores. Pregunto le mas que
me dizes delas sa<n>grias. Ella le respo<n>dio. La sangria
es noble cosa enel tie<m>po q<ue> es menester: porque desem-}
[fol. 7r]
{CB1.
barga & alimpia el cuerpo d<e>los malos humores. Pregunto le mas: qual es la cosa que mas enuegesce al ho<m>-
bre antes de tiempo. Respo<n>dio la do<n>zella: el dormir
mucho con mugeres. Ca dize Aristoteles: fablando
delos luxuriosos: que toda su obra era ponçoñosa: por
que los hombres daua<n> la meyor sangre d<e> su cuerpo: &
que las mugeres daua<n> la peor que tenia<n>. E pregunto
le mas el sabio. Que me dizes d<e>l baño. respo<n>dio le la
donzella. El baño es mucho menester para alimpiar
se el hombre / o la muger antes que vaya a hazer oracion. & para ento<n>ces es bueno. Empero es menester q<ue>
salga luego d<e>l / que no este mucho deleyta<n>do se dentro.
E pregunto le mas el sabio. di me donzella / que me dizes d<e>la carne d<e>la vaca. La donzella le respondio & dixo q<ue> era muy buena & sabrosa. & dixo le mas el sabio: q<ue>
me dizes d<e>la carne d<e>la oueja vieja La do<n>zella le respo<n>-
dio. sabed señor q<ue> la carne d<e>la oueja vieja es el cuero /
en que esta escrita la ley de dios: & el prouecho es el go-
uierno & ma<n>tenimie<n>to. E dixo le mas el sabio ala donzella. que me dixzes d<e>la carne gorda. respo<n>dio le la do<n>-
zella La carne gorda endreça el cuerpo d<e>las personas
& siente el cuerpo co<n> ella gra<n> holgura. E pregunto le
mas que me dizes d<e>la carne magra & flaca. & respo<n>dio
la do<n>zella bie<n> sabes q<ue> esta la be<n>dicio<n> d<e> dios en<e>lla. & re-
spo<n>dio el sabio & dixole: di me do<n>zella q<ua>l es la cosa mas
calie<n>te enel cuerpo d<e>l ho<m>bre. & ella respo<n>dio & dixo. la
cosa mas caliente es la sangre & la vianda que la persona come. E dixo el sabio. bie<n> has dicho do<n>zella. Pregunto le mas el sabio. Di me donzella: qual es el mejor dormir co<n>la muger amenudo o qua<n>do esta en razo<n>
En oye<n>do esto la do<n>zella: abaxo su cabeça: & puso sus
ojos co<n> muy gra<n> vergue<n>ça abaxo fasta la tierra. E des-}

[fol. 7v]
{CB1.
q<ue> esto vio el sabio / leua<n>to se apriessa & dixo al rey. Señor sabed q<ue> esta do<n>zella no sabe ya responder ala pre-
gu<n>ta que le fago: & podeys creer sin duda que la te-
go vencida. & ma<n>do el rey ala do<n>zella que fablasse. E
luego fablo la donzella al rey muy humildosamente: &
dixo assi. Uuestra alteza sabra la verdad: & no plega a
dios q<ue> yo sea ve<n>çida d<e>l / ni d<e> otro sabio / q<ue> sepa mucho
mas que no el: & como quiera que yo sea muger / sabed
q<ue> le respo<n>dere bien si yo q<u>i`ero: mas q<ue> sepa v<uest>ra alteza &
d<e>la noble caualleria hauer le de respo<n>der ala tal razo<n>
por qua<n>to yo soyo pequeña & d<e> pocos dias & virge<n>: que
nu<n>ca en mi vida conosci varo<n> en juego: ni en veras: ni
en sueños nu<n>ca houo q<ue> ver comigo Esto<n>ces al rey plugo mucho d<e>la vergue<n>ça d<e>la do<n>zella & d<e> su respuesta &
ma<n>do le q<ue> respo<n>diesse / & no houiesse verguença alguna
E la do<n>zella le dicho q<ue> le plazia d<e> buena volu<n>tad de le
respo<n>der. & dixo luego sin detardar al sabio. Sabed señor maestro: q<ue> la muger ge<n>til es muy donosa & sabrosa: emp<er>o no es d<e> dormir co<n> muger: saluo q<ue> la escoja el
o<m>bre el q<ue> hazer lo pudiere. & d<e>ue la buscar q<ue> sea garça
q<ue> dize el sabio Aristoteles: trata<n>do d<e> aquesta materia;
que la muger garça para dormir el ho<m>bre con ella / ha
menester q<ue> este parida: & te<n>ga la criatura a sus pechos
o que este preñada. Otrosi el ho<m>bre q<ue> asi co<n> ella quiere dormir ha menester q<ue> sea sabio & sotil & engenioso
q<ua>ndo dormiere conella. E el sabio le pregunto: di me
do<n>zella en q<ue> manera. & ella dixo señor maestro:> sabed
q<ue> si la muger fuere tardia en su volu<n>tad deue el ho<m>bre
q<ue> dormiere co<n> ella ser sabio: como dicho te<n>go: & conoscer su co<m>plexio<n>: & deue se detardar co<n>ella: burla<n>do se
co<n> ella / & hazie<n>do le d<e>las tetas & apreta<n>do gelas: & a
vezes poner le la mano enel papagayo: & otros vezes}
[fol. 8r; sig. b I recto]
{CB1.
tener la encima de si / & a vezes de baxo. & haga por tal
manera que las volu<n>tades d<e>los dos vengan a vn tie<m>-
po: & si por ventura la muger veniere a co<m>plir su volu<n>-
tad mas ayna q<ue> el ho<m>bre: deue el co<n> discrecion ente<n>der
la: & iugar vn rato co<n> ella: porq<ue> la haga co<m>plir otra vez
& vengan juntas las volu<n>tades d<e> amos: como d<e>suso

dixe: & haziendo lo desta manera: amar le ha mucho la
muger. Ento<n>çes le respo<n>dio el sabio. Digo te do<n>zella
q<ue> muy bie<n> has respo<n>dido. E pregu<n>to le mas el sabio
Di me do<n>zella: qual tie<m>po & hora es mas clara & mas
prouechosa para dormir el ho<m>bre co<n> la muger. respondio le la do<n>zella. Maestro señor el tiempo & la hora q<ue>
es mas prouechosa para el hombre q<ue> ha de dormir co<n>
muger: & mas sano ha d<e> ser despues d<e> pasados los dos
tercios d<e>la noche: & enel postrer tercio esta el stomago
d<e>l ho<m>bre vasio & limpio d<e>la vianda: & la muger en aq<ue>l
tiempo tiene la madre caliente: & tiene ella mayor plazer en si para lo reçebir. respo<n>dio el sabio & dixo le. muy
bie<n> has dicho do<n>zella. E pregu<n>to le el sabio: di me do<n>-
zella d<e>las edades d<e>las mugeres / en q<ue> es preciada cada vna: la de veynte años q<ue> me dizes della. Digo vos
maestro q<ue> quando es gentil q<ue> paresce bien alas gentes
especialme<n>te alos ho<m>bres. E la muger d<e> trenta años
que me dizes della. Digo os señor maestro que es tal
& tan sabrosa: como quando ho<m>bre come p<er>dizes: o carnero co<n> limones. E la d<e> quare<n>ta años q<ue> me dizes. essa
señor tiene seso entero & para dar lo a otras q<ue> no lo tienen. Dela d<e> cinque<n>ta años q<ue> me dizes. Essa vos digo señor maestro: que es para el cuchillo. E la d<e> sesenta años que me dizes. En essa no hay bien ninguno E
la de setenta años q<ue> me dizes. Essa os digo señor ma-}
[fol. 8v; sig. b I verso]
{CB1.
estro q<ue> es tierra: & fuera de toda razon. E d<e>la ochenta
años / q<ue> me dizes. Essa os digo q<ue> no me la menteys. &
d<e>las vnas & d<e>las otras renegad d<e>la mejor. Ento<n>çes
respo<n>dio el sabio & dixo le Digo te q<ue> has hablado bien
en todo q<ua>nto has respo<n>dido E dixo le mas el sabio / dime do<n>zella: q<ue> señales ha d<e> hauer vna muger par ser
muy fermosa. Ella le respo<n>dio: ha de tener diez & ocho
señales: & son estas q<ue> yo os dire: ha de ser leu<n>ga en tres
lugares: & corta en tres lugares: & a<n>cha en tres lugares
v<er>meja en tres lugares: y prieta en tres lugares: & bla<n>-
ca en tres lugares: & rogo le mucho el sabio q<ue> le dixiesse en q<ue> manera: & q<ue> gelo co<n>tasse todo por menudo: cada vna cosa por si. E ella dixo le asi: señor maestro sabed q<ue> ha d<e> ser lue<n>ga en tres lugares: en esta man era para ser d<e>l todo fermosa: ha d<e> tener el cuello lue<n>go: & los

dedos lue<n>gos: & el cuerpo lue<n>gȯ. E ha de ser pequeña
en tres lugares. pequeñas las narizes & la boca & los
pies: & ha de ser bla<n>ca en tres lugares: ha d<e> ser blanca
enel cuerpo: & bla<n>ca enla cara: & bla<n>cos los die<n>tes. E
ha de ser prieta en tres lugares. los cabellos prietos:
& las pestañas prietas & lo prieto d<e>los ojos. E ha de
ser vermeja en tres lugares: vermejos los labrios de
la boca: & vermejas las enzias: & vermeja en medio d<e>
los carillos. Ha d<e> ser ancha en tres lugares: ancha en
las muñecas d<e>los braços: & ancha d<e>los ho<m>bros: & ha
de ser ancha enlas espaldas. % E despues q<ue> todo esto
huuo fablado la discreta do<n>zella: el sabio maestro se le-
ua<n>to luego en pies: & dixo al rey & a todos los sabios &
maestros / & a toda caualleria q<ue> ay estaua: por ver la disputa d<e>la do<n>zella co<n> los sabios: por v<er>dad vos digo señor rey & a vosotros señores q<ue> presentes estays / q<ue> esta}
[fol. 9r; sig. b II recto]
{CB1.
do<n>zella sabe mas q<ue> yo: & es muy sabia: & no podria p<re>-
guntar cosa q<ue> a todo no me diesse buena salida & respuesta: & digo desde aqui: & dire q<ue> sabe mas q<ue> qua<n>tos sabios son por todo el mu<n>do. & q<ue> es por d<e>mas ningu<n> sabio
disputar co<n> ella: porq<ue> a todos los ve<n>cera E d<e>sque esto
oyo el rey: plugo le mucho d<e>llo: porq<ue> bie<n> se penso q<ue> ya
era suya: & q<ue> ya la donzella era enamorada d<e>l rey: por
lo q<ua>l la q<u>i`so mas de alli adela<n>te / & dese[a]ua mucho q<ue> ho-
uiesse vençido al terçero sabio. Lo qual la discreta donzella supo mas q<ue> los sabios ni el rey: & hizo co<n> su saber
& co<n> la gracia d<e> dios todo lo q<ue> complia a su señor / q<ue> la
hauia comprado & para co<n> que el saliessa d<e> trabajos &
pobreza.
{RUB. % Titulo dela disputa que houo la do<n>-
zella Teodor co<n> el terçero sabio: al qual llamaua<n> abraam el trobador & maest[r]o enla musica.}
{IN3.} Dize la estoria que desque vido
el terçero sabio q<ue> los otros dos eran ve<n>çidos
por vna donzella tan pequeña que houo por
ello gran pesar & terrible enojo. & touo en su coraçon
que se hauian dado para poco; porque se dexaron asi
vençer de aquella donzella tan simple / & tan pequeña
niña de tan pocos dias: & touo los por muy nesçios /
& de poco saber: porque el bien pensaua dela vençer.

E leuantose muy soberuio sabio en pie: & dixo le assi.
Tu donzella responder me has a todo lo que te preguntare. Cumple que te apercibas a responder me de-
rechamente / que tu has de saber que no so you tan simple como eran los otros maestros con quien tu has
disputado: & tan malame<n>te ve<n>çido co<n> tus argume<n>tos}
[fol. 9v; sign. b II verso]
{CB1.
falsos. E desque houo el iudio acabado su razon: leua<n>-
to se la donzella & respondio le muy humilme<n>te & con
gran verguença: & dixo le assi. Señor & discreto maestro: dezis vos q<ue> soys mas sabio & mayor letrado q<ue> todos los otros: asi los q<ue> comigo ha<n> disputado: como los
otros señores & maestros & discretos sabios q<ue. delante
son. Alo q<ua>l los respo<n>do fabla<n>do en reuere<n>cia d<e> mi señor
el rey que esta presente: & d<e>lante toda caualleria & gentiles ho<m>bres q<ue> aqui estan ayuntados ala nuestra disputa: digo os q<ue> me marauillo mucho d<e> todo lo q<ue> haueys
hablado d<e> tener en poco saber & por nesçios alos sabios a<ue> comigo han disputado: & como dezis q<ue> co<n> argu-
me<n>tos falsos los venci. E pues q<ue> vos os loays por ta<n>
grande & discreto sabio: ruego vos q<ue> hagays como yo
agora os dire. & sea fecha vuna co<n>ueniencia entre vos &
mi: enla presencia d<e. su alteza d<e>l rey mi señor & d<e> toda
la caualleria: sabios & ge<n>tiles ho<m>bres & maestros soti-
les enlas sabidurias q<ue> a esta nuestra disputa son allega-
dos. E la co<n>uene<n>ncia sea en esta manera: q<ue> si vos venci-
eredes a mi: luego enesse pu<n>to me d<e>snude & me dispon-
ga & dispoje d<e> todos mis paños & la camisa: & todo q,ua>:n-
to sobre mi esta: d<e> manera q<ue> d<e>l todo desnuda / assi
como el dia en que nasci: & yo vos lo d<e> todo: & sea todo
vuestro. & si por ventura venciere yo a vos q<ue> vos faga
yo esso mismo: & q<ue> vos me deys todos vuestros paños
por manera q<ue> quedeys desnudo como el dia en que nacistes / si yo os ganare. E co<n> esta razon q<ue> dixo la do<n>ze-
lla plugo mucho al sabio judio / porq<ue> la pe<n>saua amen-
guar & auergo<n>çar creyendo q<ue> la tenia vençida. & resp<n>-
dio que le plazia. E esto fue asi otorgado por e<n>tramas
las partes en p<re>sencia d<e>l señor rey & d<e>la noble caualle-}
[fol. 10r; sig. b III recto]
{CB1.
ria & sabios / & de toda la otra gente que alli eran ayu<n>-

tados por ver la disputa: por manera que pidio la do<n>-
zella por merced al rey a<ue> passasse por acto de notario:
porque ninguno se puediesse llamar a ygnora<n>cia. E el
sabio consentio en todo ello: porque se creya que la tenia vençida. & al rey plugo mucho dello & mandolo
assi guardar E complir: & fue el mismo fiador de todo
ello para pagar ala parte que ganasse & fazer pagar ala
que perdiesse: & fizo su seguro real.
{RUB. % Titulo de las pregu<n>tas que fizo abra-
ha<m> el trobador ala do<n>zella. & de las respuestas q<ue> le dio}[44]
{IN 3.} Pregunto el sabio ala donzella
di me qual es la cosa mas pesada d<e> todo el mu<n>-
do respondio la donzella: que era la deuda.[45] &
dixo el sabio que era la verdad. E preguntole mas / q<ue>
qual era la cosa mas aguda en todas las cosas. respo<n>-
dio la donzella que la lengua del ho<m>bre / o de la muger
Pregu<n>tole mas que qual era la cosa mas apressurada
que saeta. E dixo la donzella que era el pensamiento[46]
E pregu<n>tole mas que qual era la cosa mas apressurada & mas ardiente & quema<n>te que el fuego: & dixo que
era el coraço<n>.[47] Pregu<n>tole mas q<ue> qual era la cosa mas

---

[44] The following sections incorporate several didactic *quaestiones* not attested in the manuscript witnesses of the Teodor material. In particular, the Toledo imprint conflates Versions A, B, and C of the *Diálogo de Epicteto y el emperador Adriano*. These versions share affinity with the fourteenth-century Catalan redaction of the "Dialogue of Epictetus" derived from the Provenzal version of *L'Enfant Sage*. It is possible that these dialogues were known to Hagenbach through manuscript sources or now-lost printed editions.

[45] MS Egerton 939 offers a source for this *quaestio*: "La cosa más pesada del mundo es la debda" (Bizzari 114: 92).

[46] MS Egerton 939 offers an interesting variant for this *quaestio*: "El ojo es más apresurado que saeta, que abriéndole le pone en vn punto donde quiere" (Bizzari 114: 93).

[47] The *quaestio*, missing from Version A and B of the Castilian *Diálogo*, is found in MS Egerton 939: "El coraçón del omne es más ardiente que el fuego quando está ayrado e enbuelto en sanna""(Bizzari 114: 95).

dulce que la miel. Respo<n>dia la do<n>zella que era la gran
bien quere<n>cia que tenia el padre & la madre con sus fijos.[48] E pregu<n>tole mas q<ue> qual era la cosa mas amarga
mas que la hiel. Respo<n>diole la donzella & dixo q<ue> era
el mal fijo o la mala fija. Pregu<n>tole mas q<ue> qual era la
dole<n>cia sin medicina que era incurable. Respo<n>diole la
donzella q<ue> era la mala fija loca & de poco seso & poca
verguença.[49] E pregu<n>tole mas q<ue> qual era la deuda que}
[fol. 10v; b III verso]
{CB1.
nu<n>ca se pagaua Respo<n>dio la do<n>zella q<ue> era la locura.
Pregu<n>tole mas q<ue> qual era la cosa mas dura q<ue> azero.
Respondio le q<ue> era la verdad.[50] Preguntole mas q<ue> q<ua>l
era la cosa mas deleytosa para vna hora. Respo<n>dio la
do<n>zella q<ue> a ella era gra<n> vergue<n>ça respo<n>der atal d<e>man-
da: por qua<n>to soy do<n>zella virgen: q<ue> nu<n>ca cognosci varon: mas porq<ue> no penseys q<ue> no se respo<n>der. digo que
deleyte de vna hora / es dormir & co<m>plir ho<m>bre su volu<n>-
tad con ge<n>til do<n>zella: o muger q<ue> es graciosa: ala
q<ua>l ho<m>bre ama & quiere mas q<ue> a todas las cosas d<e>l mu<n>-
do & duerme co<n> ella desnudo seguramie<n>te & sin temor
porque en aq<ue>lla hora es muy ence<n>dido el amor espe-
cialme<n>te si se ha sido penado de amores por ella mucho: & nu<n>ca la ha hauido fasta en aquella hora: enel q<ua>l
tie<m>po esta ho<m>bre tan encendido: q<ue> co<m>portaria la muerte por co<m>plir aq<ue>l plazer.[51] Pregu<n>tole mas q<ue> q<ua>l era d<e>leyu-

---

[48] This *quaestio* is found in the *Arabian Nights*: "Now that which is sweeter than honey is the love of pious children to their two parents" [*Arabian Nights*, IV:193]. The redaction from Granada contains: "¿Qué es más dulce que la miel...? --Más dulce que la miel es el amor que tienen los padres a los hijos..." ["Una versión del cuento" 362]. MS. Egerton 939 of the *quaestio* offers the variant: "La ganança es más dulce que la miel" (Bizzari 114: 96).

[49] The Arabic version sheds some light on the *quaestio*: "the disease that may not be healed is an ill nature, and the shame that may not be wiped away is an ill daughter""[*Arabian Nights*, IV:194].

[50] MS. Egerton 939 offers a variant for this *quaestio*: "La verdat es más fuerte que el azero" (Bizzari 114: 99).

te de vn dia. Respo<n>dio la do<n>zella q<ue> era la gana<n>çia que
gana el ho<m>bre o la muger q<ue> venden: o co<m>pra<n> mercaderias de cadeldia: sabed que aq<ue>llo es muy gra<n> deleyte
& gran alegria.[52] Pregu<n>tole mas q<ue> q<ua>l era deleyte d<e> vna
semana: & ella dixo q<ue> era el nouio con su esposa: quando vien se aman.[53] Pregu<n>tole mas q<ue> q<ua>l era deleyte d<e> vn
mes. Respo<n>dio la do<n>zella q<ue> q<ua>ndo ho<m>bre viene de lue<n>-
go camino / do<n>de se ha mucho detenido vien con bien
a su casa co<n> prosperidad y ganancia delo q<ue> ha trabaja-
do. y halla sanos & allegres a su muger & hijos & parie<n>-
tes: & a todos los q<ue> bie<n> quiere. Pregu<n>tole mas di me
do<n>zella: q<ua>l es vn aue q<ue> a<n>da en los mo<n>tes: en la q<ua>l hay
ocho señales las q<ua>les tiene<n> las gra<n>des animalias Re-
spo<n>dia la do<n>zella assi. sabed q<ue> aq<ue>lla aue q<ue> dezis: es la
la<n>gusta la q<ua>l tiene los cuernos como cieruô y el cuello}
[fol. 11r; sig. b IIII recto]
{CB1
de toro: y los pechos de cauallo: y el rostro de vaca: y
las alas de aguila: & el rabo de vibora: y los pies de
cigueña: y los ojos d<e> vna bestia q<ue> ha no<m>bre marcel la
q<ua>l bestia es muy bra<n>de & fiera y es lexos destas tierras[54]

---

[51] The question derives from the Arabic versions of the material. In *The Glory*, the following appears: "In his commentary on The Assemblies, Ibn 'Abdul-ul-Mu'min writes: The Chosroes Parvitz was once asked, 'What is delight for an hour?' 'Coitus,' he replied." [*The Glory* 175]. The *Arabian Nights* offers a similar observation: "...the delight of a moment is carnal copulation" [*Arabian Nights*, IV: 193].

[52] Compare the following analogue from the *Arabian Nights*: "...the pleasantest of three days is that of profit on merchandise" [*Arabian Nights*, IV:193]. The version from Granada offers the observation: "...la alegría de un día es la ganancia de los comerciantes..." ["Una versión del cuento" 362].

[53] The original tale of Tawaddud displayed a keen interest in aspects of Koranic law and doctrines associated with Islam. The *quaestio* in the Arabic version reflects that social-cultural concern: "And for a year?" "Marriage with a virgin." "And for ever?" "To talk with friends in this world and the pleasures of Paradise in the next." [*The Glory* 175]; "...el gozo de una semana es la desposada..." ["Una versión del cuento" 362].

% El sabio le pregu<n>to[55] q<ue> cosa es el ho<m>bre. la do<n>zella le respo<n>dio: ymagen de nuestro señor dios.
% % El sabio le pregu<n>to: donzella q<ue> cosa es la muger. la do<n>zella le respo<n>dio: arca d<e> mucho bie<n> & d<e> mucho mal ymagen d<e>l ho<m>bre: bestia q<ue> nunca se farta.[56]
% % El sabio le p<re>gu<n>to: do<n>zella que cosa es sueño. la do<n>-zella respo<n>dio: ymagen d<e> muerto.
% % El sabio le p<re>gunto: donzella q<ua>l fue el q<ue> murio & no mascio: la do<n>zella le respo<n>dio: nuestro padre adam.
% % El sabio le pregu<n>to. do<n>zella qual es la cosa d<e>la q<ua>l el ho<m>bre no se puede ver farto: la do<n>zella respo<n>dio: d<e> ganar riquezas.
% % El sabio le pregunto: donzella di me que cosa es ho<m>-bre mancebo la do<n>zella respondio: cand<e>la encendida que luego se mata.[57]
% % El sabio le p<re>gu<n>to: q<ue> cosa es ho<m>bre viejo. la do<n>zella

---

[54] This particular question has a riddling quality and reflects the Oriental context of the tale. The source for this riddle is the *Arabian Nights*, IV:194. An excellent overview of the use of riddles in *HDT* can be found in Goldberg (63-75).

[55] The following sequence of 11 *quaestiones* comes from the Version C of the Castilian *Diálogo Epicteto*. See Bizzari 109: 8-10; 12-13; 16-21.

[56] This *quaestio*, missing from Versions A and B of the Castilian *Diálogo*, is attested in several of the Latin texts associated with the *Joca Monachorum* tradition: "Quid est mulier formosa? --Cupiditas prava, incensio luxurie" [Suchier 1955, JM AE2 #84] or "Adr.d.: Quid est mulier formosa? Ep.r:Sicut templum super fluvio edificatum" [Suchier 1955, JM AE1a #69]. The *Secundus* dialogues offers the following variant: "Quid mulier? Hominis confusio, insaturabilis bestia, continua sollicitudo, indesinens pugna, cotidianum dampnum, domus tempestas, sollicitudinis impedimentum, viri incontinentis naufragium, adulterii vas, preciosum proelium, animal pessimum, pondus gravissimum, aspis insanabilis, humanum mancipium" [*Secundus* 96]. The Old Spanish version of *Secundus* offers the following exchange: "¿Que es la mugier?" "Confondimiento dell omne, bestia que numqua se farta, cuydado que no a fin, guerra que numqua queda, periglo dell omne que no a en si mesura"[PCG 147; similar in Knust 503; *De vita* 381].

[57] This *quaestio* is missing from Version A and B of the Castilian *Diálogo Epicteto*.

le respo<n>dio: mal desseado vestidura d<e> dolores.[58]
% % El sabio le pregu<n>to: do<n>zella q<ue> es la cosa mas incierta: la do<n>zella le respondio: la vida del ho<m>bre.
% % El sabio le p<re>gunto: do<n>zella q<ua>l cosa es mas cie(t)[r]ta la
donzella le respo<n>dio: la muerte d<e> las p<er>sonas.
% % El sabio le pregu<n>to do<n>zella por qua<n>tas cosas o maneras mienten los hombres: la donzella le respondio
señor el ho<m>bre mie<n>te por tres maneras. la primera o
por deleyte de fablar: la segu<n>da: o por dezir bien de
quien bien qui[e]ren: la terçera: o por dezir mal de quien
mal quieren.}
[fol. 11v; sig. b IIII verso]
{CB1.
% % El sabio le pregu<n>to: do<n>zella quie<n> fuel el q<ue> puso nombre a todas las cosas que dios crio. la do<n>zella le respo<n>-
dio: nuestro padre adam.
% % El sabio le p<re>gu<n>to: do<n>zella q<ua>l es la cosa del mu<n>do mas
graue & pejor de saber: la donzella le respo<n>dio: el coraçon del ho<m>bre: & los pensamie<n>tos: que no hay persona
enel mu<n>do que los pueda saber sino solo dios: & aq<ue>llos
a quien el ho<m>bre lo quiere reuelar.
% % El sabio le pregu<n>to: donzella qual es la cosa mas ligera del mu<n>do. la do<n>zella le respondio. El coraço<n> del
ho<m>bre & el pensamie<n>to. que en vn punto lo pone do quiere. ahun que sea en cabo del mundo.
% % El sabio le p<re>gu<n>to. do<n>zella q<ua>l es la cosa q<ue> el ho<m>bre
vee & no puede llegar a ella: ni la puede tocar. la do<n>ze-
lla le respo<n>dio: el sol & la luna & las estrellas.
% % El sabio le p<re>gunto: do<n>zella que faze el sol de noche.
la do<n>zella le respo<n>dio. Oras hay q<ue> alu<m>bra alos infier-
nos & horas hay q<ue> alu<m>bra & da lu<m>bre al purgatorio. E
oras hay q<ue> alu<m>bra a todo el mu<n>do & se pone al ponie<n>te
% % El sabio le p<re>gunto: do<n>zella quie<n> sostene la tierra. la
donzella le respo<n>dio los quatro elemie<n>tos. Fuego en-
fernal & los abismos que son de yuso dela tierra.

[58] This *quaestio* is missing from Castilian Versions A and B of the Castilian *Diálogo Epicteto*. The *Secundus* tradition offers the following variant: "Quid senectus? Optatum malum, viventium mors, incolumis languor, spirans mors, Veneris expers, mors expectata, mors communis" [*Secundus* 97].

% % El sabio le p<re>gu<n>to do<n>zella quie<n> sustene los abysmos
que son de yuso dela tierra. la do<n>zella le respondio el
aruol q<ue> fue pla<n>tado en<e>l parayso: q<ue> la rayz del yua enel
inferno ante de la passion de iesu christo.[59]
% % El sabio le p<re>gu<n>to: do<n>zella que cosa es la noche la
donzella le respo<n>dio: descanso delos trauajadores en-
cobridora delos malfechores.
% % El sabio le pre(p)[g]u<n>to: do<n>zella quales fueron q<ue> nasci-
eron & no muriero<n> ni morira<n> fasta la fin del mundo. la}
[fol. 12r]
{CB1.
donzella le respondio. Helias & Enoch q<ue> fueron leua-
dos & traidos en cuerpo & en alma al parayso terrenal
& estan ay & estaran fasta q<ue> venga el antecristo: & ento<n>-
ce saliran a pelear conel.[60]

---

[59] This *quaestio* topic is extant in the *JM/AE* tradition: "Ad.d.: Qui sustinent abyssum? -- Ep.r.: Arbor qui ante initium mundi ad radice positus est et omnia continet; ipse est Dominus Deus noster" [Suchier 1955, JM AE1a #19] and "Quid sustinet abyssum -- Arbor qui ab inicio positus est ipse est Dominus noster Iesus" [Suchier 1955, JM AE2 #63]. The Catalan *Epitus* translates the *JM/AE* version: "Que soste abis?' L'infant respos: Lo abre que fon plantat en parais en lo començment, que es nostre senyor deus" [Suchier 1910, E, #65]. Suchier gives the following variant: "Quien sostiene los abismos y los ynfiernos dela tierra? -- El arbol que fue plantado en parayso; enlas rrayses d'el estavan los patriarcas y profetas, que yvan al ynfierno antes dela pasion de nuestro señor Jesu Christo." [Suchier 1910, Spanish N # 34]. Madrid BN 17657 lacks part of the *quaestio*: "¿Qué sostiene al bismo? --rrespondió el ynfante--El [ ] fue plantado en el paray|so" [*Tratado del ynfante* 28].

[60] The *quaestio* reflects a topic derived from scripture (*Genesis* 5:24; *Hebrews* 11:5; *Malachias*, 4:5). According to Cross (143), medieval exegetical traditions associated Henoch and Elias with the "two witnesses of Apocalypse 11:3 against whom 'the beast that ascendeth out of the abyss shall make war'(11:7)." The topic appears in the *AE* tradition: "Adrianus Quis fuit natus et non mortuus? -- Respondit: Elyas et Enoch" [Suchier 1910, Latin AE #17]. The Catalan *Epitus* follows the Apocalyptic tradition: "Quals son aquells qui son nats e no morran entro ala fi del mon? — L'infant respos: Elies e Enoch, que stan ala porta de paradis e staran entro al dia del juhi" [Suchier 1910, E #73]. MS Egerton 939 matches the Catalan version: "Los que nasçieron e non murieron nin murirán fasta la fin del mundo, fueron Elías e Enoc, que fueron levados biuos en cuerpos e en ánimas a parayso terrenal e

% % El sabio le p<re>gunto: do<n>zella qual fue el primer rey
la donzella le respondio. Mombet.[61]
% % El sabio lo pregu<n>ta: do<n>zella qual fue la primera ci-
bdad. la do<n>zella le respo<n>dio la ciudad de Niniue.
% % El sabio le p<re>gu<n>to: do<n>zella qual es q<ue> anduuo eneste
mundo en dos ve<n>tres. la donzella le respondio Jonas
profeta: que anduuo en el ve<n>tre de su madre: & enel vie<n>-
tre dela vallena tres dias & tres noches.[62]
% % El sabio le p<re>gunto: do<n>zella qual fue el mayor con-
quistador del mu<n>do que en menos tie<m>po mas tierra ganasse. la donzella respo<n>dio. Alexa<n>dre que en dos años
gano & co<n>quisto todo el mu<n>do: quando murio hauia
quarenta & seys años.[63]

---

estan ay'y estaran fasta que venga el antichristo, que pelee con ellos" [Bizzari 111:37]. In Madrid BN 17657, the *quaestio* makes no mention of eschatology and reflects the *AE* tradition: "¿Quién fueron los que naçieron e non morirán fasta la fyn del mundo? --rrespondió el ynfante—Elias e Enoch" [*Tratado del ynfante* 29].

[61] The *princeps* does not reflect Version C of the *Diálogo* which has: "El primero rrey que ouo fue Nenbrot" [Bizzarri 111:39].

[62] This topic derives from Biblical authority and reflects a commonplace in the Middle Ages: "Quis tres dies et tres noctes jejunavit, nec celum vidit nec terram tetigit? --Jonas in ventre ceti"[Suchier 1910, Latin AE #53]. Juan Ruiz makes similar reference to Jonah in the *LBA*:

> A Jonas el profeta del vientre de la ballena,
> en que moró tres días, dentro en la mar ll[ena],
> sacaste lo tú sano, así commo de casa buena.
> *LBA*, 5a-c

The Catalan redaction of *Epitus* includes a *quaestio* on this topic: "Qual fon aquell que dejuna tres dies e tres nits, e no veu lo cel ni toqua la terra? L'infant respos—Jonas en lo cors dela balena""[Suchier 1910, E #80]. Madrid BN 17657 follows the Catalan version: "¿Quién fue aquel que ayunó tres días e tres noches que non vio çielo nin tierra? Péticus rresponde —Jonas, en el vientre de la vallena" [[Bizzari 50:87]. MS Egerton 939 offers the version found in *HDT*: "El profeta Jonás andouo en este mundo en dos vientres: en el vientre de su madre e después andouo en el vientre de la vallena tres días e tres noches" [Bizzari 111:47].

% % El sabio le pregu<n>to: donzella qual fue q<ue> en este mu<n>-
do mayor sente<n>cia dio. la donzella respondio. Pilato
que mando a matar nuestro señor jesu cristo que es verdadero dios & verdadero hombre que sabia el bie<n> que
era sin culpa.[64]
% % El sabio le pregu<n>to: donzella qual fue el mejor luchador que enel mundo huuo. la donzella le respondio el
patriarcha iacob / que lucho toda la noche co<n> el angel[65]
% % El sabio le p<re>gunto: donzella qual fue la primera fusta que anduuo por la mar. la donzella le respondio el
arca de noe.[66]
% % El sabio le pregunto donzella qual es ho<m>bre de mas
conplida bondad la donzella le respondio el que priua su ira & su voluntad.}[67]
[fol. 12v]
{CB1.
% % El sabio le p<re>gunto qual es la cosa q<ue> endeuda al que
no deue nada. la donzella respondio: el q<ue> discubre su
secreto a otro ho<m>bre o muger.
% % El sabio le p<re>gunto: donzella qual fue el ho<m>bre mas
rezio enel mundo: la donzella le respondio: en fuerça
sanson. mas etor en armas.[68]

---

[63] This *quaestio*, missing from Castilian Versions A and B of the *Diálogo*, is present in MS Egerton 939 (Bizzari 112:57).

[64] This *quaestio*, missing from Castilian Versions A and B of the *Diálogo*, is present in MS Egerton 939 (Bizzari 112:63).

[65] This *quaestio*, missing from Castilian Versions A and B of the *Diálogo*, is present in MS Egerton 939 (Bizzari 113:74).

[66] This *quaestio*, missing from Castilian Versions A and B of the *Diálogo*, is present in MS Egerton 939 (Bizzari 113:75).

[67] This *quaestio* is missing from Version A and B of the *Diálogo*. A variant of this *quaestio* occurs in *Bocados*: "¿Quál es el de más complida voluntad? E dixo: El que apremia su ira, e lidia con su voluntad""(*Bocados* 97).

% % El sabio le pregunto donzella por que persona fueron mas muertes. la donzella respo<n>dio. por la reyna
encuba sobre troya.
% % El sabio le pregu<n>todonde fue mayor ayu<n>tamie<n>to d<e>
gentes enel mu<n>do. la do<n>zella le respo<n>dio: sobre troya
ca viniron gentes d< e> todo el mu<n>do: vnos para d<e>struyr
& otros para guareçer.
% % El sabio le pregu<n>to donzella quales son las mejores
cosas que el ho<m>bre puede hauer en si. La do<n>zella le respondio: la verdad & la vergue<n>ça.[69]
% % El sabio le pregunto: donzella qual es mayor mal
q<ue> los ho<m>bres cobdicia<n>: la do<n>zella le respo<n>dio. la vejez.[70]
% % El sabio le pregunto: donzella qual es la cosa mas
aguda que nauaja: la donzella le respondio: la lengua
d<e>la muger quanto esta ayrada.[71]
% % El sabio le pregunto donzella qual es la cosa mas
ardiente q<ue> el fuego: la do<n>zella le respo<n>dio: el coraço<n> d<e>l
hombre quando esta yrado embulto en saña.[72]
% % El sabio le pregunto donzella qual es la cosa mas
dulce q<ue> la miel: la do<n>zella le respo<n>dio la ganancia.[73]

---

[68] This *quaestio* and the next two are missing from Version A and B of the *Diálogo*.

[69] This *quaestio*, missing from Version A and B of the *Diálogo*, is similar to the central topic of *Exemplo* 50 of *El Conde Lucanor*. See Bizarri 127:87.

[70] This *quaestio*, missing from Version A and B of the *Diálogo*, occurs in the Latin versions of the *Secundus* dialogues: "Quid senectus? Optatum malum, viventium mors, incolumnis languor, spirans mors, Veneris expers, mors expectata, mors communis" [*Secundus* 97].

[71] Several analogues exist for this *quaestio*; see footnote 25 above.

[72] This *quaestio*, missing from Version A and B of the *Diálogo*, is related to an earlier *quaestio* in Teodor (see page 13).

[73] MS. Egerton 939 offers the following variant: "La ganança es más dulce que la miel" (Bizzari 114: 96).

% % El sabio le pregunto. donzella qual es la dolencia
sin sanidad: la donzella le respondio: la locura.[74]
% % El sabio le pregunto. donzella qual es la cosa mas
rezia q<ue> azero: la donzella respondio: la verdad.[75]
% % El sabio le p<re>gu<n>to: do<n>zella qual es mejor plazer de}
[fol. 13r]
{CB1.
los plazeres: la donzella le respondio: el vençimiento
d<e> su enemigo.[76]
% % El sabio le pregu<n>to: donzella quales son los peores
& mas principales pecados: la do<n>zella le respo<n>dio en
no creer la santa fe catholica. & desesperar d<e>la misericordia de dios.[77]
% % El sabio le pregu<n>to: donzella: quales son las cosas
mas ciertas que lleuan el ho<m>bre al parayso. la do<n>zella
le respo<n>dio Obra. Spera<n>ça. & Caridad.[78]
% % El [s]abio le p<re>gu<n>to: donzella
% % El sabio le pregu<n>to do<n>zella qual es la mejor cosa & pe-
or del mundo. la donzella le respondio: la palabra: ca
con esta puede fazer mucho mal & mucho bien.[79]
% % El sabio le pregunto: donzella qual es el mejor dia
la do<n>zella respondio; el viernes por cinco razones:[80] la

---

[74] This *quaestio* is missing from Version A and B of the *Diálogo*. MS. Egerton 939 offers an interesting variant: "La locura es dolençia syn sanidat" (Bizzari 114: 97).

[75] This *quaestio* is missing from Version A and B of the *Diálogo*.

[76] This *quaestio* is missing from Version A and B of the *Diálogo*.

[77] This *quaestio* is missing from Version A and B of the *Diálogo*.

[78] This *quaestio* reflects Version C of the *Diálogo* (Bizarri 114:105).

[79] The material here follows the Version B of the *Diálogo* (Bizzari 93:36).

[80] This *quaestio* has several analogues. The topic reflects the medieval view of the ages of man as well as traditional beliefs associated with the days of the week. Although the question appears in the printed redactions of the *HDT*, the topic is at-

tested quite early in medieval texts and has basis in Biblical authority. See, for example, Genesis 2:7, Matthew 27:46, and Mark 15:34-42. Exegesis of this topic connects Adam's fall with Christ's crucifixion and his Harrowing of Hell as a series of interrelated events which dramatize the nature of God's divine plan. Rabanus Maurus offers the following exposition: "Nam sicut in illa sexta die primus homo Adam de limo terrae ad imaginem Dei formatus est, sic in ista saeculi aetate secundus Adam, id est, Christus in carne de Maria virgine natus est, ille in anima vivente, hic in spiritu vivificante. Et sicut in illa die fit anima viva, sic in isto saculo vitam desiderat aeternam; et in illa sexta die serpentium et ferarum genera terra produxit, ita in hac sexta aetate saeculi, gentes vitam appetentes aeternam Ecclesia generavit" [Rabanus col. 470]. The *Collectanea* makes the following observations: "Adam vixit annos quindecim in paradiso, Eva quatuordecim, alii dicunt septem, sine uxore quadraginta dies. Die sexto manducavit Adam de ligno scientiae boni et mali, decimo quinto anno aetatis suae" [*Collectanea* col 547D]. A *JM* text edited by Suchier has the following information "--A. In qua die clamavit diabolus de ligno in paradiso quando seduxit Evam? -- E. In sexta feria hora sexta et in ipsa die conceptus est et crucifixus est Christus" [Suchier 1955, AE1b, #101]. The same question appears in vernacular works. The Old English *Adrian and Ritheus* offers the following exhange:

> Saga me on hwilcne daeig he gesingode.
> Ic _e secge, on frydaeig and on _one daeig he was aer gesceapen, and on _am dæge he eft asweolt and for _am crist eft _rowede on _am dæg. [Cross, *Adrian and Ritheus*, #2]

A similar exchange occurs in the Old English *Solomon and Saturn*:

> Saga me hu lange lyfde adam on neorxenawange.
> Ic _e secge...and on _am...[h]e abyrgd[e] _a
> farbodenan fictrewæs blæda, and _æt on frigdæg and _urh _æt he was on helle v _usend wintra and iic wintra and viii and xx wintra. [Cross, *Solomon and Saturn*, #16]

Jacobus de Voragine comments on the importance of Friday: "It was fitting from the point of view of the time, because Adam was created and fell into sin in the month of March, on Friday the sixth day of the week and at the sixth hour of the day, and Christ chose to suffer on the day in March on which his coming was announced and on which he was put to-death-the sixth day, Friday at the sixth hour" [Jacobus de Voragine, I: 209-10.]. A French text repeats this concept of outlining the progress of man's fall and salvation: "A la tierce houre si donna Ada- nous a

primera porq<ue> en el dia sancto d<e> viernes fizo dios a nuestro padre adam: la segu<n>da porq<ue> enel viernes vino a tomar carne el fijo d<e> dios en la virge<n> santa maria: y nascio d<e>lla verdadero dios & ho<m>bre sin simiente d<e> varon & sin ningun corro<m>pimie<n>to. la terçera porq<ue> enel viernes fue bautizado nuestro señor d<e> los manos d<e> san iuan bautista: la quarta fue porq<ue> en el dia sa<n>to d<e> viernes fue crucificado nuestro señor iesu cristo & tomo muerte & passion por saluar la humanal linage. E la quinta porq<ue> en el dia santo d<e> viernes verna nuestro señor jesu christo a juzgar viuos & muertos: y alos buenos dara gloria. y alos malos dara pena para siempre yamas sin fin.[81]

---

toutes bestes, e la siste houre si manga la femme la poume e en dona a sun baroun e il en manga pur lamur de li, e a houre de noune si furent gette hors de paradis""[Kemble 208, note 1].

Berceo outlines a similar sequence of events in *Los loores*:

> Viernes fue aquel día, siempre sera nomnado,
> en essi día misme fue Adán engannado,
> fue por salvar el mundo / Christo crucificado,
> cerca d'El dos ladrones del un e'l otro lado.
>
> Berceo, *Los loores de Nuestra Señora*, copla 66

[81] The comments concerning Christ's baptism occur only in the printed editions of the *HDT* which reproduces information found in Version B of the *Diálogo*, the *Tratado del ynfante* (BN MS 17657[Dutton MN39]): "¿Por quántas cosas deue omne ayunar en el parayso? Rrespondió el ynfante--Por nueve. La primera, por que en tal día formó Dios Adán en el parayso. La segunda, que en viernes mató Cayn Abel. La tercera, que en tal día mató Dauid a Golías. La quarta, que en tal día vyno Jhesu Christo en la Virgen María. La quinta, que en tal día fue babtizado Nuestro Señor Jhesus Christo e sant Juan Babtista en la fuen Jordan. La sesta, que en tal día fue apedreado Sant Esteuan. La séptima, que en tal día fue descabeçado Sant Juan Babtista. La ottaua, que en tal día fue cruçificado Nuestro Señor Jhesu Christo. La novena, que en tal día verá a juzgar en el postimero día a la tierra e dará sentençia contra buenos y malos en el Val de Josafat, y dará a los buenos gualardón y a los malos pena" [*Tratado del ynfante*, 29]. This late fifteenth-century Castilian version derived from a fourteenth-century Catalan redaction offers the following variation: "L'infant respos: Per viiii: la primera cosa es perque en dia de divendres nostre seyo

% % El sabio le pregunto donzella: que condicion tiene
el ho<m>bre: la donzella respondio. el ho<m>bre tiene en si todas las condiciones & virtudes que tienen todas las
aues & otras bestias & anemalias que dios crio: q<ue> so<n>}
[fol. 13v]
{CB1.
estas que se pudieron fallar.
% % Es brauo como leon. Fra<n>co como gallo. Ardit como furon. Alegre como ximio. Callado como pece.
Suzio como puerco. Ma<n>so como oueja. Ligero como cieruo. Artero como raposo Fermoso como pauo<n>
Tragon como lobo. Casto como abeja. Leal como
cauallo. Perezoso como xaxo. Escaso como can. Couarde como lebre. Triste como araña. Parlador co-
mo tordo. Limpio como cisne. Nescio como el asno.
Feo como erizo. Ayunador como topo. Fornicador
como chinche. Falso como sierpe.
{RUB. % Titulo octauo como se dio por ven-

---

deus feu e forma Adam; la segona cosa, que en aquell dia mata Caym son germa Abel; la terça cosa es que en lo dit dia David profeta mata Golies; la quarta cosa, per tal com en dia de divendres nostre senyor deus vench en la gloriosa verge Maria; la quinta cosa es que en dia de divendres nostre senyor deus e sent Johan foren batejats en flum Jorda..." [Suchier, Catalan E, 299-300]. The source for the Catalan redaction is a family of Provenzal texts dated by Suchier as late thirteenth century. The Provenzal offers the following: "...la primeira, car a divenres fes dieus e formet Adam; la segonda, car a divenres vene en ela carn human e nasquets d'ela vers dieus e vers homs; la v, car a divenres nostre senhor dieu Jhesu Crist e sant Johan Baptista foron batejatz el flum Jorda" (Suchier, Provenzal A B C, 328-29). Other vernacular texts of the *L'Enfant Sage* offer the similar reasons. The *Wyse Chylde* (London: Wynkyn de Worde, 1530) provides the following: "And the chylde answered hym: For viii reasons pryncypally. The fyrste for that on frydaye our Lorde Jesu Chryst formed Adam. The seconde for that that in the fryday Saynt Joh Baptist baptysed our Lorde in the Flome Jordayn. the thirde is for that that on the fryday David, the prophete, slewe the grete Golyas. The IIII is for that that on the frydaye our Lodre toke humayne flesshe in the wombe of the gloryouse vyrgen Marye. The .V. is for that that on the frydaye saint Steven, the fyrst martyr, was stoned. The .VI. for that that on the frydaye our Lorde Jesus Chryst was crucified. The .VIII. for that that on the frydaye our Lorde Jesus Chryst shall descende from heven for to holde his jugement in the vale of Josepath" [*The Wyse Chylde* 21).

cido el terçero sabio el qual llamauan abraha<n> el trobador & maestro enlas otras scie<n>cias}
{IN3.} Dize la estoria que aquel sabio
tercero desque vido las respuestas q<ue> la donzella teodor le daua a todas tan concertadas
& dando su co<n>clusion por muy acabada: & le hauia re-
spo<n>dido muy sesudame<n>te atodo qua<n>to le hauia pregu<n>-
tado: & miro bien en si q<ue> creya que no hauria cosa enel
mu<n>do que le p<re>gu<n>tasse q<ue> no desse salida a todo & buena
co<n>clusio<n>. leua<n>tose de donde staua & fizo su reuerencia
al rey: & dixole a gra<n>des bozes. yo os digo señor cier-
tamie<n>te que esta do<n>zella sabe mas q<ue> yo. E desde aqui
os digo que ella es basta<n>te de disputar con todo el mu<n>-
do: & quedar ve<n>çedora. & q<ue> v<uest>ra alteza le deue dar señaladas mercedes & mucha honrra. E desque el sabio
houo su razon acabada a<n>te el rey. leua<n>tose la do<n>zella
dela<n>te del rey co<n> gran reuere<n>cia: & beso le las manos &
los pies: & catta<n>dole como a su rey & señor dixole assi.}
[fol. 14r]
{CB1.
dar luego a este vuestro sabio que luego sin tarda<n>ça se
desnude aq<u>i' en p<re>sencia d<e> vuestra alteza & d<e> todos estos
grandes señores & discretos varones: todos sus pa-
ños: & me los entregue luego sin otra detardança: sin
poner en ello otra escusa ni lo<n>gueria. & vista por el rey
la peticio<n> q<ue> la buena & discreta do<n>zella le fazia & conosciendo su alteza la razo<n> & iusticia q<ue> para ello tenia: se-
gu<n> el co<n>trato q<ue> entre ellos hauia passado: d<e>lo q<ua>l el era
fiador por amas las partes. ma<n>do al sabio por sente-
cia que luego enesse pu<n>to se desnudasse d<e> todos sus paños: & los diesse & entregasse ala donzella. E vie<n>do el
sabio q<ue> el rey ma<n>daua iusticia & razo<n>: luego enesse punto se asento a desnudar todos sus paños: co<n> gra<n> verguença: & dio los ala do<n>zella / & q<uan>do desnudo sin ropo nin-
gu<n>a: por tal manera q<ue> no tenia en todo su cuerpo sino
los paños co<n> q<ue> cobria las partes vergo<n>çosas. E qua<n>-
do la do<n>zella le vido todo desnudo: & q<ue> tenia los paño[*s]
menores calçados & no otra cosa ningu<n>a: dixo le la do<n>-
zella a gra<n>des bozes: porq<ue> el rey & toda la caualleria
& discretos ho<m>bres q<ue> alli estaua<n> lo oyessen: q<ue> luego de[*s]
calçasse los paños menores: & gelos diesse & entregas-
se luego: pues q<ue> asi estaua enla co<n>ueniencia: q<ue> el q<ue> per-

diesse q<ue> hauia d<e> q<ue>dar desnudo como la hora en q<ue> nacio
E pues q<ue> el sabio assi hauia causado ante el rey & ante
toda la caualleria & discretos varones q<ue> alli estaua<n>: pidio al rey a altas bozes q<ue> le ma<n>dasse dar los paños menores: pues q<ue> todo era suyo: & lo hauia ganado segun
la co<n>ueniencia. E el rey ma<n>do luego al sabio q<ue> se descalçasse & gelos diese ala do<n>zella so pena d<e>la su merçed
porq<ue> otro dia se auisasse & mirase como apostaua. E el
sabio respondio al rey & ala do<n>zella q<ue> no lo faria: ahu<n>-}
[fol. 14v]
{CB1.
q<ue> supiesse morir por ello por qua<n>to no podia fazer ora-
çio<n> sin ellos: segu<n> lo ma<n>daua su ley. E dixo la do<n>zella
reuere<n>do maestro: yo os mostrare como hagays ora-
çio<n> sin ellos: & alca<n>seis lo <ue> iustame<n>te dema<n>daredes a
n<uest>ro señor dios: q<ua>nto mas q<ue> otros teneys en v<uest>ra casa:
o los podeis ma<n>dar hazer. E respo<n>dio el sabio: bie<n> es
do<n>zella lo q<ue> dezis: mas porq<ue> son q<u>i`tados do<n>de soy av<er>-
go<n>çado: no los puedo mas calçar. Ento<n>çes le respon-
dio la do<n>zella: maestro todo esso es alargar en razo<n>es
q<ue> yo os mostrare como los podais tornar a calçar & podais hazer oraçio<n> a nuestro señor: & por ta<n>to plega os
de me los dar. & vie<n>do el sabio q<ue> no tenia remedio sino
hauer gelos d<e>dar finco las rodillas ante ella: & tomo
le las manos & beso gelas: & echose a sus pies q<ue>riendo
gelos besar: roga<n>dola muy afincadame<n>te q<ue> no le hiziesse passar tan gra<n> verguença ante el señor rey & ante tan
noble caualleria & discretos ho<m>bres & gra<n>des señores
como alli estaua<n> & q<ue> el le q<ue>ria dar diez mill doblas de
bue<n> oro: porq<ue> no le fiziesse descalçar sus paños menores. E la do<n>zella houo piadad d<e>l pues q<ue> ya se rescataua & co<n>cebio el ruego d<e>l sabio. co<n> q<ue> el ganasse licencia
d<e>l rey: & q<ue> el lo ma<n>dasse a ella. E esto<n>çes el rey dio liçe<n>-
cia ala do<n>zella & agradescio gelo mucho. & el rey man-
do al sabio q<ue. luego en esse punto embiasse a su casa por
las diez mill doblas: & las diesse ala do<n>zella & el sabio
hizolo asi & dio gelas luego. E el rey dixo ala do<n>zella
q<ue> demandasse en merçed todo qua<n>to ella q<u>i`siesse: q<ue> el ge-
lo daria. E ella le beso los pies & las manos. E d<e>ma<n>-
de le en merçed q<ue> la dexasse tornar co<n> su señor el mercadero. & q<ue> la venda sea ningu<n>a q<ue> de mi tiene fecha a v<uest>ra
alteza: porq<ue> señor el ha gastado por mi qua<n>to tenia / &}

Universidad de Salamanca Library — MS 1866
Spine title "Coleccion de sentencias"

The Teodor chapter starts at 91vb19.

[fol. 91vb19]
{CB2.
{IN2.} [A]uia en babilonia vn mercador muy rrico & bueno
& muy linpio & oraçion<er>o enlas
ci<n>co oraçion<e>s E fazedor de bondades alos men<e>sterosos & alas biudas & auia muchos algos E tenia muchos h<er>manos & muchos
parie<n>tes & no<n> tenia fijo ni<n> fija}
[fol. 92r]
{CB2.
E acaesçio vn dia q<ue> me<r>co vna
donzella & dio por ella muchas
doblas & muchos florin<e>s E le
uola asu casa E demostrole todas las artes & sabidurias q<ua>n-
tas pudo saber E dende a t<ien>po
llego el mercador a gra<n>t men<e>st<e>r
E dixo ala donzella sabet que
me ha dios traydo a gra<n>t me-
n<e>ster q<ue> no<n> he algo ni<n> co<n>sejo &
no<n> se me escusa q<ue> vos no<n> aya
de vender & pu<e>s datme co<n>se-
jo por onde aure bie<n> & mejoria E abaxo la donzella los
ojos & la cabeza co<n>tra t<ie>rra comidiendo E despu<e>s alço los ojos
arriba & dixo no<n> auedes q<ue> rreçelar co<n>la me<r>ced de dios E
dixole yt vos agora al alcaçeria delos buticarios & traed
me afeytamie<n>tos p<ar>a mug<e>r &
nobles vestiduras E leuadme
al alcaçar del rrey abomeliq<ue> al-
ma<n>çor E q<ua>ndo vos p<re>guntare

por v<uest>ra venido dezilde q<ui>ero vos
vender esta donzella & pedil-
de por mi diez mill doblas de
buen oro fino E sy dixiere q<ue>}
{CB2.
es mucho dezilde señor sy conoçiesedes la donzella no<n>lo terniades por mucho E fuese el
m<er>cador al alcaçeria alos buticarios & fue a vno q<ue> dezia<n> mahomad & saluolo & el buticario
le dixo me<r>cador q<ue> auedes me-
n<e>ster E el me<r>cador le co<n>to la
rrazo<n> por q<ue> venia E dixo q<ui>ero
q<ue> me dedes fermosas vestiduras
& fermosos afeytam<i>e<n>tos p<ar>a mi
donzella E el tendero ouo del
me<r>cador gra<n>t piedat & delo q<ue>
dixo & dela donzella q<ue>la q<ue>ria ve<n>-
der E dixo amigo mucho me
ama<n>zillastes mi coraço<n> & fezistes llorar mis ojos por la v<uest>ra
pobreza & por q<ue> q<ue>redes vender
v<uest>ra donzella E la v<uest>ra dema<n>da
presta es E leua<n>tose el buticario & diole nobles vestiduras & nobles afeytamie<n>tos p<ar>a
muger E el me<r>cador tomolo
todo E leuolo ala donzella &
ella pagose dello E dixo esto
vos sera bue<n> comie<n>ço co<n>la a-
yuda dedios E leua<n>tose
la donzella & vistiose & afey-}
[fol. 92v]
{CB2.
tose muy bie<n> & dixo asu señor
leua<n>taduos & sobid comigo
al alcaçar del rrey E leua<n>-
tose su señor & fuero<n>se p<ar>a el
al[ca]çar del rrey & pidiero<n> liçe<n>çia
que entrasen al rrey E el rrey
mando q<ue> entrasen & entraro<n>

& pararo<n>se entramos ante el
rrey E q<ua>ndo el rrey los vido
com<en>ço de fablar con<e>l me<r>cador
& pregu<n>to por su venida & que
era lo q<ue> q<ue>ria E el me<r>cador
le dixo señor q<ui>ero vos vender
esta donzella E el rrey dixo
q<ua>nto es su presçio & rrespo<n>-
diole el me<r>cador & dixo señor q<ui>ero por ella diez mill
doblas de bue<n> oro finisimo
bermejo E el rrey lo touo por
estraño el p<re>sçio dela donzella
& dixo al me<r>cador mucho bos
estiendiestes ensu p<re>sçio & sa-
llistes de v<uest>ro acue<r>do o la donzella se alaba de cosas q<ue> no<n>
pueden ser E rrespondiole
el me<r>cador & dixo al rrey señor no<n> tengades por mucho
el p<re>scio dela donzella ca por}
{CB2.
co es q<ue> yo la crie de peq<ue>ña & es
moça & costome muchos aue-
res fasta q<ue> ap<re>ndio & entendio
todas las ares & los nobles
men<e>steres & esto no<n> sera çelado avos E come<n>ço el rrey a
fablar co<n>la donzella & ella abaxo el velo de v<er>gue<n>ça & el rrey
alço los ojos & vido su fermosura q<ue> semejaua el sol q<ue> rrelozia q<ue> no<n> auia en<e>se t<ien>po mas
fermosa q<ue> ella E dixole el
rrey donzella com<m>o au<e>des no<n>-
bre rrespondio la donzella &
dixo señor ami dize<n> teodor
E dixo el rrey donzella que
ap<re>ndiestes delas artes dixo
la donzella señor yo ap<re>ndi
la ley & el libro de dios &
ap<re>ndi mas los q<ua>tro vie<n>tos

& las siete planetas & las
estrellas E las leyes & los
mandamie<n>tos & el traslado
& los p<ro>metimie<n>tos de dios
& las cosas q<ue> crio en los çielos & ap<re>ndi las fablas de
las aues & delas animali-
as & la fisica & la filosofia}
[fol. 93r]
{CB2.
& la logica & las cosas p<ro>uadas
E ap<re>ndi mas el juego del
axedrez E ap<re>ndi tañer
laud & cañon & las trey<n>ta
& tres trobas E ap<re>ndi las buenas costu<n>bres de leyes E ap<re>n-
di baylar & cantar & sotar E
ap<re>ndi texer paños de peso E
ap<re>ndi labrar paños de seda
E ap<re>ndi labrar de oro & de plata & de todas las otras art<e>s
& cosas nobles E en q<ue> oyo
el rrey estas palabras dela
donzella fizose marauillado
E mando llamar los mayo-
res sabios desus cortes & dixoles q<ue> p<ro>uasen esta donzella E salliero<n> luego a ella
tres om<n>es letrados & todos
le p<re>gu<n>taro<n> espeçial me<n>te vn
fisico q<ue> le p<re>gu<n>to & dixo donzella las flores son sanas
E dixo la donzella son sanas ensu t<ien>po & dolie<n>tes en
su t<ien>po E dixo el fisico q<ua>les
son las frutas & dixo la donzella las granadas p<ar>a los
dolie<n>tes & las alme<n>dras &}
{CB2.
las ma<n>çanas E otorgo con<e>lla
el fisico E p<re>gu<n>to dela sang<ri>a
E dixo la donzella sangria

es buena en martes la lu-
na me<n>gua<n>te & el çielo esco<n>-
brado de nuues & sera el cue<r>-
po espaçioso & alegre & el figado E el sangrador avn-
q<ue> sea sabidor delas co<n>plisio-
nes delos am<n>es E otorgo
con<e>lla el fisico E dixo ala
donzella q<ua>l cosa es la que enca-
nesçe al om<n>e ant<e> de su tie<n>po
E dixo la donzella la debda
descubie<r>ta & la poridat & yazer co<n> muger vieja que es
pecado mortal E otorgo co<n>
ella el fisico E p<re>gu<n>tole de
la entrada del baño E dixo
la donzella bueno es el ba-
ño saluo q<ue> ha men<e>ster co<n>di-
çion<e>s E dixo el fisico q<ua>les
son E dixo las donzella la
vergue<n>ça & cobrir lo que es
de cobrir E q<ue> el baño sea
co<n> agua fria & dulçe & sallira luego el cue<r>po del om<n>e}
[fol. 93v]
{CB2.
alegre E otorgo con<e>lla el
fisico E p<re>gu<n>tole dela carne
qual era la mas sana E di-
xo la donzella el carn<er>o es
melezina & su carne es vianda ot<r>o`ssy la carne es ma<n>-
teca & es sanidat E oto<r>go
con<e>lla el fisico E dixo ala
donzella q<ue> dezides dela carne gorda E dixo la donze-
lla es pe<n>samie<n>to del alma
E q<ue> dezides dela carne magra & dixo la donzella es
vianda calie<n>te E otorgo
con<e>lla el fisico E dixo que
dezides del yazer co<n> las mu-

geres E la donzella co<n> gra<n>t
vergue<n>ça q<ue> ouo abaxo sus
ojos co<n> su rrostro co<n>tra t<ie>rra
E leuantose el fisico en pie
& dixo al rrey sabet señor
q<ue> es vençida la donzella
pu<e>s q<ue> no<n> rresponde a esta
demanda E dixo la donze-
lla señor no<n> lo mande dios
q<ue> yo oue ve<r>gue<n>ça de vos
porq<ue> so moça & niña & so
virgen E el rrey ouo gra<n>t}
{CB2.
amor della & mandole q<ue> rrespo<n>-
diese E dixo la donzella fisico todo yazer co<n> muge<r> es
dolençia E q<ua>ndo ouieres de
yazer con<e>lla podra ser que
sea preñada o q<ue> crie fijo
mucho a sus tetas o otra
muger q<ue> g<ua>rde & es men<e>ster
q<ue> sea el varo<n> sabidor de esto
E dixo el fisico enq<ue> ha menester q<ue> sea sabidor E dixo
la donzella sy fuere la muge<r>
tal q<ue> vinie<n>te su talente tarde & la del varo<n> ayna toller
se a el talante della ant<e> que
del varo<n> & acaesçe q<ue> non podra sanar la muge<r> dello E
ha men<e>ster q<ue> sea el yazer
co<n>la muger en<e>l te<r>çio postrimero dela noche por q<ue> sea
el coraço<n> calie<n>te & el cue<r>po
& el estomago destrauado de
la vianda E otorgo con<e>lla
el fisico E q<ue> dezides dela
hedat delas mug<er>es E dixo
la donzella la muge<r> de vey<n>-
te años es com<m>o nobleza
E la muger de trey<n>ta años}
[fol. 94r]

{CB2.
es com<m>o carne co<n> limo<n> E la muger de q<ua>ranta annols es de seso
E la muger de çi<n>q<ua>nta años
es p<ar>a el cuchillo E la muger
delos sesenta años es p<ar>a el otro
mundo E la muge<r> delos sete<n>ta
años es vieja t<ie>rra E la muge<r>
de noue<n>ta años no<n> me pre-
gu<n>tedes del infie<r>no q<ue> es la
cosa mas esq<ui>ua q<ue> ay enel
mundo todo E el fisico pre-
gu<n>to por las fermosuras delas
mug<er>es q<ua>les era E dixo la
donzella acuçioso sodes de pre-
gu<n>tar E el vno dellos era
alfaq<ui> sabidor de justiçias &
de leyes E el otro era fisico
delas cosas q<ue> p<er>ten<e>sçian ala fisica E el otro era sabidor de
la gramatica & de la logica
& dela buena fabla E el
alfaq<ui> sabidor delas leyes & del
libro de dios dixo ala donzella
rrespondet alo q<ue> vos p<re>gu<n>tare
E dixo la donzella rresponde-
re co<n>la merçed de dios & de n<uest>ro
señor el rrey abomeliq<ue> alma<n>-
çor q<ue> dios ma<n>tenga E dixo
el alfaq<ui> donzella q<ue> ordeno di-}
{CB2.
os sobre nos en n<uest>ro dia E sobre su sie<r>uo ensu dia E dixo
la donzella alas gentes & A
las animalias dixo s<er>uit me
& no<n> me menospreçiedes E
yo no<n> menospreçiare a vos
E dixo el alfaq<ui> donzella muy
bie<n> rrespondiestes E p<re>gu<n>touos
q<ua>les son los juyzios & los ma<n>-
damie<n>tos de dios E dixo la
donzella tres & ci<n>co E dixo el

alfaq<ui> glosatme q<ua>les son E dixo la donzella p<er>donat q<ua>ndo
ouieredes poder & q<ua>ndo fueredes poderoso & g<ra>nde el dia alto delante v<uest>ros ojos E dixo
el alfaq<ui> donzella muy bien
dixiestes E los tres que so<n>
çi<n>co E dixo la donzella los
tres q<ue> son çi<n>co es el testimonio q<ue> ha otro c<ri>ador sy non
dios & mu<n>dat el cue<r>po & a-
linpiadlo E otorgo con<e>lla el
alfaq<ui> en q<ua>nto dixo la donzella E estonçe dixo la donzella alfaq<ui> el sennor alto & bendito sea co<n> siete çielos E puso en<e>llos las estrellas vna
p<ar>tida dellas p<ar>a ennoblesçer}
[fol. 94v]
{CB2.
los çielos E otra p<ar>a los moros
E otra p<ar>a las gentes E otra
p<ar>a el poder del diablo maldito E dixo el alfaq<ui> donzella
muy bie<n> dixiestes E dixo estonçes la donzella alfaqui el
n<uest>ro señor alto & bendito sea co<n>
siete çielos & co<n> doze signos
E dixo el alfaq<ui> glosatme q<ua>-
les son E dixo la donzella
Acarius geminis Aries taur<us>
piscis cançer leo virgo libra
escorpi<us> sagitari<us> cap<ri>cornius
E dixo la donzella alfaq<ui> el q<ue>
fiziere oraçio<n> & no<n> fuere q<ui>to
de pecado no<n> sera oyda su ora-
çio<n> E el q<ue> es q<ui>to de pecado
sy no<n> fiziere oraçio<n> non sera
ouda su castidat E el que es
casto & fiziere oraçio<n> entrara
enla gl<or>ia de p<ar>ayso E dixo el
alfaq<ui> donzella bie<n> dixiestes

mas enq<ue> deue om<n>e ser casto
E dixo la donzella enla plata
& en<e>l t<ri>go & enla çeuada & e-
nel çe<n>teno & en la[s] frutas &
enlas azeytunas & en<e>l ganado ouejuno & vacuno & de
todas las otras cosas q<ue> dios}
{CB2.
le diere E leua<n>tose el alfaq<ui>
& dixo al rrey señor por verdat
esta donzella mas sabe que no<n>
yo & yo le do la mejoria enel
saber E el rrey ouo desto gra<n>t
plazer E mando al otro luego
q<ue> fablase con<e>lla E leuantose
el fisico & dixo ala donzella
rrespondetme alo q<ue> vos p<re>gu<n>ta-
re E dixo la donzella sy rrespondere co<n>la me<r>çed del c<ri>ador
& de n<uest>ro señor el rrey abomeli-
q<ue> q<ue> dios ma<n>tenga E dixo el
fisico donzella dezitme dela
co<n>façio<n> del cue<r>po del om<n>e E dixo la donzella al fisico assi es
q<ue> n<uest>ro señor te<n>pro la humidat
co<n>la secura & el fizo dende la
t<ie>rra & te<n>pro la secura & la humidat & fizo dende el ayre &
abafo la t<ie>rra E sy no<n> fuese por
los bafos dela t<ie>rra federia<n> n<uest>ros
fuelgos co<n>tra el çielo & enla t<ie>rra
& el om<n>e com<m>o es de q<ua>tro eleme<n>-
tos E dixo el fisico q<ua>les son
& dixo la donzella t<ie>rra & fuego
& agua & ayre En<e>l año son
q<ua>tro te<n>porales Inui<e>rno & verano & estio & otoño E en<e>stos
[catchword] q<ua>tro t<ien>pos}
[fol. 95r}
{CB2.
q<ua>tro t<ien>pos rreman<e>sçe la colora
& la maletia & la sangre &

la flema E ha men<e>ster q<ue>
sea el fisico sabidor delas co<n>-
plision<e>s & delas melezinas
q<ue> p<er>ten<e>sçen al cue<r>po & segu<n>t
fuere<n> men<e>ster al cue<r>po E o-
torgo con<e>lla el fisico E dixo donzella dezitme q<ua>les
son las señales p<ar>a la muge<r>
ser fermosa E dixo la donzella aq<ue>lla muge<r> es fermosa q<ue> es señora de diez & ocho
señales E dixo el fisico dezitme q<ua>les son estas diez &
ocho señalesE dixo la donzella la q<ue> es lue<n>ga en tres
& peq<ue>ña en tres & ancha en
tres & blanca en tres & p<ri>eta
en tres & be<r>meja en tres E
dixo el fisico dezitme com<m>o
es esto E dixo la donzella
lue<n>ga en tres q<ue> sea luenga
de estado & q<ue> aya el cuello la<r>-
go & los dedos lue<n>gos E bla<n>-
ca en tres el cue<r>po blanco
& los die<n>tes blancos & lo bla<n>-
co de los ojos blanco E p<ri>eta}
{CB2.
en tres cabellos p<ri>etos & pestañas p<ri>etas & lo p<ri>eto delos o-
jos p<ri>eto E be<r>meja en tres
mexillas bermejas & beços be<r>-
mejos & enzias be<r>mejas E
peq<ue>ña en tres boca peq<ue>ña
& nariz peq<ue>ña & los pies
peq<ue>ños E ancha en tres
ancha de caderas & ancha
de espaldas & ancha la fre<n>te
E q<ue> sea muy plaze<n>tera asu
marido & muy ayudadora
asu marido & q<ue> sea peq<ue>ña de
hedat E leua<n>tose el fisico
e dixo ala donzella dios vos

faga bie<n> q<ue> en todo fablast<e>s
bie<n> E dixo al rrey por ve<r>dat
señor yo vos digo q<ue> esta donzella q<ue> sabe mas q<ue> no<n> yo &
yo la do per ve<r>dadera E el rrey
p<re>sçiolo mucho E mando luego al otro sabidor q<ue> se leua<n>ta-
se ha fablar co<n>la donzella E
leua<n>tose luego abrahe<n> el trobador & sabidor de gramatica
& de logica E dixo donzella
aparejaduos q<ue> no<n> so yo delos
q<ue> auedes ençerrado & vençido}
[fol. 95v]
{CB2.
E p<re>gu<n>tole la donzella quie<n>
era & com<m>o auia no<n>bre E dixo
el yo so abrahe<n> el trobador E
dixo la donzella abrahe<n> yo
nu<n>ca vos conosci p<er>o asentat
vos & p<re>gu<n>tadme q<ue> yo vos
rrespondere co<n>la me<r>çed de dios
& de n<uest>ro señor el rrey q<ue> dios
mante<n>ga E luego dixo a-
brahe<n> ala donzella sy vos me
rrespondedes çie<r>ta me<n>te a todo
lo q<ue> yo vos p<re>gu tare q<ue> yo que
vos de todos los mis paños E
sy vos no<n> me rrespondedes çie<r>-
tame<n>te q<ue> vos q<ue> me dedes los
v<uest>ros paños E dixo la donzella & yo assy lo pido por me<r>-
çed a n<uest>ro señor el rrey que
nos lo mande a vos & a mi
E el rrey mandolo luego &
otorgogelo assy a amos a
dos E abrahe<n> el trobador dixo donzella qual es la cosa
mas pesada q<ue> ay enlos mo<n>-
tes & mas ap<re>surada q<ue> la
saeta & mas aguda quela
espada & mas ardiente que el

fuego & mas dulçe que la}
{CB2.
miel & lag<ri>mas de ojos & dole<n>-
çia syn melexina & mas rrezio
q<ue> el hueso & tale<n>te de vna
ora & plazer de tres dias &
plazer de vn mes & plaz<er> de
çinco dias E vna aue q<ue> se c<ri>a
enlos mo<n>tes q<ue> en<e>lla ay ocho
señales de g<ra>ndes animalias
E rrespondio la donzella apa-
rejad v<uest>ras rropas q<ue> yo vos rrespondere co<n>la me<r>çed de dios
E rrespondiole & dixo lo que
es mas pesado q<ue>los mo<n>tes es
el agua e mas ap<re>surado q<ue> la
saeta es el ojo E mas aguda
q<ue> la espada es la lengua E
mas ardiente q<ue> el fuego es el
coraço<n> E mas dulçe q<ue> la miel
es el bue<n> fijo E dole<n>çia syn
melezina es la locura E el
mas çierto es el llamamie<n>to
del señor del mu<n>do E lo q<ue> es
mas rrezio q<ue> el hueso es la
verdat E talente de vna ora
es yazer co<n>la muge<r> E solaz
de vn dia es gana<n>çia E plazer de tres dias son obras
de baño(^r) E plazer de siete}
[fol. 96r]
{CB2.
dias es el nouio los p<ri>meros
siete dias E plazer de vn
mes es el q<ue> viene desu camino E el aue q<ue> se c<ri>a enlos mo<n>-
tes q<ue> ha en<e>lla ocho man<er>as
de g<ra>ndes animalias es la
çigarra q<ue> el su pescueço es de
vaca & el su pecho es de cauallo & sus rrostros de leon
& sus alas de aguila & su

çi<n>ta de alacra<n> & la cola de sie<r>-
pe & los pies de auestruz
& el vie<n>tre de buey E abra-
he<n> el trob ador se leua<n>to en
pie & dixo al rrey señor sed
çie<r>to q<ue> sabe esta donzella
mas q<ue> no<n> yo ni<n> q<ua>ntos sabios
vos tenes & todos le deue<n>
dar la mejora en<e>l saber E
luego el rrey abemeliq<ue> dixo ala
donzella dios vos g<ua>rde de mal
& vos de su gr<aci>a por q<ue> ta<n> bie<n>
rrespondiestes a todas estas co-
sas q<ue> aq<ue>llos sabios & yo vos
p<re>gu<n>tamos & ta<n> çie<r>ta mente
rrespondiestes a ellas E lue-
go q<ue> esto ouo dicho el rrey a-
brahe<n> despojo sus paños & dio}
{CB2.
los ala donzella E luego la
donzella se leua<n>to en pie & dixo abrahe<n> datme los v<uest>ros paños menores com<m>o fue puesto
q<ue> me diesedes todos v<uest>ros paños & abrahe<n> dio ala donzella diez mill doblas de oro por
no<n> pasar tal ve<r>gue<n>ça com<m>o le
fuera sy los paños le ouiera
de dar ally dela<n>te del rrey E
luego el rrey le dixo donzella
peditme me<r>çed & dezit en q<ue>
man<er>a la q<ue>redes syla q<ue>redes
en mi casa o en bue<n> casa mia`
q<ue> sed çie<r>ta q<ue> vos lo de q<ua>l vos
demandares E luego rrespon-
dio la donzella al rrey E dixole señor ma<n>te<n>gauos dios
sy me<r>çed me auedes de faze<r>
enbiatme co<n> mi señor el me<r>-
cador q<ue> yo no<n> conosco otro
padre saluo a el q<ue> me c<ri>o q<ua>n-
to mas q<ue> fizo mucho por me

llegar a este estado & me mostro lo q<ue> se E el rrey mando
le dar luego diez mill doblas
de bue<n> oro & de p<re>sçio E la do<n>-
zella tomolas & beso al rrey
las manos & la t<ie>rra ant<e>l E}
[fol. 96v]
{CB2.
fuese co<n>su señor el me<r>cador
E casose con<e>l & fuero<n> muy
rricos dende adelante p<ar>a sie<n>-
pre jamas.}

Biblioteca Nacional, Madrid — MS 9055

The first text in this book is a list of arms (illustrated), dated 1305 "era de Cristo" within the text. The last text in the book is dated 1454 (22 July, King John died in Valladolid). This is a partial copy only of the Teodor text; pages are missing before, within, and following this fragment. The Teodor fragment begins on folio 69r.

[fol. 69r]
{CB1.
buena fabla Entonçe rrecudio el maest<r>o`
sabidor dela ley & delos Juyzios & del
libro de dios E dixo ala donzella señora rrespondet E veredes lo q<ue> yo vos p<re>-
guntare E dixole la donzella maest<r>o`
señor yo vos rrespondere conla ayuda
de dios E del rrey almaçorre Donze-
lla q<ue> ordeno n<uest>ro señor dios sobre vos
el dia q<ue> nasçistes Respondio la do<n>ze-
lla maestro señor dios ordeno sobre mi
& sobre todos los sieruos & dixo asy
a las gentes & alas almanias s<er>uid
me & no<n> me (& no<n> me) aprouechedes
q<ue> yo ap<ro>uechare avos & dixo el maest<r>o`
donzella declarad lo aquesta rrespondio
la donzella q<ua>ndo fueredes poderosos es
bien poderoso q<ua>ndo ovieredes poder
de prender prendes diablo maledicho
de ante vos & de ante v<uest>ros ojos E dixo
le el maestro se aq<ue>llos otros q<ue> son ci<n>co
Respondio la donzella & dixo yo vo
en romeria alos tres rromerajes dela
casa sancta de jh<e>r<usa>l<e>m & a sant pedro
de rroma & asantiago de galizia &}
[fol. 69v]
{CB1.
enmendar el cuerpo por penitençia & fazer deuota mente oracion & ma[n]tener castidat E preguntole el maestro & dixo
donzella en qual otra manera deue ser
om
e casto & v<er>dadero & no<n> feziese deuota-
mente oraçion com<m>o deue con grand co-

raçon ca este no<n>le sera rreçebida su castidat ni<n> su coraçon & si la feziera omildo-
sa mente & de gra<n>d coraço<n> sera rresçe-
bida en la gl<or>ia del ot<r>o` mu<n>do & sera sal-
uo com<m>o la ora q<ue>lo pario su madre & p<re>-
guntole el sabio E dixole donzella en
qual otra man<er>a deue ser om
e casto &
v<er>dadero Respondio la donzella & dixo
en la plata & en<e>l oro & en<e>l t<ri>go & enla
çeuada & enel çenteno e enlas pasas
& enlas azetunas E en el ganado ove-
Juno & en vacuno E leuanto se el maestro & paro se ante el rrey & dixole
por v<er>dat vos digo señor q<ue> esta donzella q<ue> sabe mucho mas q<ue> yo & yo la
do por v<er>dadera & le do toda mi memo-
ria E luego el rrey fuese p<ar>a la do<n>ze-
lla muy gradoso & tomo muy gra<n>d
plazer E entoçe leuanto se el segu<n>do
maestro}
[fol. 70r]
BLANK
[fol. 70v]
BLANK
[fol. 71r]
{CB1.
dela fisica delo que conuenia A cada
dolençia segu<n>d el t<ien>po & pregunto a
la donzella antel rrey & ante todos
los caualleros & escuderos & dixo le
maestro señor yo vos rrespondere co<n>
el ayuda de dios & del rrey alman-
çorre E dixol el maestro donzella p<re>-
gunto vos por las conplesiones delos
om
es com<m>o son de sçidas Et dixo
le la donzella maestro señor asy es q<ue>
el n<uest>ro señor dios con<e>l çielo & conla
t<ie>rra & conlos baos delos ayres q<ue> sy
no<n> fuesen por los baos delos ayres
que andan sobre la t<ie>rra federia<n> v<uest>ros
fuelgos q<ue> son los resullos por eso
fizo dios el çielo & la t<ie>rra por q<ue> todo

om
e es criado de q<ua>tro eleme<n>tos fue
go & ayre & t<ie>rra Asi en<e>l Año so<n>
q<ua>tro t<ien>pos Inuierno & verao & agos`-
to & otono enq<ue> A faze rremeçer e<n>
Aquestos q<ua>tro t<ien>pos la colora & la maletia & la flema & la sangre & rrespondio el sabio & dixol qual es mas
sana delas fructas rrespondio la do<n>ze-
lla & dixo señor maestro las gui<n>das}
[fol. 71v]
{CB1.
& alas mendras & los dolientes los da-
tiles & las granadas & los garuan-
ços cochos con su caldo preguntole
el maestro & dixo le donzella en q<ue>
dia es buena la sangria E la donzella rrespondio & dixo maestro e<n>
(en)<e>l dia del martes la luna mengua<n>-
te & el çielo esconbrado de nuues se
ra el cuerpo espaçiado E el maest<r>o`
le dixo qual es la cosa q<ue> ante faze
encanesçer Ant<e> de su t<ien>po rrespo<n>dio
la donzella maestro señor la debda
& descobrir poridat & Jazer conlas
viejas es ponçon<i>a mortal rrespo<n>dio
el maestro & dixo q<ue> cosa es mug<e>r de
veynte Años rrespondio la donzella mug<e>r de veynte Años p<ar>a la cama
mug<e>r de treynta Años nobleza d<e>l
q<ue> la veye & la mug<e>r de q<ua>renta Años
de sosiego & la mug<e>r de cinq<ue>nta
Años p<ar>a el cochillo & la mug<e>r de
sesenta Años vieja t<ie>rra la mug<e>r
de setenta Años ni<n> p<ar>a este mu<n>do ni<n>
p<ar>a el ot<r>o. la mug<e>r de ochenta Años
non melo preguntedes q<ue> enlos Ju-}
{RMK: some text missing here.}
[fol. 72r]
{CB1.
ha de av<er> enella tres señales E si fue
re luenga ha de av<er> enella tres señales
& sy fuere ancha ha de av<er> enella tres

señales E si fuere prieta ha de av<er> en
ella tres señales E sy fuere rruuia ha
(ha) de av<er> tres señales & v<er>meja & si fue
ancha ha de av<er> enella tres señales
& sy fuere peq<ue>ña ha de av<er> tres señales
rrespondio el maestro & dixo donzella
estas señales q<ue> son de tres entres de cla-
ras melas & aq<ue>sto rrespondio & dixo
blanca blanco el cuerpo & blancos los dientes & blanco lo blanco delos ojos la
prieto ojos prietos çejas prietas cabellos prietos E la luengo cuello lue<n>go
& cue<r>po luengo & dedos lue<n>gos & la
ruuia v<er>mejas enziuas & v<er>mejos la
bros & mexillas v<er>mejas E la ancha
anchas caderas & anchas espaldas
& muñecas anchas E la pequ<e>ña peq<ue>-
ño pie & pequeña boca & peq<ue>ña
manera & entoçe el fisico se leua<n>-
to & fue se ant<e>l rrey & dixo le por
v<er>dad vos digo señor q<ue> esta donze-}
[fol. 72v]
{CB1.
lla q<ue> sabe mucho mas q<ue> non yo. yo le do
toda mi me<m>oria & me do por vencedora
della E luego leua<n>tose abray alfatas
maestro sabidor del la gramatica & dela
buena fabla & dixole donzella aparejad vos donzella q<ue> no<n> so yo aq<ue>llos
maestros con q<ui>en vos avedes disputado & la (rresp) donzella rrespondio &
dixo maestro señor com<m>o avedes no<n>-
bre rrespondio el maestro ami dizen a-
bray alfatas E luego la donzella dixo asentadvos muy q<ueri>do q<ue> con<e>l ayuda de dios & d<e>l rrey alma<n>çorre yo vos
rrespondere a q<ua>nto vos me dema<n>dared<e>s
mas rruego Ami señor. el rrey & ato-
dos q<ua>ntos ag<en> son cauall<er>os com<m>o escuderos & fijos dalgo q<ue> aq<ui> estades
pregunto q<ue> sy vos me vençeredes q<ue>
yo vos do todos mis paños asy com<m>o

los tengo vestidos E sy por a[???]
ta yo vos vençiere q<ue> vos q<ue> me dedes
todos v<uest>ros paños asi com<m>o los tenedes vestidos E luego el maest<r>o` abray al-}
[fol. 73r]
{CB1.
fatos leuanto se enpie & otorgole todo
com<m>o dema<n>do la donze [sic] & ansi lo otor`-
garon Amos delante del Rey & ante
todos los cauall<er>os & fijos dalgo cada
vno en su lugar Et luego el maest<r>o` (^ab)
abray alfatas p<re>gu<n>to ala donzella
& dixo donzella qual es la cosa mas
pesada q<ue> los mo<n>tes & q<ua>l es la cosa mas`
aguda q<ue>l espada & qual es cosa mas`
ardiente q<ue>l fuego qual es la cosa
mas çie<r>ta que asmamie<n>to & q<ua>l es la cosa mas apresurada q<ue> saeta & q<ua>l es
la cosa mas dulce q<ue>la miel & q<ua>l es la
cosa mas amarga q<ue>la fiel E lagrimas de ojos & dolençia syn piedat
& plazer de vna ora & plazer de
dos dias & plazer de ocho dias & plazer de vn mes Et vn ave q<ue> bola por
los mo<n>tes q<ue> ay en<e>lla siete sennales &
elementos Et luego leua<n>to se la do<n>-
zella enpie & dixo abray alfatas des`-
pojas v<uest>ros paños q<ue> vençido sode<s> co<n>
la ayuda de dios & del rrey alma<n>-
çorre yo vos rrespondere Atodo aq<ue>sto q<ue>}
[fol. 73v]
{CB1.
vos aq<ui> avedes demandado & leuanto se
la donzella enpie & dixo maest<r>o` señor
la cosa mas pesada q<ue> los montes es
la debda & la cosa mas apresurada
q<ue>la saeta es la vista E la cosa mas a-
guda q<ue>l espada es la lengua & la cosa
mas ardiente q<ue>l fuego es el coraço<n> &
la cosa mas çie<r>ta q<ue>l asmamie<n>to es dios
Ela cosa mas rrezia q<ue>l hueso es la verdat & la cosa mas dulce q<ue>la miel es la

buena fija & la cosamas ama<r>ga q<ue>la
fiel es la me<n>tira & lagrimas de ojos es
el mal fijo & dolençia syn piedat es
la mala fija & plazer de vna ora dormir co<n> muger & plazer de dos oras
gana<n>çia en mercaderia & plazer de
ocho dias el nouio co<n>la nouia & plazer de vn mes el q<ue> viene con paz d<e>l
camino & vn aue q<ue> bola por los mo<n>-
tes q<ue> ay enella siete señales & eleme<n>-
tos de gra<n>des eleme<n>tos su cue<r>po es
de aue estrus & sus alas de ag<ui>la &
sus cue<r>nos de çie<r>uo & sus pechos de
vaca & sus çancas de alcaraua<n> & su}
[fol. 74r]
{CB1.
cabeça de buey & su cola biuora &
este es el çigaro<n> que anda por los
montes & entonçe abray alfatas se
leua<n>to & fuese ant<e>l rrey & dixo le
por v<er>dad vos digo señor q<ue> esta do<n>-
zella q<ue> sabe mucho mas q<ue> yo E yo le
do toda mi me<j>oria & la do por ven-
çedora E entonçe leua<n>tose la donzella & dixo maest<r>o` señor dad me
v<uest>ros paños q<ue> vençido sodes Et entonçe leua<n>to se el maestro & diol todos sus paños asy com<m>o los tenie
vestidos & q<ue>daron los paños menores & la donzella dixo maest<r>o` señor
tened en lo q<ue> posistes Et despues el
maestro por non le dar los paños menores diole diez mill doblas de oro
v<er>mejo q<ue> vale vna dobla diez doblas
Et ento<n>çe p<re>gunto el rrey ala donzella sy q<ue>ria quedar con<e>l osi q<ue>ria
yr conel me<r>cador & la donzella dixo señor mas q<ui>ero yr con<e>l mercador q<ue> me ha criado fasta agora}

Biblioteca Nacional, Madrid — MS 17822

Spine title "Bocados de oro"

The Teodor section begins at 117vb 18.

[fol. 117vb18]
{CB2.
{RUB. Capitulo que fabla de
los enxenplos de teodor
donzella.}
{IN4.} Auia en vauilo-
nia vn merca-
der muy rrico
& muy linpio
& oraçionero enlas çi<n>-
co oraçiones & fazedor
de bondades alos me-
nesterosos & alas biu-}
[fol. 118r]
{CB2.
das & ama muchos algos
& tenia muchos hermanos`
& muchos parientes & no<n>
tenia fijo nin fija % E aca-
eçio vn dia que merco vna
donzella & dio por ella
muchas doblas & muchos`
aueres % E leuola asu
casa & mostrole todas
las artes & sabidurias
quantas pudo saber & de<n>-
de atienpo allego el mer-
cador a gra[n]d menester
& dixo ala donzella sabed
que me a traydo A gra<n>
menester que non e algo
nin consejo & non se me
escusa que vos non aya
de vender. % Pu<e>s dadme
consejo por onde aya me-

joria & bien % E abaxo
la donzella los ojos &
la cabeça contra tierra
comidiendo % E despu<e>s
alço los ojos arriba
& dixo non auedes q<ue>
Reçelar con la merced
de dios & dixo ydvos}
{CB2.
agora al alcaçeria de
los boticarios & traed
me afeitamientos p<ar>a
muger & nobles vestidu-
ras & lleuadme al al-
caçar del Rey abomeliq<ue>
almançor % E quando
vos preguntare por v<uest>ra
venida dezilde quiero
vos vender esta donze-
lla & pedit le por mi di-
ez mill doblas de bue<n>
oro fino % E si dixere q<ue>
es mucho dezilde sen<n>or
si conoçiesedes la don-
zella nonlo terniades
por mucho % E fuese
el mercador al alcaçe-
ria delos boticarios
& fue avno que dezia<n>
mahomad & saluolo
& el boticario le dixo
mercador que auedes
menester % E el mer-
cador le conto la Ra-
zon por q<ue> venia &
dixo quiero que me
dedes fermosas vesti-
duras}
[fol. 118v]
{CB2.
& fermosos afeitami-
entos para mi do<n>zella

% E el tendero ouo del
grand piadad & delo q<ue>
dixo de la donzella que
la queria vender % E
dixo Amigo mucho me
amjvazillastes mi cora-
con & fezistes llorar
mis ojos por la v<uest>ra pobreza & por que q<ue>redes
vender la v<uest>ra donzella
& la v<uest>ra demanda presta es & leuantose el bo-
ticario & diole las nobles`
vestiduras & nobles a-
feitamientos para mu-
ger & el mercadero to-
molo todo & lleuolo a
la donzella & ella pa-
gose dello & dixo esto
vos sera buen comienço
conla ayuda de dios
% E leuantose la do<n>ze-
lla & vistiose & afeytose
muy bien % E dixo asu
sen<n>or leuantad vos &
sobid comigo al alcaçar}
{CB2.
del Rey. E leuantose su se-
n<n>or & fuero<n>se para el alcaçar del Rey & pidieron liçençia que entrasen al Rey
& el Rey mando q<ue> entrase<n>
& entraro<n> & pararonse a-
mos antel Rey % E q<ua>ndo
el Rey los vido començo
de fablar conel merca-
dor & preguntole por
su venida & que era lo q<ue>
queria & el mercador le
dixo sen<n>or quiero vos
vender esta donzella &
el Rey le dixo qua<n>to es

su preçio & el mercador
le dixo sen<n>or quiero por
ella diez mill doblas
de buen oro finisymo
bermejo & el Rey lo to-
mo por estran<n>o el pre-
çio de la donzella & dixo
al mercadero mucho vos
estendistes en su preçio
o ssallistes de v<uest>ro acuerdo % O la donzella se
alaba de cosas que no
pueden ser & Respo<n>dio}
[fol. 119r]
{CB2.
el mercadero & dixo al Rey
sen<n>or non tengas por mucho el precio de la donzella. ca poco es que yo la
crie de pequen<n>a & es
moça & costome muchos
aueres fasta que apre<n>-
dio & entendio todas
las artes & los nobles
menesteres & esto non
sera çelado avos % E
començo el Rey a fablar
conla donzella % E ella
abaxo el velo de vergue<n>-
ca & ella abaxo el ve-
lo de verguença & el Rey
alço los ojos & vido su
fermosura que semeja-
ua al sol quando salia
que non auia en ese t<ien>po
mas fermosa quella /
dixole el Rey donzella
que auedes nonbre &
Respondio la donzella
& dixo sen<n>or ami dizen
teodor % E dixole el
Rey donzella que apre<n>-

distes delas artes & di-}
{CB2.
xo la donzella sen<n>or yo
aprendi la ley & el libro
& aprendi los quatro li-
bros & las siete plane-
tas & las estrellas &
las leyes & los man-
damientos & el tras-
lado & los prometi-
mientos & las cosas q<ue>
crio en los cielos % E
aprendi las {AD. [^fablas delas]} aues. &
de las animalias & la
fisyca & filosofia & la logica & las cosas proua-
das & el juego del a-
xedrez& aprendi taner
laud & cañon & las tre-
ynta & tres trobas &
aprendi las buenas cos-
tumbres deleyes & apre<n>-
di baylar & cantar & so-
tar & aprendi texer pa-
ños de peso & aprendi
labrar de oro & de pla-
ta & de todas las otras`
artes & cosas nobles
% E en que oyo el Rey
estas palabras de la do<n>-
zella}
[fol. 119v]
{CB2.
fizose marauillado & ma<n>-
do llamar los mayores sa-
bios de sus artes & dixo
les que prouasen esta
donzella % E salleron
luego a ella tres om<ne>s letrados & todos le pre-
guntaron espeçial me<n>te
vn fisico quele pregu<n>-

tarion & dixo donzella
las flores son sanas
& dixo la donzella so<n>
sanas en su tienpo & do-
lientes en su tienpo % E
dixo el fisico quales so<n>
las frutas & dixo (el) (^fi-
sico) las almendras &
las mançanas & otor-
go conella el fisico % E
pregunto dela sang<ri>a
& dixo la sangria es
buena en martes &
la luna menguante
& el çielo ascondido
de nuues & sera el
cuerpo espaçioso &
alegre el figado % E
el sangrador avn q<ue> sea}
{CB2.
sabidor de las conplisio-
nes de los om<n>es & otorgo conella el fisico % E
dixo a la donzella q<ua>l
cosa es la que encane-
çe al om<n>e ante de su
tienpo & dixo ala don-
zella la debda descubi-
erta & la poridad & ya-
zer con muger vieja q<ue> es
pecado mortal & otor-
go conella el fisico % E
pregunto dela entra-
da del vaño & dix bu-
eno es vaño saluo que
a menester condiçiones
& dixo el fisico quales
son & dixo la donzella
la verguença & cobrir
lo que es de cobrir & q<ue>
sea el vaño con agua
fria & dulce & saliria

luego el cuerpo del o-
m<n>e alegre & otorgo
conella el fisico % E pre-
guntaro<n> le dela carne
qual era las mas sana
& dixo la donzella el}
[fol. 120r]
{CB2.
carnero es melezina &
su carne es vianda & ot<ro>-
si la carne es manteca &
es sanidad & otorgo co-
nella el fisico & dixo a
la donzella que dezides
de la carne & dixo la
donzella es pensamie<n>-
to del alma & que dezi-
des dela carne magra
& dixo la donzella es
vianda caliente & otor-
go conella el fisyco % E
dixo que dezides del
yazer con las mugeres
& la donzella con gra<n>
verguença que ouo a-
baxo sus ojos consu
Rostro contra t<ie>rra & leuantose el fisico en pie
& dixo al Rey sabed se-
ñor que es vençida la
donzella. pu<e>s que no<n>
rresponde a esta dema<n>-
da % E dixo la donze-
lla señor no<n> lo mande
dios. ca yo oue vergu-
ença de vos por q<ue> so y<o>}
{CB2.
niña pequeña & so v<ir>ge<n>
& el Rey ouo muy gra<n>
amor della & mandole
que le Respondiese % E
dixo la donzella fisico

todo yazer con muger
es dolencia & quando
ouieres de yazer cone-
lla podra ser q<ue> sea pre-
ñda o que crie fijo
macho a sus tetas o
otra muger q<ue> gu-
arde & es menester q<ue>
sea el varon sabidor
desto % E dixole el
fisico en que a menes-
ter que sea el (^s) varo<n>
sabidor dixo la don-
zella si fuere tal q<ue> viniere ala muger su
talento tarde & la
del varon ayna toller
sea el talente della a<n>-
te que del varon & po-
dra ser q<ue> sane la mu-
ger dello & a menester
que sea el yazer co<n>la
muger en el terçio pos-
trimero}
[fol. 120v]
{CB2.
dela noche por que sea
el coraçon caliente & el
cuerpo & el estomago des-
trauado dela vianda &
otorgo conella el fisi-
co % E que dezides de
la hedad delas muge-
res & dize la donzella
que la muger de veyn-
te años es com<m>o noble-
za & la muge[r] de tre-
ynta años es co<mm>o
carne con limon % E
la muger de quare<n>ta
años es de seso % E la
muger de cinque<n>ta es

para el cuchillo % E la
muger de setenta años
es para el otro mundo
% E la muger de sete<n>ta
años es vieja t<ie>rra % la
muger de noue<n>ta años
non me preguntedes
del ynfierno que es la
cosa mas esquiua de
todo el mundo % E el
fisico pregunto por las
fermosuras de las mu-}
{CB2.
geres quales eran & dixo
la donzella acuçioso sodes
de preguntar % E el vno
dellos era alfaqui sabi-
dor de justiçias e de leyes
& el otro era fisico de las
cosas que perteneçen a
la fisica & el otro era sabidor de la gramatica
& de la logica & de la buena fabla % E el alfaq<ui>
sabidor de las leyes &
del libro de dios dixo a
la donzella Responded
me alo que vos pregun-
tare & dixo (^a) la donzella
rresponderé conla mer-
çed de dios & de ṅ<uest>ro señor el Rey abomeliq<ue> almançor que dios man-
tenga & dixo el alfaq<ui>
donzella que ordeno di-
os sobre nos en n<uest>ro dia
& sobre su syeruo en su dia
& dixo la donzella alas
gentes & a las anima-
lias dixo seruid me &
non me menospreçides}
{CW. E yo no<n>}

[fol. 121r]
{CB2.
E yo non menosprecia-
re avos & dixo el alfa-
qui donzella muy bie<n>
rrespondistes % E pre-
gunto vos los juizios`
& los mandamientos
de dios % E dixo la
donzella son tres &
çinco & dixo el Alfa-
qui glosadme quales
son % E dixo la don-
zella perdonar qua<n>-
do ouieres poder &
quando fueredes po-
deroso & grande el
dia alto delante v<uest>ros
ojos & dixo el alfa-
qui muy bien dexistes
& los tres que son çin-
co & dixo la donzella
los tres que son cinco
es el criador & el testi-
monio que non ha otro``
criador sy non dios
& mundad el cuerpo &
alinpiadlo & otorgo
conella el fisico en qu-
anto dixo la donzella}
{CB2.
% E estonçe dixo la do<n>ze-
lla alfaqui el señor alto
& bendito sea con syete
çielos & puso enellos
las estrellas vna parti-
da dellas para ennoble-
çer los çielos & otra pa<ra>
los moros & otra p<ar>a
las gentes & otra pa<ra>
el poder del diablo mal-
dito & dixo el alfaqui

muy bien dexistes % E
dixo estonçes la donze-
lla alfaq<ui> el n<uest>ro Señor
alto & bendito sea con
siete çielos & con doze
signos & dixo el alfaq<ui>
glosadme quales son
% E dixo la donzella
acarius geminis aries
taurus geminis pisçis
cançer leo virgo libra
escorpius sagitarius
capicornius % E dixo
la donzella alfaqui el
q<ue> fiziere oraçion & no<n>
fuere quito de pecado
non sera oyda su oraçio<n>}
[fol. 121v]
{CB2.
& el que es quito de pecado
si non fiziere oraçion no<n>
sera oyda su castidad &
el que es casto & fiziere
oraçion entrara enla
gloria de paraiso % E
dixo el alfaqui donzella
bien dexistes mas en q<ue>
deue om<n>e de ser casto
& dixo la donzella enla
plata & en el trigo & en
la Ceuada & enel çente-
no & en las frutas & en
las azeytunas & en el
ganado ouejuno & va-
cuno & de todas las o-
tras cosas que dios les
diere % E leua<n>tose el
alfaqui & dixo al Rey
señor por uerdad mas
sabe esta donzella que
non yo &.yo le do mejo-
ria enel saber % E el rrey

ouo desto grand plazer
& mando al otro que fa-
blase conella & leua<n>to
se el fisico & dixo ala
donzella rresponded}
{CB2.
me alo que vos pregu<n>-
tare & dixo ala donzella
si Respondere conla merçet
del criador & de n<uest>ro señor
el rrey abomeliq<ue> que dios mantenga % E dixo
el fisico donzella dezit
me dela confaçion del
Cuerpo o del om<n>e &
dixo la donzella asi
es que n<uest>ro señor dios
tenplo la humanidad
con la secura % E el fi-
zo dende la tierra & te<n>-
pro la secura e la hu-
nidad & fizo dende el
ayre & abafo la t<ie>rra
% E sinon por los {AD. [^ba]}fas
de la tierra federian
nuestros fuelgos co<n>tra
el çielo & la tierra % E
el om<n>e es de quatro
elementos & dixo el
fisico quales son & di-
xo la donzella tierra
& agua & ayre & enel
ayre son quatro tempo-
<ra>les ynuierno & verano}
[fol. 122r]
{CB2.
& estio & otoño & enestos
quatro tienpos rrema-
neçe la colora & la ma-
letia & la sangre & la
flema & a menester q<ue> sea
el fisico sabidor delas

conplisiones & delas
melezinas que perte-
neçen al cuerpo & segu<n>
fueren menester al cu-
erpo & otorgo conella
el fisico % E dixo donze-
lla quales son las seña-
les para la muger ser
fermosa & dixo la do<n>-
zella a aquella muger
es fermosa que es sseño-
ra de diez & ocho seña-
les & dixo la donzella
la que es luenga en
tres & pequeña en tres
& ancha en tres & ber-
meja en tres & prieta
en tres % E dixo el fi-
syco dezidme com<m>o es
esto & dixo la do<n>zella
luenga en tres que sea
luenga de estado & q<ue>}
{CB2.
aya el cuello largo & los
dedos luengos blac-
ca en tres el cuerpo bla<n>co
& los dientes blancos
& lo blanco de los ojos.
blanco % Prieta en tres
cabellos prietos & lo
pri[e]to de los ojos prieto
% E bermeja en tres me-
xillas bermejas & beços
bermejos & ensias ber-
mejas % E pequeña
en tres boca pequeña
& nariz pequeña & los
pies pequeños % E an-
cha en tres ancha de ca-
deras & ancha de (^caderas)
la fruente & que sea muy
placentera a su marido

& muy ayudadora & q<ue>
sea pequeña de hedad
% E leuantose el fisico
e dixo ala donzella di-
os vos faga bien que e<n>
todo fablastes bien % E
dixo al Rey por verdat
Señor yo vos digo q<ue> esta}
[fol. 122v]
{CB2.
(que esta) donzella que sabe
mas que non yo & yo la
do por verdadera & el Rey
preçiolo mucho & man-
do luego al otro sabidor
q<ue> se leua<n>tase a fablar co<n>
la donzella % E leuan-
tose luego abrahan el
trobador & sabidor de
gramatica & de logica
& dixo donzella apa-
rejaduos que no<n> so yo
de aquellos que aue-
des ençerrado & venci-
do & preguntole la do<n>-
zella que quien era
& como auia nonbre
& dixo el yo so abraha<n>
el trobado(do)r % E di-
xo la donzella abra-
han yo nunca vos co-
noci. pero asentadvos
& yo vos rrespondere
con la merced de dios
& de n<uest>ro señor el Rey
que dios mante<n>ga
% E luego dixo abra-
han a la donzella sy}
{CB2.
vos me rrespondierdes
çiertamente a todo lo
que vos preguntare q<ue>

yo que vos de todos
los mis paños % E sy
vos non me Respondi-
erdes çiertamente q<ue> (^yo)
que vos de los v<uest>ros paños & dixo la donzella
& yo asi lo pido por mer-
çed a nuestro señor el Rey
que nos lo mande a vos
& a mi & el Rey mandolo
luego & otorgolo a sy
a amos ados % E abra-
han trobador dixo do<n>-
zella qual es la cossa
mas pesada que ay en
los montes & mas a-
presurada que la saeta
& mas aguda q<ue> espada
& mas ardiente q<ue>l fuego e mas dulce que
la miel % E lagrimas
de ojos & dolençia sy<n>
melezina & mas Rezio
quel hueso & talante
de vna ora & plazer}
[fol. 123r]
{CB2.
de tres dias & plazer de
un mes & plazer de cinco
dias & vna aue que se
cria en los montes q<ue>
ay enella ocho señales
de grandes animalias
% E rrespondio la don-
zella aparejad v<uest>ras
rropas que yo vos rres-
pondere con la merçed
de dios & Respondiole
& dixole lo que es mas
pesado quelos montes
es el agua & mas apre-
surado que la saeta es

el ojo & mas aguda q<ue>
la espada es la lengua
& mas ardiente quel
fuego es el coraçon.
% E mas dulce q<ue> la
miel es el buen fijo &
dolençia syn melezina
es la locura % E el
mas çierto es el llama-
miento del señor del
mundo % E lo que es
mas Rezio quel hueso
es la verdad % E tala<n>-}
{CB2.
te de vna ora es yazer
con la muger & solaz
de vn dia es ganancia
& plazer de tres dias so<n>
obras de vaño % E pla-
zer de tres dias es el
nouio los primeros syet<e>
dias & plazer de vn mes
es el que viene de su ca-
mino % E el aue que se
cria enlos montes que
a enella ocho señales
de grandes animales
es la çigarra quel su
pescueço es de vaca % el
su pecho es de cauallo
& sus rrostros de leon
& sus alas de a`guila &
su çinta de alacran & la
cola de sierpe & los pi-
es de avestruz & el vie<n>-
tre de buey % E abra-
an el trobador se leuanto
en pie & dixo al Rey se-
ñor sed çierto que sabe
esta donzella mas q<ue>
non yo & avn nin qua<n>-
tos sabios vos tenedes}

[fol. 123v]
{CB2.
& todos les deuen dar la
mejoria en el saber % E luego el Rey abomeliq<ue> dixo
ala donzella dios vos
guarde de mal & vos de
su gracia por que tan bie<n>
vos rrespondistes a todas
aquellas cosas a estos sabios q<ue>llos & yo vos preguntamos & tan çierta
mente vos Respondistes
a ellas % E luego q<ue> esto
ouo dicho abrahan des-
pojo sus paños & dio
los a la donzella % E
luego la donzella se
leuanto en pie & dixo
abraan dadme v<uest>ros
paños menores com<m>o
fue puesto q<ue> me diesedes
todos v<uest>ros paños &
abraam dio a la don-
zella diez mill doblas`
de bue<n> oro por no<n> pasar tal uerguença co-
m<m>o le fuera sylos paños`
[^me]nores le ouiera de dar
Alli delante del Rey}
{CB2.
% E luego el Rey le dixo do<n>-
zella pedidme merçed &
dezidme en q<ue> manera la q<ue>-
redes sila queredes en mi
Casa en buen Casamie<n>to
.ca sed çierta que vos lo
dare qual vos deman-
dardes % E luego Respo<n>-
dio la donzella al Rey &
dixo señor mantenga vos
dios & si merçed me aue-

des de fazer enbiadme
con mi señor el mercador
% Ca yo non conosco otro
padre saluo a el que me
crio & fizo mucho por
me allegar en este estado
& me mostro lo que se &
el Rey mandole luego dar
luego diez mill doblas de
buen oro & de preçio.
% E la donzella tomolas
& beso al Rey las manos
& la tierra antel Rey &
fuese con su señor el mercador % E casose con el
& fueron muy Ricos de<n>de
en adelante
Deo gracias}

Biblioteca Nacional, Madrid — MS 17853
Spine title "Dichos de los filósofos"

The Teodor section begins at 112ra5.
[fol. 112ra5]
{CB2.
Capitulo q<ue> fabla delas pre-
gu<n>tas q<ue> fiziero<n> ala donzella {AD. [^teo-
dor]}
{IN.3} Auia en bauilon<i>a vn
mercador muy rri-
co & bueno muy li<n>-
pio & oraçionero en las
çinco oraçiones & faze
dor de bondades alos me-
nesterosos & a las biudas'
% E auia muchos algos'
& thenia muchos herma-
nos & muchos parientes'
& non auia fijo nin fija
E acaesçio vn dia q<ue>
merco vna do<n>zella & dio
por ella muchas doblas
& muchos florines &
[l]euola asu casa. & demostrole todas las artes &
sabidurias qua<n>tas pudo
saber & dende atienpo llego el mercador a grant
menester & dixo ala do<n>-}
{CB2.
zella sabed q<ue> me ha dios traydo a grand menester q<ue> non he
algo nin consejo & non se me
escusa q<ue> vos aya de vender. pues dadme consejo por donde a-
vre mejoria & bien % E
abaxo la donzella los ojos
& la cabeça contra tierra comidiendo % E despu<e>s al-

ço los ojos arriba. & dixo no<n>
auedes que rreçelar con la
merçed de dios & dixo yt
vos agora al alcaçeria de
los boticarios & traet me
afeytamientos p<ar>a muger
& nobles vestiduras. & leuad me al alcaçar del rrey a-
bomelique almançor que dios mantenga % E quando
vos preguntare por v<uestr>a venida dezilde quiero vos ve<n>-
der esta donzella & pedidle por mi diez mill doblas
de buen oro fino & si di-
xere que es mucho dezilde
señor sy conoçiesedes la donzella non lo terniades por
mucho & fuese el mercador}
[fol. 112v]
{CB2.
al alcaçeria a los boticarios
& fue a vno q<ue> dezian mahmad & saluolo el boticario
le dixo mercador q<ue> auedes
menester & el mercador le
conto la rrazon porq<ue> venia
& dixo quiero q<ue> me dedes fer
mosas vestiduras & fermos-
sos afeytamientos para
mi donzella & el tendero o-
uo del mercador grand pi-
adad & de lo que dixo dela
donzella que la queria vender & dixo amigo mucho
me mauzillastes mi cora-
con & feziste llorar mis
ojos por la v<uest>ra pobreza &
por q<ue> queredes vender la do<n>-
zella & la v<uest>ra demanda p<re>s-
ta es & leuantose el botica
rio & diole nobles vestiduras`

& nobles afeytamie<n>tos p<ar>a
muger & el mercador tomo
lo todo & leuolo ala donzella & ella pagose della & dixo esto vos sera buen comienço con la ayuda de dios % E
leuantose la donzella & vis-}
{CB2.
tiose & afeytose muy bien
& dixo a su señor leuantad
vos & subit comigo al alcaçeria del rrey & E leuanto
se su señor & fueron se para
el alcaçar del rrey & pidie-
ro<n> liçençia que entrasen al
rrey & el rrey mando que
entrasen & entraro<n> & pararonse entramos antel
rrey & E quando el rrey
los vido començo de fablar
con el mercador & pregun-
to por su venida & q<ue> era lo
q<ue> queria % E el mercador
le dixo señor quiero vos ve<n>-
der esta donzella & el rrey
le dixo quanto es su pre-
çio & el mercador rrespo<n>-
dio & dixo señor quiero
por ella diez mill doblas`
de bue<n> oro bermejo fin[i]-
symo & el rrey tomo [p]or
estraño el precio de la d[on]-
zella & dixo al merca-
dor mucho bos estendis-
tes en su precio o sallistes`
de v<uest>ro acuerdo o la do<n>zella}
[fol. 113r]
{CB2.
se alaba de cosas que non
pueden ser % rrespondiole
el mercador & dixo señor
non tengas por mucho

el precio de la donzella ca
poco es. ca yo la crie de pe-
q<ue>ña & es maça & costo
me muchos aueres fas-
ta q<ue> aprendio los nobles
menesteres & todas las
artes & esto non sera çe-
lado a vos % E començo
el rrey afablar con la do<n>-
zella & ella abaxo el ve-
lo de verguença & el rrey
alço los (^l) ojos & vido su
fermosura que semeja
com<m>o el sol que rreluzia
que non auia enese t<ien>po
otra mas fermosa q<ue> ella
% E dixole el rrey don-
zella com<m>o auedes non-
bre & rrespondio la do<n>-
zella & dixo sabed señor
que ami dizen (^sy) teodor
% E dixo el rrey donze-
lla q<ue> aprendistes de las artes & dixo la donzella se-}
{CB2.
ñor yo aprendi la ley & el libro
& aprendi mas los quatro
vientos & las siete planetas`
& las estrellas & las leyes
& los mandamientos & el
translado & los prometi-
mientos de dios & las co-
sas q<ue> crio en los çielos % E
aprendi las fablas de
las aues & de las anima
lias & la fisica & la filosofia & la logica & las cosas`
prouadas % E aprendi
mas el juego del axedres
& aprendi tañer laud ca-
non & las treynta {AD. [^& tres]} trobas`
& aprendi las buenas costu<m>-

bres de leyes & aprendi baylar & cantar & sotar & apre<n>-
di texer paños de peso(^s) &
aprendi labrar paños de
seda & aprendi labrar de
oro & de plata & de todas
las artes & cosas nobles
% E en que oyo el rrey estas palabras & cosas no
bles de la donzella fizo
se marauillado & mando}
[fol. 113v]
{CB2.
llamar los mayores sabios
de sus artes & dixoles que prouasen esta donzella % E salieron a ella luego tres om<n>es letrados & todos le pregu<n>taro<n>
espeçial mente vn fisico q<ue> le
pregunto & dixo donzella
las flores son sanas & dixo
la donzella son sanas en su
tienpo & dolientes en su t<ien>po
% E dixo el fisico quales so<n>
las frutas & dixo la donzella las granadas para los
dolientes & las almendras
% las ma<n>çanas & otorgo
con ella el fisico & pregu<n>-
to de la sangria % dixo la
donzella la sangria es buena martes & la luna men-
guante & el çielo esconbrado de nuues & sera el cuerpo espaçioso & alegre &
el figado % E el sangra-
dor avnq<ue> sea sabidor de las
conplisiones delos om<n>es
& otorgo conella el fisyco
& dixo a la donzella qual
cosa es la q<ue> caneçe al om<n>e a<n>te}
{CB2.

de su tiempo (& dixo [^a`] la donze-
lla qual cosa es la que encaneçe al om<n>e ante de su t<ien>po)
& dixo la donzella la debda
descubierta & la poridad
& yazer con muger vieja
que es pecado mortal &
otorgo con ella el fisico
% E preguntole de la
entrada del baño & dixo
la donzella bueno es
baño saluo q<ue> ha menester condiçiones & dixo
el fisico quales son & dixo la donzella la vergu-
ença & cobrir lo q<ue> es de
cobrir & quel baño sea
con agua fria & dulçe
& salira luego el cuerpo
del om<n>e alegre & otor-
go con ella el fisico % E
preguntaronle de la car-
ne qual era la mas sana
& dixo la donzella el carnero es melezina & su
carne es vianda. otro
sy la carne es manteca &
es sanidad & otorgo co<ne>lla}
[fol. 114r]
{CB2.
el fisyco % E dixo a la donzella q<ue> dezides de la carne gorda dixo (a) la donzella es pensamiento del alma & que
dezides dela carne magra
& dixo la donzella es via<n>-
da caliente & otorgo con
ella el fisyco & dixo q<ue> dezides del yazer con las mu-
geres & la donzella con
grand vergue<n>ça q<ue> ouo
abaxo los ojos con su rros-

tro contra tierra & leua<n>to
se el fisyco en pie & dixo
al rrey sabed señor que es`
vençida la donzella pu<e>s
q<ue> no<n> rresponde a esta demanda & dixo la donzella
señor no<n> lo mande dios q<ue> yo
oue verguença deso por
q<ue> soy moça & niña & so v<er>ge<n>
& el rrey ouo muy grant
amor della & mandole q<ue>
le rrespondiese & dixo la
donzella fisico todo ya-
zer con muger es dole<n>-
çia & qua<n>do ouieres de
yazer con ella podra ser}
{CB2.
que sea preñada o q<ue> crie fijo
macho a sus thetas o otra muger q<ue> guarde & es menester
que sea el varon sabidor desto & dixo el fisico en q<ue> ha menester q<ue> sea sabidor & dixo
sifuere la muger tal vi-
niere a su talante tarde & la
del varon ayna toller sea
el talente della ante q<ue> del
varon & acaeçe q<ue> no podra
sañar la muger dello &
ha menester q<ue> sea el yazer
con la muger en el terçio pos-
strimero de la noche por q<ue> sea
el coraçon caliente & el cuerpo & el estomago destrauado
del(^l)a vianda & otorgo con
ella el fisico & que dezides de
la hedad de las mugeres &
dixo la donzella la muger
de veynte años es com<m>o nobleza % la muger de trey<n>-
ta años es com<m>o carne con
limon % la muger de q<ua>renta

años es de seso la muger
de çinque<n>ta años es para
el cuchillo & la muger de se-
se<n>ta}
[fol. 114v]
{CB2.
años es para el otro mundo
% la muger de setenta años
es vieja tierra % la muger de
noue<n>ta años non me pregu<n>-
tedes delas cosas del ynfierno
que es la cosa mas esquiua de
todo el mundo % E el fisico
pregunto por las fermosu-
ras de las mugeres quales
eran & dixo la donzella acuçioso sodes de preguntar . el
vno dellos era el alfaqui sabidor de justiçias & de leyes
& el otro era fisyco de las cosas que perteneçen ala fisica
el otro era sabidor de la gramatica & de logica & de buena
fabla % E el alfaqui sabidor
de las leyes & dell libro dixo
a la donzella rrespondedme
a lo que vos preguntare &
dixo la donzella rresponde
re con la merçed de dios & de
nuestro señor el rrey abome-
liq<ue> almançor q<ue> dios ma<n>ten-
ga % E dixo el alfaqui donzella que ordeno dios en n<uest>ro
dia sobre su sieruo en su dia}
{CB2.
a las gentes & a las animalias % Dixo seruit me &
no<n> me menospreçiedes &
yo non menospreçiare a
vos % E dixo el alfaq<ui>
donzella muy bie<n> rrespo<n>-
distes & pregunto vos qu-

ales so<n> los juizios & los
mandimientos de dios &
dixo tres & çinco & dixo
el alfaqui glosad me qua-
les son % E dixo la do<n>ze
lla (^y) perdonar q<ua>ndo ouieres poder & quando fuere-
des poderoso & grande el
dia alto delante v<uest>ros ojos
& dixo el alfaqui donzella
muy bien dexistes. los tres
que son çinco dixo la do<n>zella
los tres q<ue> son çinco es el testimonio que no<n> ha otro criador sy non dios & mundat
el cuerpo & alinpiadlo &
otorgo con ella en qua<n>to
dixo la donzella % E
entonçe dixo la do<n>zella
alfaqui el señor alto &
bendito sea con syete çielos}
[fol. 115r]
{CB2.
& con doze signos & dixo el alfaqui glosadme quales son & dixo la donzella acarius ge-
mi[ni]s aries tauros gemines
piscis cançer leo. virgo libra
escorpius sagitarius capi-
Cornius % E dixo la don-
zella alfaqui el que fiziere oraçion & non fuere qui
to de pecado sy non fiziere
oraçion non sera oyda su
castidad & el q<ue> es casto &fi-
ziere oraçion entrara en la
gloria de parayso % E di-
xo el alfaqui donzella bien
dexistes mas en q<ue> deue om<n>e
ser casto % E dixo la donzella en la plata & en el trigo
& en la çeuada & en el çen-

teno & en las frutas & en
las azeytunas & en el ga-
nado ouejuno & vacuno
& de todas las otras cosas`
vedadas & el alfaqui dixo
al rrey señor por verdad
esta donzella mas sabe q<ue>
(q<ue>) no<n> yo & yo le do mejoria
en el saber % E el rrey ouo}
{CB2.
desto grand plazer & man-
do al otro que fablase co<ne>lla
& leuantose el fisyco & dixo
a la donzella rrespondedme
a lo que vos preguntare &
dixo la donzella sy rrespondere con la merçed del criador
& de n<uest>ro señor el rrey abome-
liq<ue> que dios mantenga % E
dixo el alfaqui donzella dezidme dela confuçion del om<n>e
& dixo la donzella al fisico
asy es que nuestro señor tenpro la humanidad con la secura & el fizo dende la tierra
& te<n>pro la secura & la humidad & fizo dende el ayre & a-
baho la tierra % E sy non
fuese por los bahos de la tierra
fedrian los huelgos contra
el çielo & en la tierra & el om<n>e
es de quatro elementos & dixo el fisyco quales son & dixo
la donzella t<ie>rra & agua & a-
yre & en el año son quatro te<n>-
porales ynuierno & verano &
estio & otoño & en estos quatro
tienpos rremaneçe la colora}
[fol. 115v]
{CB2.
& la maletia & la sangre & la
flema & ha menester que sea

el fisico sabidor delas compli-
siones & de las melezinas q<ue>
perteneçen al cuerpo segun
fueren menester al cuerpo
% E otorgo con ella el fisyco & dixo donzella dezit me
quales son las señales para
la muger ser fermosa & dixo la donzella aq<ue>lla muger
es fermosa q<ue> es señora de diez & ocho señales % E di-
xo el fisyco dezitme quales
son estas diez &ocho señales`
& dixo la donzella. la q<ue> es lu
enga en tres & pequeña en
tres & ancha en tres & bla<n>ca
en tres & prieta en tres & bermeja en tres % E dixo el
fisyco dezit me com<m>o es esto
& dixo la donzella luenga en
tres que sea luenga de estado
& que aya el cuello largo &
los dedos luengos . blanca
en tres el cuerpo blanco & los
dientes blancos & lo blanco de los ojos blanco % P<ri>e}
{CB2.
ta en tres. cabellos prietos
& lo prieto de los ojos prieto & las çejas prietas % E
Bermeja en tres mexillas`
Bermejas & beços berme-
jos & enzias bermejas &
pequeña en tres. boca pe-
q<ue>ña & naris peq<ue>ña & los`
pies peq<ue>ños % E an-
cha en tres ancha de caderas & ancha de espaldas
& ancha la fruente & q<ue>
sea muy plazentera a su
marido & muy ayudadera
& que sea pequeña de he-

dad & leuantose el fisyco
& dixo a la donzella dios
vos faga bien q<ue> en todo
fablastes bie<n> % E dixo
al rrey por verdad señor
esta donzella mas sabe
que non yo & yo la do por
verdadera & el rrey pre-
çiolo mucho & mando lue-
go al otro sabidor que se
leuantase a fablar con la
donzella % E leua<n>-
tose luego abrahen el}
[fol. 116r]
{CB2.
trobador sabidor de gramatica & de logica & dixo donzella aparejad vos que non so
yo delos que auedes ençerrado & vençido % E pregun-
tole la donzella que quien
era & com<m>o auia nonbre &
dixo ell yo so abrahen el tro-
Bador & dixo ella abrahe<n>
yo nunca vos conoçi. Pero
asentadvos & preguntad
me q<ue> yo vos rrespondere co<n>
la merçed de dios & de n<uest>ro
señor el rrey que dios ma<n>-
tenga % E luego dixo a
brahen ala donzella sy
vos me rrespondedes çiertamente a todo lo que vos preguntare que yo que vos
de todos los mis paños
& sy vos no<n> me rrespondierdes sçiertamente q<ue> vos me
dedes los v<uest>ros paños & dixo la donzella & yo asi lo
pido por merçed a nuestro
señor el rrey que nos lo ma<n>-
de a vos & a mi % E el rrey

mandolo luego & otorgo}
{CB2.
gelo asy a amos a dos & a-
brahen el trobador dixo do<n>-
zella qual es la cosa mas
pesada que ay enlos montes`
& mas apresurada q<ue> la saeta
& mas aguda q<ue> espada & mas`
ardiente q<ue> el fuego & mas
dulçe que la miel & lagrimas
de ojos & dolençia syn melezina & mas rrezio q<ue>l hueso & talante de vna ora & plazer de tres dias & plazer de
vn mes & plazer de cinco dias % E vna aue que se cria
en los montes que enella ay
ocho señales de grandes an-
nimalias % E rrespondio
la donzella aparejad v<uest>ras
rropas que yo vos rrespondere con la merçed de dios
% E rrespondiole & dixo
le lo que es mas pesado q<ue>
los montes es el agua & mas`
apresurado que la saeta es
el ojo & mas aguda q<ue> la espada es la lengua & mas
ardiente q<ue> el fuego es el coraçon & mas dulçe q<ue> la miel}
[fol. 116v]
{CB2.
es el buen fijo & dolençia
syn melezina es la locura &
el mas sçierto es llamami-
ento del señor del mu<n>do & lo q<ue>
es mas rrezio q<ue>l hueso es la
verdad & talante de vna o-
ra es yazer con la muger
& solas de vn dia es ganançia & plazer de tres dias so<n>
obras de baño % E pla-

zer de syete dias es el no
uio los primeros syete dias
% E plazer de vn mes es el
que viene de camino & el a-
ue que se cria en los mo<n>tes q<ue>
ha en ella ocho señales de gra<n>
des animalias es la çigara
quel su pescueço es de vaca
& el su pecho es de cauallo
& sus rrostros de leon & sus
alas de aguila & su çinta
de alacran & la cola de syer-
pe & los pies de abestruz &
el vientre de buey % E a-
brahem el trobador se leua<n>-
to en pie & dixo al rrey señor
sed sçierto que sabe esta donzella mas q<ue> non yo ni<n> q<ua>ntos}
{CB2.
sabios vos tenedes & todos
le deuen dar la mejoria
enel saber % E luego el
rrey abomeliq<ue> dixo a al do<n>-
zella dios vos guarde de
mal & vos de su graçia por
que tan bien rrespondistes`
a todas aquellas cosas q<ue>
yo & todos estos sabios vos
preguntamos & tan çierta
mente rrespondistes a ellas`
% E luego q<ue> esto ouo dicho
el rrey abrahan despojo sus`
paños & diolos a la do<n>zella
% E luego la donzella
se leuanto en pie & dixo
brahen dadme v<uest>ros paños`
menores com<m>o fue pues-
to que me diesedes todos
v<uest>ros paños % E abrahen dio a la donzella diez
mill doblas de oro por no<n>
pasar tal verguença com<m>o

le fuera sy los paños me-
nores ouiera de dar alli
delante el rrey & luengo el
rrey le dixo donzella pe-
ditme merçed & dezitme}
[fol. 117r]
{CB2.
en que manera la q<ue>redes sy
la q<ue>redes en mi casa en buen
casamiento q<ue> sed sçierta que
vos lo de qual vos demandardes % E luego rrespo<n>dio
la donzella al rrey & dixo señor mantenga vos dios & sy
merçed me auedes de fazer
enbiat me con mi señor el
mercador que yo non conosco otro padre sy non a el qua<n>-
to mas que fizo mucho por
me llegar a este estado & me
mostro lo que se & el rrey
mandole luego dar diez mill
doblas de buen oro e de preçio % E la donzella tomo
las & beso al rrey las manos`
& la tierra antel rrey & fue
se con su señor el mercador
% E casose con el & fue
ron muy rricos dende en
adelante
deo graçias}

El Escorial — MS h-III-6
Spine title "Bocados de oro"

The Teodor section begins at folio 118v15.

[fol. 118v15]
{CB1.
spondio enel tienpo dela saña Capitulo que fabla
delos enxemplos & castigos de teo`dor la donzella
auia en babilonia vn mercader muy rryco & bueno & muy lynpio & oraçionero enlas cinco ora
ciones & fazedor de bondades alos menesterosos & alas bybdas & auia muchos algos & muchos
hermanos & muchos parientes & no<n> tenia fijo ni<n>
fija & acaesçio vn dia que merco vna donzella & dio por`
ella muchas doblas & florynes & leuole asu casa &
enseño le todas las artes & sabidurias quantas pudo saber & dende a poco llego el mercader a grand
menester & dix ala donzella sabed que me ha dios`
traydo a gra<n>d menester que ni<n> he algo ni<n> consejo & no<n>
se me escusa que vos no<n> aya menester & de uender pues}
[fol. 119r]
{CB1.
dadme consejo por do abre mejoria & bien % E abaxo la
donzella los ojos & la cabeça contra la tierra & despues`
alço los arriba & dixo no<n> auedes de rresçelar con la
merçed de dios % E dixo yd vos agora ala alcaçeria
de los boticarios & traed me afeytamientos para muger & nobles vestiduras & leuadme al alcaçar del rrey
abomely que es almançor & quando vos preguntare
que es v<uest>ra venida dezidle quiero vos vender esta donzella
& pedidle por mi diez mill doblas de buen oro fyno &
sy dixere ques mucho dezidle señor sy conosçiesedes la
donzella no<n> lo avryades por mucho % E fuese el mercader ala alcaçeria alos boticarios & fue a vno que dezia<n>
mahomada & saluolo & el boticario le dyxo mercader q<ue>
auedes menester & el mercado[r] le conto la rrazon porq<ue>
venia & dixo quiero que me dedes fermosas vestiduras
& fermosos afeytamientos para mi donzella % El tendero ouo del mercador grand piedat delo que dixo
de la donzella que la queria vender & dixo amigo mu-

cho me manzillastes mi coraçon & fezistes llorar mis`
ojos por la v<uest>ra pobreza % E por que queredes vender
la v<uest>ra donzella que la v<uest>ra demanda presta es % E
leuanto se el boticario & dio le nobles vestiduras & afeytamiento de muger & el mercador tomolo todo & leuolo
ala donzella & paguose dello & dixo estos vos sera<n> bue<n>
comienço conla ayuda dedios % E louanto se la donzella & leuantose & adobose & afeytose muy bien & dixo le
uantad vos & sobid comigo al alcaçar del rrey % E leua<n>
tose su señor & fuero<n> al alcaçar del rrey & pedieron liçençia}
[fol. 119v]
{CB1.
que entrasen al rrey & el rrey ma<n>doles que entrasen & entraron & apartaro<n> se anbos conel rrey & quando el rrey los vido començo a fablar conel mercador & pregunto por su venida & que era lo que queria & el mercador le dixo señor
quiero vos vender esta donzella & dixo el rrey quanto es
su prescio & dixo el mercador señor diez mill doblas de bue<n>
oro fyno bermejo & el rrey lo tomo por estraño el presçio de
la donzella & dixo al mercador mucho vos estendistes
en su presçio & salistes de v<uest>ro acuerdo (^o la donzella) o la
donzella(^s) se alaba mas de lo que sabe & rrespondiole
el mercador & dixo señor non tengas por grande el presçio dela donzella que yo la crye de pequeña & es moça
& costome muchos aueres fasta que aprendio todas las`
artes & los no[n]bres menesteres & esto no<n> sera negado
a vos % E començo el rrey afablar conla donzella y e-
lla abaxo el velo de verguen<ç>a & el rrey alço los ojos & vy-
do su fermosura que rrelunbraua com<m>o el sol que non
auia eneste tienpo mas fermosa quella % E dixo el rrey
donzella com<m> auedes no<n>bre & rrespondio & dixo theodor & E dixo el rrey donzella que aprendistes delas artes
& dixo la donzella señor yo aprendy la ley & el libro & a-
prendy mas los quatro vyientos & las syete planetas %
las estrellas & las leyes & los mandamientos & el traslado & los prometimientos de dios & las cosas que cryo
en los çielos & aprendy las fablas delas aues & delas
animalias & la fisyca & la filosofia & las cosas prouadas & aprendy mas el juego del axedes &
aprendy tañer laud & cañon & las treynta & tres trobas}
[fol. 120r]
{CB1.

E aprendy las buenas costunbres de leye`s & aprendy
vaylar & sotar & cantar & aprendi labrar panos de seda & aprendy texer panos de oro & de peso & aprendy labrar de oro & de plata & aprendy todas las cosas nobles`
% E quando el rrey ayo estas palabras de la(^s) do[n]zella
fizose marauillado & mando llamar los mayores sabios`
de su[s] corte & dixoles que prouasen aquella donzella
% E saliero<n> luego a ella tres onbres letrados & todos
tres le preguntaro<n> speçialmente vn fisyco le pregunto
% dixo donzella las flores son sanas % la donzella le rrespondio son sanas ensu tienpo & dolientes ensu tienpo %
E dixo el fisico quales son las frutas & dixo la donzella
para los dolientes (^&) las mançanas & las almendra[s] &
otorgo conella el fisyco & pregunto dela sangrya & dyxo la donzella la sangria es buena en martes & luna
menguante & el çielo esconbrado de nubes & sera el cuerpo espaçioso & alegre el figado & el sabidor aunq<ue> sea sabidor delas conplisiones de los onbres otorgo conella
el fisico % & dixo ala donzella qual es la cosa que enca-
nesçe al onbre ante de su tienpo & dixo la donzella la debda & la porydat descobierta & dormir con muger vieja
que es pecado mortal que otorgo conella el fisyco % E
preguntole dela entrada del vaño % dixo la donzella es`
bueno el vaño & saluo que ha menester condiçiones &
dixo el fisico quales son & dixo la donzella la verguença
& cobryr lo que es de cobryr & que el vaño sea con agua
frya & dulçe & salira leugo el cuerpo del onbre alegre &
otorgo conella el fisico % E preguntole dela carne qual}
[fol. 120v]
{CB1.
era la mas sana & rrespondio la donzella el carnero es melezina & su carne es vyanda otro sy la carne es sanidad
& otorgo conella el fisyco % E dixo l(a)[e] donzella que dizes
dela carne gorda & dixo la donzella es pesamiento de la
alma & que dizes de la carne magra & dixo la donzella
es vyanda callyente & otorgo conella el fisyco & dixo
que dezides del yazer con las mugeres & la donzella
con grand verguença que ouo abaxo sus ojos a tierra &
leuantose el fisico en pie & dixo sabed señor que es vençida la donzella pues que non rresponde a esta dema<n>da &
dixo la donzella señor no<n> lo ma<n>de dios que yo oue verguença de vos porque so niña & vyrgen el rrey ouo gra<n>

amor della & ma<n>dole que rrespondiese & dixo la donzella fisyco todo yazer con muger es dolença quando ayas de yazer conella podra ser que sea preñada
o que crye fijo a sus tetas o otra muger es menester que`
el varo<n> guarde & sea sabidor & dixo el fisico sy fuere tal
la muger dixo la donzella sy la muger fuere tal que sepa o vyniere el su talente tarde & la del varo<n> ayna toller sea el talente della ante que del varon & acaesçe q<ue>
no<n> podra la muger sanar dello & ha menester que sea
el tienpo de yazer conla muger el postrymero de la noche
por que sea el coraçon calyente & el cuerpo & el estomago de
stranado de la vyanda & otorgo conella el fisico % E que
dezides de la hedat de las mugeres & rrespondio la donzella la muger de veynte años es com<m>o nobleza la
muger de treynta años es com<m>o carne con lymon & la
muger de quarenta años es de seso & la muger de qu[a]-}
[fol. 121r]
{CB1.
renta años es para el cuchillo & la muger de (^a) sesenta
años es para el otro mundo la de setenta años es vieja
tierra la muger ochenta años no<n> me preguntes del infierno es que es la cosa mas esquiva de todo el mundo %
el fisico pregunto por las fermosuras de las mugeres quales eran & dixo la donzella acuçioso (^d) soys de preguntar & el vno dellos era alfaquy sabidor de justicias & de
leyes & el otro era fisico de las cosas que pertenesçian ala
fisica & el otro era sabidor de gramatica & logica & de la
buena fabla % E el alfaqui sabidor de las leyes & delos`
libros de dios dixo ala donzella rrespondedme alo q<ue>
vos preguntare & dixo la donzella con la merçed de dios
n<uest>ro señor & del rrey obomenaliq<ue> almançor que dios ma<n>-
tenga & dixo el alfaqui donzella que ordeno dios sobre nos en n<uest>ro dia & sobre su sieruo en su dia & dixo
la donzella alas gentes & alas animalias & dixo seruid & non menos presçiedes & yo no<n> (menospresçiare
des & yo non) menospresçiare a vos & dixo el alfaquy
donzella muy bien rrespondistes % E pregunto vos
quales son los mandamientos & juyzio des dixo la
donzella tres & çinco & dixo el alfaquy glosad me q<ua>les
son & di(^d)xo la donzella perdonad quando ouierdes
poder & quando fuerdes poderosos & grandes el dia ante
v<uest>ros ojos & dixo el alfaquy muy bien dexistes & los

tres que son çinco & dixo la donzella los tres que son çinco es el testimonio que no<n> ho (^toro) otro cryador syno<n> dios
& mondat el cuerpo & alynpiadlo & otorgo conella el alfaqui en quanto dixo la donzella % Estonçes d[i]xo la}
[fol. 121v]
{CB1.
donzella (^l) alfaqui el señor alto bendito sea con syete çielos
& puse enellas las estrellas & una partida dellas para
ennobleçer los çiellos & otro para los moros & otra para
las otras gentes & otra para el poder del diablo maldy-
to & dixo el alfaqui muy bien dexistes & dixo estonçes
la donzella alfaqui el n<uest>ro señor alto bendito sea con sye[te]
çielos & con doze sygnos & dixo el alfaqui glosad me
quales son & dixo la donzella acayus geminis ari<e>s
taurus geminis piçis cancer leo vyrgo libra scorpius sa-
gitaryus caprycornius % e dixo la donzella alfaqui
el que fiziere oraçion & no<n> confesare sus pecados no<n> sera
oyda su oraçion el que es quito de pecado sy no<n> fiziere
oraçion no<n> sera oyda su castidat el que es casto & fiziere
oraçion entrara en la gloria del parayso & dixo el alfaqui
donzella bien dexistes mas en que deue onbre ser casto
& dixo la donzella en la plata & en el trygo & en la ceuada & enel çenteno & enlas (las) frutas & enlas azetunas &
enel ganado ouejuno & vacuno & de todas cosas que dios`
le diere & leuantose el alfaqui & dixo al rrey por verdat
señor esta donzella sabe mas que no<n> yo & yo le do mejori`a
enel saber & el rrey ouo desto muy gran plazer & mando
el rrey que fablase el otro conella & leuantose el fisio &
dixo donzella rrespo`ndedme alo que vos preguntare & di-
xo la donzella sy rrespondere con la merçed de dios & de n<uest> ro
señor el rey abomeneliqu(^i)e que dios mantenga & dixo el
fisyco dezid me donzella dela confaçion del cuerpo del
onbre & dixo la donzella asy es que n<uest>ro señor tenpro
la humidad conla secura & el fizo dende la tierra &}
[fol. 122r]
{CB1.
tenpro la secura & la humidad & fizo dende el ayre & abafo
la tierra & sy no<n> fuese por los vafos de la tierra federan
n<uest>ros fuelgos contra tierra & contra el çielo & lonbre es
de quatro elementos & dixo el fisio quales son & dixo la
donzella tierra & agua & ayre & fuego & dixo la donzella
en el año son quatro temporales yuyerno verano estio otoño

enestos quatro tienpos rremanesce la colora & la maletia
& la sangre & la flema & es meneste<r> que sea el fisio sabidor
de las cosas & delas melexinas que pertenescen al cuerpo
& segu,n.de que pertenesçen al cuerpo & otorgo conella el fisyco & dixo donzella dezidme quales son las señales para la muger ser fermosa & dixo la donzella la muger
es fermosa que es señora de deziseys señales o deziocho
& dixo la que es luenga en tres & pequeña en tres & ancha
en tres & angosta en tres & blanca en tres & negra en tres
& vermeja en tres & dixo el fisico dezidme com<m>o es esto &
digo que luenga en tres que sea luenga destado & que
aya el cuello largo & los dedos luengos % blanca en
tres el cuerpo blanco & los dientes blancos & lo blanco
de los ojos blanco & pryeta en tres a cauellos p<r>yetos &
las cejas pryetas & lo (^blanco) delos ojos negro que (^s) sea
pryeto % Vermeja en tres labros maxillas enzias % &
pequeña en tres boca pequeña narizes pequenas &
los pies pequeños % & ancha en tres ancha de caderas
& espaldas & ancha a la fruente & que sea muy plazentera a su marydo & muy ayudadera & que sea pequeña
de hedat & leuantos el fisico & dixo a la donzella dios
vos faga bien que en todo fablastes vien % E dixo al rrey por}
[fol. 122v]
{CB1.
verdat señor yo vos digo que esta donzella que sabe mas
que no<n> yo & yo la do por verdadera & el rrey presçio lo mucho & mando al otro sabydor que se leuantase a fablar
con la donzella % E leuantose luego abrahen el trobador & sabidor de gramatica & logica & dixo donzella apa-
rejadvos que non so yo de los que vencidos o enterrados
auedes & preguntole la donzella que quien era & com<m>o
auia nonbre & dixo el yo so abrahen el trouador & dixo e-
lla abrahen yo nu[n]ca os conosci mas asentadvos & preguntad que yo vos rrespondere con la merçed de dios & de el
rrey n<uest>ro señor que dios mantenga % E luego dixo abrahe<n>
a la donzella que si vos me respondierdes a todo lo q<ue>
yo vos preguntare que (^qo) yo os de todos los mis paños
& que sy vos no<n> rrespondierdes sçierta mente que vos q<ue>
me dedes v<uest>ros paños & dixo la donzella & yo asy lo py-
do por merçed a n<uest>ro señor el rrey que lo mande de vos a
mi & el rrey mandolo luego & otorgojelo asy a anb[o]s a dos`
& abrahun trobador dixo donzella qual es la cosa mas`

pesada que ay en los montes & mas apresuada que la
saeta & mas aguda que la espada & mas ardiente que el
fuego & mas dulçe que la miel & lagrymas de ojos &
dolençia syn melezina & mas rrezio que el hueso & talante de vna ora & plazer de tres dias & plazer de
vn mes & plazer de çinco dias & Vna aue que se crya en los
montes que ay en ella ocho señales de grandes anima-
li`as % E rrespondio la donzella aparejad v<uest>ras rropas
que yo vos rrespondere con la merçed de dio % E rrespo<n>-
dio & dixole lo que es mas pesado que los mo<n>tes es el a-}
[fol. 123r]
{CB1.
gua & mas apresurado que la saeta el ojo & mas aguda q<ue>
la espada la lengua & mas ardiente que el fuego es el coraçon & mas dulçe que la miel el buen fijo & dolençia syn
melezina es la locura & el mas çierto es el llamamiento del señor del mundo lo que es mas rrezio que
el hueso es la verdad & talente de vna ora es yazer
co<n> la muger & solaz de vn dia es ganançia & plazer de
tres dias son obras de vaño & plazer de syete dias es el
nouio los prymeros syete dias plazer de un mes el q<ue>
vyene de camino E el aue que se crya en los montes
que ay enella ocho señales de grande[s] alymañas e(l)[s]
la çigarra que el su p[e]scueço es de vaca & el su pecho
es de cauallo & sus rrostros de leo<n> & sus alas de aguila
& su çinta de alacran & la cola de sierpe & los pies de a-
uestruz & el vientre de buey % E [a]brahen trobador se
leuanto en pie & dixo al rrey señor sabed que esta donzella sabe mas que no<n> yo nin quantos sabios tenedes
& todos le deuen dar la mejory[a] & yo gela do enel saber
% E luego el rrey abomeliq<ue> dixo ala donzella dios
vos guarde de mal & vos de su graçia por que tan bie<n>
rrespondistes a estos sabios & ta[n] çiertamente rrespondiste a todas las preguntas % E luego que esto ouo dicho el rrey abomeniq<ue> abrahen desnudo sus paños &
abrahen dio ala donzella diez mill doblas de oro por
que non pasase tal verguença com<m>o sy los Paños
menores ally delante el rrey le ouieran de quitar % &
luego el rrey le dixo donzella pedidme merçed & dezidme en que manera la querres sy queredes en mi}
[fol. 123v]
{CB1.

casa en buen casamiento que sed çierto que vos lo dare qual vos quesyerdes % E luego rrespondio la donzella al rrey & dixo le señor(a) mantenga vos dios & sy merçed me auedes de fazer enbiad me con my señor el mercador que yo no<n> conosco a otro padre sy no<n> ael que me cryo % quanto mas que fizo mucho por me llegar a este estado & me enseño lo que se & el rrey mandole luego diez mill doblas de bue<n> oro & de presçio E la donzella tomolas & beso al rrey las manos & la tierra ante el & fuese con su señor el mercador % E casose conel & fueron muy rrycos dende en adelante
deo graçias}

Biblioteca Nacional, Madrid — Incunable R 10688

Hystoria de la do<n>zella Teodor [Zaragoza, 15 May 1540]

This book contains 16 folios, 19 woodcuts, plus title page and printers' mark (see colophon on folio 16v). Collation: A 16. Lines 33 (=sig. A1v).

[fol.1r = sig. A1 recto]
{CB1.
% hystoria de
la do<n>zella theo-
dor.}[82]

[fol. 1v = sig. A1 verso]
{CB1.
{IN10.}[83]En los reynos de Tunez hauia vn
mercader delas p<ar>tes de Ungria: el
q<ua>l era el mas rico q<ue> enel mu<n>do se ha-
llase: y vn dia passando por la plac'a
vido vender vna donzella christiana
queera delas partes de España: yel
viendola ser muy hermosa compro
la al moro que la traya: y conosciendo en su gentil disposicion y criança
que deuia ser hijadalgo: hizole mos-
trar a leer y escreuir: y todas las ciencias que deprender pu-
diese: la qual se dio tanto ala virtud que sobrepuyo a todos
hombres y mugeres que en aquel tiempo se hallassen: assi en
ciencia como en musica: y como todas las cosas enesta vida
sean mudables fue la voluntad de nuestro señor de dar tal re-
ues al mercader que cargando vnas naues de mercaderias

[82] The title page utilizes a four-piece border to evoke a classical archway. Within the border is a group of factotum woodcuts consisting of a king seated on a throne on the right, a young woman in the center, and an older man on the left. The title appears below the factotum figures followed by a Maltese cross.

[83] The initial E is decorated in a vine motif.

de grandissimo valor con mucha fortuna fuero<n> enla mar per-
didas: de manera que se hallo tan perdido y en tierras estra-
ñas que no sabia darse remedio ala grandissima pobreza en
que hauia quedado: y hallando se en tanta miseria que cosa
ninguna no tenia para se mantener. acordo dedezir ala do<n>-
zella lo siguiente. ya sabes como corre sobre mi fortuna en
tanta manera que no me ha quedado cosa de quanto solia tener: de todos mis thesoros ya no tengo cosa q<ue> venda ni em-
peñe: y esto es por los mis pecados que yo he hecho y come-
tido co<n>tra n<uest>ro señor dios: de que ya no me queda otra cosa sino vos: por lo qual hija me sera forçado que hos aya de vender: dios sabe qua<n>to por ello me pesa: emp<er>o vos ya conoceys
q<ue> yo no puedo mas hazer. Por esso mucho hos ruego hija q<ue>
vos me querays consejar delo q<ue> a v<uest>ro entendimiento mas le
paresciere q<ue> yo deuo hazer: q<ue> segun la muchaciencia vuestra
yo tengo gran confiança q<ue> con vuestro consejo yo sere remediado: y aure manera con que pueda mantenerme y salir de}
[fol. 2r = sig. A2 recto]
{CB1.
mis trabajos: y la donzella theodor como esto oyo hablar
a su señor: houo dello mucha tristeza y pesar: y abaxo sus o-
jos en tierra començo de llor: y estuuo assi vna gran pieça que
no hablo pensando en su coraçon. E despues que houo bien
pensado: y mirado en su entendimiento el cobro que podria
dar a su señor: el qual la auia criado y gastado co<n> ella sus thesoros en le mostrar todo lo q<ue> sabia alçola cabeça y dixole. Esforçad señor mio y no tomeys cuydado de cosa alguna y tened buena esperança en nuestro señor dios q<ue> el vos ayudara
y vos dara buen consejo con q<ue> salgays deste trabajo y dela
gran pobreza en q<ue> aora estays: y no cureys de mas pensar
sobre esto q<ue> dios hos porna cobro: porende leuantadvos luego & ydos para losjoyeros y traedme co<m>postura y afeytes
con q<ue> se ageytan las mugeres y traedme paños de fina color
para q<ue> vista: y vestirlos he y componerme he con ellos: y despues q<ue> yo sea afeytada yco<m>puesta lleuarme eys al rey Miramolin Almançor: y dezid que me quereys vender: y quando
el hos preguntare que es lo que por mi quereys. Respondelde enesta manera. Señor yo vengo a vuestra alteza co<n> gran
menester que tengo con esta donzella: sivos plaze de me la co<m>-
prar yo hos la vendere por lo que justo sea: y si el rey vos preguntare por quanto precio me la dareys dezid que quereys
por mi diez mil doblas de buen oro bermejo. E si el rey se ma-

rauillare del precio que por mi demandays: dezi assi. Señor
no se marauille vuestra alteza porque hos demande este precio por esta donzella que verdaderamente mucho mas vale
delo que yo hos demando por ella: y despues que el mercader houo oydo el consejo que la donzella le dio: conoscio que
era muy bien camino para su remedio: y fue luego para los
mercaderes que vendian joyas: y hablo con vn moro que llamauan Mahoma que era grandissimo amigo suyo: el qual
Moro vendia de todas maneras de mercadurias. Assi de}
[fol. 2v = sig. A2 verso]
{CB1.
paños como de seda como de joyeria y especeria y contole
sus trabajos y miseria en q<ue> era venido por sus pecados: y el
doliendose del le respondio assi. Verdaderamente mi gran a-
migo quebra<n>tado has mi coraçon: y mis ojos has heccho llorar por la gran cuyta y trabajo que tienes. Empero demanda agora delo que yo tengo: y sepas de cierto q<ue>no te sera negado que yo te lo dare de muy buena voluntad: y con lo q<ue> yo
te dare plega a n<uest>ro señor q<ue> tu y tu donzella ayays buen pro-
[ue]cho y ventura: y dixole el mercader. Amigo sepas q<ue>yo he menester vnos pannos de muy fina color y afeytes muy escogidos para esrostro: y esto quiero para mi donzella para la atauiar: y despues sepas amigo que yo la quiero lleuar avender
al rey porque yo pueda salir de trabajo: y despues que el mercader ouo acabado su razon el joyero le dio los paños y afeytes tales y tan buenos como se los hauia demandado: y el
mercader despues que los tomo dio muchas gracias a dios
por ello: porque hauia hallado tan buen recaudo en aquel su
amigo de todo lo que hauia menester para su donzella: y dixo en su coraçon. Si al señor dios pluguiesse esto seria buen
comienço: y vinose luego para su casa con sus paños y afeytes y diolo todo a su donzella: y ella se alegro mucho co<n> ellos
por quanto ella era muy hermosa: y los paños y afeytes era<n>
muy buenos: por lo qual dixo a su señor alegrad vos señor
y haued plazer queesto sera començo de vuestro bien si al señor dios pluguiere: y la donzella tomo los paños y vistiosse
los: los quales levenian tambien como si fueran cortados a
su medida. E tomo los afeytes y afeytosse con ellos lo mejor
que pudo: y qua<n>do la donzella fue vestida y afeytada parescio la mas gentil y bella que se pudiesse hallar enel mundo: y
entonces lleuola el mercader ante el rey Miramamolin Almançor: el qual se contentaua mucho de ver gentiles muge-

res y hermosas donzellas.}
[fol. 3r = A 3 recto]
{CB1.
% {RUB. Capitulo primero que habla de como
lleuo el mercader a su donzella delante del rey Almançor a su
alcaçar y delo que dixo el rey ala donzella: y la respuesta que
dio la donzella al rey.}
{MIN=.}[84]
{IN4.}La historia dize que aquel mercader lleuo su donzella Theodor ante el rey Miramolin Almançor a su alcaçar donde estaua: y hablo con el portero rogandole mucho que le abriesse y le dexasse
entrar: porque queria hablar con el Rey. El portero le abrio
luego la puerta diziendole que entrasse en buen hora: y el mercader entro luego y fuesse con su donzella para la camara do<n>-
de estaua el rey: y saludo al rey Miramamolin Almançor y
a todos los que estauan: y humillandose a el hizole gran reuerencia y beso la tierra ante el rey y llegaron se mas: y besaron
le las manos. y el rey pregunto al mercader. Di amigo que
te plaze o que quieres: y luego el mercader le respondio y dixole. Señor traygo a vuestra alteza esta donzella si le plaze
de mela comprar: y el rey le dixo que si compraria y q<ue> dixesse
quanto queria por ella: y el mercader le dixo que queria diez}
[fol. 3v = sig. A3 verso]
{CB1.
mil doblas de buen oro bermejo: y el marauillosse mucho del
mercader: porque tal precio demandaua: y el le dixo. Amigo
mucho demandas porella o tueres fuera de seso ola donzella se alaba de grandes cosas que por ventura no saber hazer:
y el mercader respondio al rey diziendo. Señor nolo tengas
a marauilla: porque yo he demandado tal precio por esta do<n>-
zella. Que haueys de saber que sabe tantas maneras de cien
cias que no ay sabio que la pueda vencer hombre ni muger.
Porque yo señor despendi con ella gran thesoro por la hazer enseñar lo que ella ha aprendido: y tiene muy bien estudiado todas maneras de ciencias que pueden serescritas y sabios letrados puedan escreuir por todo el mundo assi hombres

84 Factotum strip, from left to right: a castle, a king seated on a throne, an old man, and a young woman.

como mugeres. El rey quando esto oyo miro mucho ala donzella: y mando quese tirasse el manto que traya puesto sobre
los ojos: y que se alçasse el velo y lo pusiesse enla cabeça: y la
donzella lo tiro luego y hizo todo quanto el rey le mando: y
alli vio ell rey la gran hermosura y beldad quela donzella tenia: y le parescio las mas hermosa que visto hauia en toda su
vida: y plugole mucho con su vista y preguntole que dixesse
como hauia nombre. La donzella le respondio con muy gra<n>
verguença: y humilmente le dixo. Muy esclarecido señor
vuestra alteza sabra que a mi llaman Theodor: y el rey le dixo
Theodor plegate de me dezir que es la ciencia que aprendis-
te de todos los saberes deste mundo. y la donzella le respondio y dixole. Tu real alteza sabra que el primer saber que yo
deprendi fue todas las siete artes liberales: y el arte dela as-
trologia: y las propiedades delas piedras y delas aguas: y
de yeruas: y delas propiedades que tienen todas las maneras de animales o aues que nuestro señor dios crio enel mundo: y se la musica ca<n>tar tañer y baylar mas que ninguna persona deste mundo.}
[fol. 4r = sig. A4 recto]
{CB1.
% {RUB. Capitulo segundo Como se marauillo
el rey delas cosas que dixo la donzella Theodor que sabia hazer: por la qual razon ma<n>do luego que llamassen a todos los
sabios que d[i]sputassen con ella.}
{=MIN=.}[85]
{IN4.} UEnidos que fueron los sabios mando el rey que
disputassen muy bien con la donzella Theodor
pues que ella tanto se loaua que sabia por ver si
era assi aquello que dezia. E de todos aquellos
sabios que alli fuero ayuntados mando el Rey
que fuessen escogidos tres los quales sabian mas que todos
los otros sabios. Los quales hablaron luego con la donzella en razon de disputa. el vno era gran sabio en todas las leyes. y enlos mandamientos de nuestro señor dios: y el otro
era muy gran sabio y discreto y muy gran letrado enla cie<n>cia}
[fol. 4v = sig. A4 verso]

---

[85] Factotum strip with same elements as the previous strip (sig. A3 recto). Decorative border appears on top and bottom of strip.

{CB1.
dela logica y dela cirurgia: y era muy gran astrologo philosopho: y en todas las otras artes era muy entendido: conoscia bien en todas las naturalezas y cosas deste mundo: sabia obrar de todas cosas. El tercero era sabidor en philosophia gramatica logica: y era maestro en ttodas las siete artes liberales. Entonces el primero delos sabios hablo con la donzella: y dixole assi por manera de desden teniendola por simple y nescia. Tu donzella responderme has alo que yo te preguntare: y la donzella respondio. Señor y discreto sabio yo respo<n>dere con ayuda de dios y plaziendo a mi señor el rey q<ue> dios mantenga: el qual presente esta co<n> toda su caualleria y nobles hombres dela su corte real y con su licencia y mandamiento: y entonces dixo el sabio que le respondiesse a todo lo q<ue> le preguntasse a priessa y sin mas tardar. La donzella le respondio que le plazia: y començo por la manera siguiente.
% {RUB. Capitulo tercero dela primera disputa que houo el primero sabio con la donzella.}
{=MIN=.}}[86]
[fol. 5r = sig. A5 recto]
{CB1.
{IN4.} EL sabio le pregunto donzella plazete de no te enoojar pues que aqui estamos delante del señor rey conuiene que cada vno sea examinado con dilige<n>cia que seamos bien determinados por sabios o por letrados qual de nosotros ha de ser vencido tu o yo: y la donzella le dixo que a ella le plazio mucho. Preguntole el sabio: donzella responderme has a esto que te dire: dime quales son las cosas que crio el alto poderoso dios enlos secretos y muy altos cielos. A esta pregu<n>ta le respondio luego la sabia donzella y dixole assi. Señor maestro deueys saber que nuestro señor crio enlos sus altos cielos siete planetas: los quales son estos que agora yo hos dire. El sol la Luna las estrellas Saturno Jupiter Mars Uenus Mercurius. Otro si compuso .xii. signos: los quales son. Aries Taurus Geminis ca<n>cer Leo Uirgo Libra Scorpius Sagitari<us> Capricorn<us> Aquarius Piscis: y mas crio n<uest>ro señor dios en sus altos cie-

[86] Factotum strip, from left to right: house, old man, young woman, king seated on throne (same figure as title page).

los los siete cielos: compuso las quatro partes del mundo.
{MIN=.}[87] % El sabio le pregunto: dime do<n>zella en q<ue> mes
reyna cada signo y q<ue> propiedad es la que tiene
o en que parte del cuerpo esta señoreada la figu-
ra de cada vno delos signos que tal es. La donzella le respondio y dixole.[88] En el mes de Enero
reyna Aquarius y reyna enlas espenillas de las piernas: y este signo Aquarius es assignado al planeta Saturno porq<ue> el
sol entra en aqueste signo a .xi. de Enero y quando entra el sol
es el dia de .ix horas y media: y dende que entra eneste signo
hasta que sale crece el dia vna hora es de natura de ayre: y su
calidad es caliente y humida: y el q<ue> nasciere eneste signo sera
hombre pequeño y triste de condicion y amara bien las mugeres:[89] y mas te digo que eneste mes deues vsar los manjares y
potajes claros y calientes de su natura: y no deues sufrir que
se leuante el estomago dela mesa con sed.}[90]
[fol. 5v = sig. A5 verso]
{CB1.
{MIN=.}[91] % El sabio le pregu<n>to: dime del mes de Febrero que signo es: la donzella le respondio es vn
signo llamado Pisces y reyna por los pies y a-
q<ue>ste signo llamado Piscis es assignado al planeta Jupiter porque el sol entro a .x. de Febrero
quando entra enel primer grado son los dias de diez horas y

---

[87] Text cut illustrating Aquarius.

[88] The calendar section that follows differs from the section found in the *princeps*. The material in the Zaragoza 1540 is derived from the edition published at Seville in 1526-28 by Juan Cromberger. As in the *princeps*, the source text for this information remains Andrés de Li's *Reportorio*. The selections, however, are taken the Zodiac section of the *Reportorio*. This change may reflect practices utilized by editors and publishers in the early years of printing to ensure success of their books.

[89] Li2 folio 26 recto.

[90] Li2 sig D 1 verso.

[91] Text cut illustrating Pisces.

media eneste signo cresce el dia vna hora y media: es de natura de agua: y su qualidad es fria: el que nasciere eneste signo sera gentil hombre de cuerpo:[92] y digo te mas quel sangrar qualquier persona es peligroso yel mal enlos pies.[93]
{MIN=.}[94] % El sabio le pregu<n>to: dime do<n>zella del mes de
Março: enel mes de Março reyna Aries y se-
ñorea e<n>la cabeça: es assignado al planeta mars
porque qua<n>do el sol primero nascio parescio en
la quarta parte deste signo: en[e]l qual entra comunmente a .xi. dias de Março entrando enel primero grado son los dias yguales con las noches: y desque entra eneste signo hasta q<ue> sale cresce el dia hora y media: y es signo mo-
uible y demuestra fuego: y su calidad es caliente y seca: por esto los que eneste signo nascen por minima causa se ayran supi-
tamente:[95] y mas te digo que eneste mes se engendra<n> malos humores enlos cuerpos: son peligrosas las dolencias dela cabeça: y delos oydos mas que de otra parte.[96]
{MIN=.}[97] % El sabio le pregu<n>to: dime del mes de Abril:
la donzella le respondio: en aqueste mes reyna
vn signo llamado Taur<us>: aq<ue>ste signo llamado
Taurus es assignado al planeta Uenus: porq<ue>
entra el sol eneste signo o casa comunmente a
onze dias de Abril: y reyna enel cuello y entrando enel primer grado son los dias de treze horas y media: y dende que

---

[92] Li2 folio 26 verso.

[93] Andrés de Li includes the following: "Es tiempo dispuesto para reconocer las colmenas por si se ponen arnas en ellas o si qieren enxambrar: et para sangrar qualquier miembro dela persona. E en aqueste mes es peligroso el mal enlos pies" (Li2 sig. D2 verso).

[94] Text cut illustrating Aries.

[95] Li2 sig. C 6 verso.

[96] Li2 sig. D2 verso.

[97] Text cut illustrating Taurus.

entra hasta que sale cresce el dia vna hora: y es de natura de
tierra: y es Signo estable y fixo: y su qualidad es fria y se-}
[fol. 6r = sig. A6 recto]
{CB1
ca: ylos que eneste signo nascieren muchas vezes adolescera<n>
y no ternan dicha en mugeres:[98] y aun mas te digo que quando
en [a]queste mes cresce mucho la sangre: purgarse es salutifero:
y qualquier mal enla garganta es peligroso.[99]
{MIN=.}[100] % El sabio de pregunto donzella dime del mes
de Mayo: la do<n>zella le respondio: enel mes de
Mayo reyna vn signo llamado Geminis: y tiene morada enlos braços: y aq<ue>ste signo llamado
Geminis es assignado al planeta Mercurio
porque entra el sol eneste signo a .xii. del mes de Mayo: y son
los dias de .xiiii. horas y media: y es aqueste signo de natura
de ayre: y su qualidad es caliente y humida: y el q<ue> nasciere en
aqueste signo sera ho<m>bre franco y seguira corte de rey o palacio de gra<n>des señores:[101] y mas te digo q<ue> en aqueste mes las dolencias enlos braços son peligrosas: y si tuuieres mal enlas
manos no consientas que te sean labradas con hierro.[102]
{MIN=.}[103] % El sabio le pregu<n>to do<n>zella dime del mes de
Junio. La do<n>zella le respo<n>dio en el mes de Junio reyna vn signo llamado Cancer: y aqueste signo es assignado al planeta Luna: y entra el sol co-
mu<n>mente en aqueste signo a .xii. de Junio: y qua<n>-
do entre enel primer grado son los dias de quinze horas. E
luego comiençan a menguar: y mengua el dia dende que en-

---

[98] Li2 sig. C 6 verso

[99] Li2 sig. D 4 verso.

[100] Text cut illustrating Gemini.

[101] Li2 folio 23 recto.

[102] Li2 sig. D 5 verso.

[103] Text cut illustrating Cancer.

tra el sol eneste signo hasta q<ue> sale media hora: y es de natura
de agua: y su calidad es fria y humida: y el que nasciere eneste
signo sera hombre muy valiente de cuerpo y esf orçado por su
persona:[104] y mas te digo que las dolencias enlos pechos pul-
{MIN=.}[105] mon y enel higado son muy peligrosas porq<ue> se
ñorea el signo eneste mes enlos pechos.[106]
% El sabio le pregunto. di donzella dime del
mes de Julio. La donzella le respondio: el signo del mes de Julio es llamado Leo y tiene}
[fol. 6v = sig. A6 verso]
{CB1.
fuerça enel coraçon y es assignado al sol: porque entra el sol
en aqueste signo comunmente a .xiiii. de Julio: y quando entra enel primer grado son los dias de .xiiii. horas y media y
desque entre el sol en aqueste signo hasta que sale mengua el
dia vna hora y es de natura de fuego: y su calidad es caliente
y seca: el que nasciere eneste signo sera hombre caluo y muy
honrado y acatado: y de gran coraçon altiuo:[107] y mas te digo
que es tiempo muy peligroso para sangria o purgarse y es
muy dañoso el sueño d<e> medio dia y no te deues bañar: y el ajo
y la saluia son medicinales: las dolencias en el coraçon o estomago son muy peligrosas.[108]
{MIN=.}[109] % El sabio le pregunto do<n>zella dime del mes d<e>
Agosto: la donzella le respo<n>dio en aqueste mes
reyna vn signo q<ue> llaman virgo: y tiene su fuerça
enel vientre: y es assignado al planeta Mercurio: porque entra el sol a .xiiii. de Agosto y qua<n>-

---

[104] Li2 23 verso.

[105] Text cut illustrating Leo.

[106] Li 2 folio 32 verso.

[107] Li2 folio 24 recto.

[108] Li2 folio 33 verso.

[109] Text cut illustrating Virgo.

do entra el sol enel primer grado son los dias de .xiiii. horas
y media: y dende q<ue> entra el sol en aqueste signo mengua el dia
vna hora y media: y es de natura de tierra: el que nasciere en a-
queste signo sera hombre gran gastador y musico:[110] y mas te digo que la co<m>pañia delas mugeres es dañosa mas que en ningun tiempo del año: y tambien el sueño de medio dia yel bañar es dañoso: y el mucho comer y no se d<e>ue nadie sangrar sin
gran necessidad: ni tomar medicina alguna.[111]
{MIN=.}[112] % El sabio le pregunto donzella dime del mes
de Setiembre. La donzella le respondio enel
mes de Setiembre reyna vn signo que se llama
Libra: y es assignado al planeta Uenus porque
el sol entra en aqueste signo a .xiii. de Setie<m>bre: y
quando entra enel primer grado son los dias yguales con
las noches: dende que entra eneste signo hasta que sale mengua el dia vna hora y media: y es de natur(e)[a] de agua: y su qua-}
[fol. 7r = sig. A 7 recto]
{CB1.
lidad es calie<n>te y humida: el que naciere en este signo sera ho<m>-
bre de buena criança y gran trabajador: y terna muchos ami-
gos:[113] y mas te digo que eneste mes la leche es muy prouechosa: y puedes te sangrar sin peligro: mas las dolencias delos
riñones o delas nalgas son peligrosas.[114]
{MIN=.}[115] % El sabio le pregunto: donzella dime del mes
de octubre: la donzella le respondio enel mes de
octubre señorea un signollamadoScorpius y
mora enlos genitales: aqueste signo Scorpius

---

[110] Li2 folio 24 verso.

[111] Li2 folio 34 verso.

[112] Text cut illustrating Libra.

[113] Li2 folio 24 verso.

[114] Li2 sig. E 1 verso.

[115] Text cut illustrating Scorpio.

es assignado al planeta Mars porque el sol en-
tra eneste signo a .xiiii. de octubre: y quando entra enel primero grado son los dias de .x. horas y media: y dende q<ue> entra el
sol eneste signo hasta q<ue> sale mengua el dia vna hora y es de natura de agua: y su qualidad es fria y humida: y el que nasciere
en aqueste signo sera hombre parlero y vizco y enamorado[116] y
mas te digo que en aqueste mes las aues son muy prouechosas para comer. Empero qualquier llaga es dificultosa de sanar enlos miembros ocultos.[117]
{MIN=.}[118] % El sabio le pregu<n>to: dime donzella del mes d<e>
Nouie<m>bre: la donzella le respo<n>dio enel mes de nouiembre reyna vn signo que se llama Sagitari<us>
y tiene su fuerça enlas piernas: y es assignado al
planeta Jupiter porque el sol entra en aqueste
a treze dias del mes de Nouiembre: y quando entra enel primer grado son losdias de .x. horas y media: y de<s>de que entra
el sol en aqueste signo hasta que sale mengua el dia vna hora
y es de natura de fuego y su calidad es caliente y seca: y el q<ue>
en aqueste signo nasciere sera hombre que sus hijos seran in-
clinados a no serle obedientes a el. E sera hombre vergonço-
so y de buena criança:[119] y mas te digo que en aqueste mes si tu
tuuieres mal enlas piernas es muy peligroso: y es muy seguro el sangrar y entrar enlos baños.}[120]
[fol. 7v = sig. A7 verso]
{CB1.
{MIN=.}[121] % El sabio le pregu<n>to: dime do<n>zella del mes de
Deziembre: la donzella le respo<n>dio enel mes de

---

[116] Li2 folio 25 recto.

[117] Li2 sig. E 2 verso.

[118] Text cut illustrating Sagittarius.

[119] Li2 folio 25 verso.

[120] Li2 sig. E 3 verso.

[121] Text cut illustrating Capricorn.

Deziembre reyna vn signo que se llama Capri-
cornus y tiene su fuerça enlas rodillas: es assignado al planeta Saturno: porque el sol entra en
aqueste signo a .xii. de Deziembre y quando entra en el primer grado son los dias de nueue horas y luego comiençan
de crescer: y desque entra el sol en aqueste signo hasta que sale
cresce el dia media hora: y es de natura d<e> tierra y su qualidad
es fria y seca: y el que nasciere en aqueste signo seran inclina-
dos sus hermanos a quererlo mal y terna buena criança: sera
franco y muy malenconico:[122] y mas te digo que eneste mes todas las cosas que son calientes de natura son buenas: mas
las dolencias enlas rodillas o heridas son peligrosas.[123]
% El sabio le pregunto[124]: donzella qual fue el mayor pecado q<ue>
hombre hizo eneste mundo: la donzella le respondio el que hizo Judas escariot que vendio a nuestro señor Jesu christo y
desespero dela misericordia de dios. % El sabio le pregunto
dime donzella en tiempo d<e> qual emperador nascio Jesu christo: la donzella le respondio en tiempo de Octauiano cesar.
% El sabio le pregu<n>to: do<n>zella en tiempo d<e> qual emperador
murio Jesu christo: la donzella respo<n>dio en tie<m>po de Tiberio
cesar. % El sabio le pregunto quales son las cosas mas ciertas que lleuan el hombre a parayso. La donzella le respondio
obra esperança y caridad[125]: y desque esto oyo el sabio leuantos-

---

[122] Li2 folios 25 verso-26 recto.

[123] Li2 sig. E 4 verso.

[124] The 1540 redaction incorporates several didactic *quaestiones* not found in the manuscript witnesses of the Teodor materials. The *quaestiones* derive from Version C of the *Diálogo de Epicteto y el emperador Adriano* (Ms. Egerton 939). See Bizzari 112:52-54, 105. An early imprint entitled *Las preguntas que el emperador Adriano hizo al infante Epitus* (Burgos: Juan de Junta, 1540) is of interest since it reproduces a version of the *Diálogo*. It is possible that the publisher of the 1540 Zaragoza was aware of this imprint or of other now-lost editions.

[125] This topic was quite common in the *quaestio* literature of Middle Ages. The Latin *AE* offers the following: "Quod res sunt que ducunt hominem ad regnum celorum? — Tres: cogitatio sancta, verbum bonum, opus perfectum" [Suchier 1910, AE #76]. The Catalan *Epitus* follows the *AE* tradition: "Quantes son les coses que porten al hom a parais? — L'infant respos: .iii.: bona cogitacio, bona paraul,

se luego y dixo assi al rey y a todos los caualleros a muy altas bozes. O muy alto rey por verdad vos digo que esta gentil donzella que ante vos esta ella sabe mas que yo. Por lo
qual yo me doy por vencido y digo que sabe mas que yo.
% {RUB. Capitulo quarto dela disputa
del segundo sabio.}}
[fol. 8r =sig. A8 recto]
{CB1.
{MIN=.}[126]
{IN4.} DEspues quel primer sabio fue vencido leuantose
el segundo y dixo assi. Donzella apercibete bien
que yo no soy tan simple como esse sabio que as
vencido. La donzella le respondio acatandole co<n>
mesura como a hombre viejo y letrado que era: y dixo
Señor yo vos respondere con licencia de mi señor el rey que
esta presente y de toda la caualleria. Ento<n>ces el sabio le pregunto: dime donzella qual delos doze signos y(o)[a] nombra-
dos es subjeto cada miembro que es enel cuerpo humano
y en que signos o meses son buenas o malas: las purgas y
las sangrias. La donzella le respondio maestro yo vos pin-
tare[127] vn hombre en que vereys toda manera de experiencia de
los miembros del cuerpo humano: de qual signo es regido
cada vno dellos. Otro si vos escriuire vna tabla en que vereys las purgas y las sangrias quando son buenas o malas o

---

bona obra""[Suchier 1910, E #26]. Madrid BN 17657 follows the Catalan version: "¿Quántas son las cosas que lleuan al onbre a parayso? Rrespondió el ynfante — Tres Buena cogitaçión e buena palabra e buena obra." In Egerton 939 , the *quaestio* offers an enumeration: "Las obras mas çiertas que lievan a onbre a parayso, es la fe con obra y esperança y caridad" [Suchier 1910, Spanish N #115; Bizzari 114: 105].

[126] Factotum strip, from left to right: castle, seated king (repeated from sig. A3 recto), young woman (repeated from sig. A4 verso), and old man/scholar (repeated sig. A3 recto).

[127] The printed text inludes a woodcut of a *homo signorum* which visualizes for the reader the relationships between the Zodiac and the body. It should be noted that Juana Milián, the publisher of the Zaragoza 1540, follows the *mise-en-page* utilized by Cromberger in the Seville 1526 edition. The woodcuts in each imprint are quite different.

indiferentes: empero muy sabio y discreto maestro. Aueys de notar que no se deue sangrar aquel miembro o particula quanto la luna esta puesta en aquel signo de donde te deues sangrar y este es el hombre que aqui vereys con todas sus significaciones.}
[fol. 8v = sig A8 verso]
{CB1.
{DIAG=}.[128]
Aries la cabeça.
Taurus el pescueço.
Geminis los braços.
Cancer los pechos.
Leo el coraçon.
Virgo el vientre.
Libra las ancas.
Scor. los genitales.
Sagita. las piernas.
Capri. las rodillas.
Aq<ua>ri<us> las espinillas.
Piscis los pies.
Signos Purga Sangria.
Aries. Indifferente Buena.
Aries. Indifferente. Buena.
Aries. Indifferente. Buena.
Taurus. Mala. Mala.
Taurus. Mala. Mala.
Geminis. Indifferente. Indifferente.
Geminis. Indifferente. Indifferente.
Cancer. Buena. Indifferente.
Cancer. Buena. Indifferente.}
[fol. 9r = sig. A9 recto]
{CB1.
Leo. Mala. Mala.
Leo. Mala. Mala.
Leo. Mala. Mala.
Virgo. Mala. Mala.
Virgo. Mala. Mala.
Libra. Buena. Buena.

---

[128] Text cut illustrating *homo signorum*.

Libra. Buena. Buena.
Scorpius. Buena. Indifferente.
Scorpius. Buena. Indifferente.
Sagitarius. Buena. Buena.
Sagitarius. Buena. Buena.
Sagitarius. Buena. Buena.
Capricornius. Mala. Mala.
Capricornius. Mala. Mala.
Aquarius. Buena. Buena.
Aquarius. Buena. Buena.
Piscis. Buena. Indifferente.
Piscis. Buena. Indifferente.
Piscis. Buena. Indifferente.
{IN4.} DEsque el sabio vido el hombre pintado y la tabla
delante si marauillose mucho: y dixo que verda-
deramente no auria cosa enel mundo que le pre-
guntasse que no diesse razon de todo.
% El sabio le dixo. Donzella bien has dicho y preguntole
mas. Dime donzella delas edades delas mugeres: y en que
es preciada cada vna. La de veynte años que me dizes della
Digo vos señor maestro que quando es gentil que paresce
bien alas gentes: especialmente alos hombres que son de
su complixion. La muger de treynta años que me dizes
della. Digo maestro que es tal y tan sabrosa como perdizes
por nauidad. La muger de quarenta años que me dizes d<e>lla
essa señor tiene seso entero: y para darlo a otras que no lo
tienen. Dela de cincuenta años que me dizes: essa vos digo
señor que es para el cuchillo: y la de sesenta años q<ue> me dizes
en essa señor no ay bien ninguno: y la de setenta años que
me dizes: essa vos digo señor ques tierra y fuera de to(do)-}
[fol. 9v = sig. A9 verso]
{CB1.
da razon: y la de .lxxx. años que me dizes: essa vos digo q<ue> no
me menteys: delas vnas y dela[s] otras reniego dela mejor. Entonces respondio el sabio y dixole q<ue> has hablado bien
en todo qua<n>to has respondido: dixole mas el sabio: dime donzella que señales ha de auer vna muger para ser hermosa: ella
respondio ha de tener .xviii. señales son estos que yo os dire: a
de ser luenga en tres lugares: y corta en tres lugares: vermeja en tres lugares: y ancha en tres lugares: y prieta en tres lugares y blanca en tres lugares: y rogandole mucho el sabio q<ue>
le dixesse en q<ue> manera y que selo co<n>tasse todo por menudo ca-

da cosa por si: ella le dixo que era co<n>te<n>ta de lo hazer y dixole assi
Señor maestro luenga en tres lugares enesta manera p<ar>a ser
del todo hermosa ha de tener el cuello luengo: y los dedos lue<n>-
gos y enel cuerpo luengo: ha de ser pequeña en tres lugares
pequeñas las narizes: la boca y los pies: y a de ser blanca en
tres lugares: ha de ser blanca enel cuerpo blanca enla cara:
blanca enlos dientes: y ha de ser prieta en tres lugares: las cejas prietas: las pestañas prietas: y lo prieto delos ojos: y a
de ser vermeja en tres lugares vermejos los labios dela boca
vermejas las enzias: vermeja en medio delos carrillos. y
ha de ser ancha en tres lugares: ancha enlas muñecas de los
braços: y ancha delos hombros: y ha de ser ancha enlas caderas. E despues que todo esto ouo hablado la discreta donzella el sabio se leuanto luego en pie: y dixo al rey y a todos los
ho<m>bres sabios y a toda la grande caualleria que ay esta por
ver la disputa dela donzella con los sabios. En verdad vos digo señor rey y a vosotros señores q<ue> presentes estays q<ue> esta do<n>-
zella sabe mas que yo: y es muy sabia y no le podria preguntar cosa q<ue> a todo n o diesse buena respuesta: y dixo desde aqui
yo dire q<ue> sabe mas q<ue> quantos sabiosay enel mu<n>do y q<ue> es por
demas ningun sabio disputar con ella: porq<ue> a todos los ven-
cera: y desque esto oyo el rey plugole mucho por ello: porque}
[fol. 10r]
{CB1.
bien se penso que ya era suya: y que la donzella era enamorada del rey: por lo qual la quiso mas de alli adela<n>te: y desseaua
mucho que houiesse vencido al tercero sabio: la qual donzella
supo mas que los sabios ni el rey y hizo con su saber y con la
gracia de dios todo lo q<ue> cumplia a su señor q<ue> la hauia co<m>pra-
do: y para con que el saliesse de trabajos y pobreza.
% {RUB. Capitulo .v. Dela disputa que houo la
donzella Theodor co<n> el tercero sabio: al qual llamaua<n> Abrahan el trobador y maestro enla musica.}
{IN2.} DIze la historia q<ue> desque vido el tercero sabio q<ue> los dos
eran vencidos por vna pequeña donzella houo grande
enojo en su coraçon q<ue> era para poco pues assi se hauia<n> dexa-
do vercer de vna do<n>zella ta<n> simple: el bie<n> pensaua dela vencer
y leuantosse muy soberuio en pie y dixo assi: tu do<n>zella responderme has alo q<ue> te preguntare: porq<ue> yo no soy tan simple como los otros sabios co<n> quien tu has disputado y tan malame<n>-
te vencido con tus argumentos falsos: y acabada el judio su
razo<n>: respo<n>dio la do<n>zella con grande verguença y dixole. Se-

ñor maestro vos dezis que soys mas sabio y letrado que los
otros que comigo han disputado y mayor que los discretos
sabios q<ue> delante son: alo qual respondo con reuerencia de mi
señor el rey de toda la caualleria que delante estan ajunta-
dos a n<uest>ra disputa. Digo que me marauillo de vos delo que
haueys hablado de tener un poco alos maestros que comigo
han disputado y dezir que con argumentos falsos los venci-
y pues que vos os loays por tan gran sabio hagamos entre
yo y vos esta conueniencia delante del rey mi señor y de toda
su caualleria y sabios hombres q<ue> aqui estan: q<ue> si vos me ven-
cieredes que me aya de desudar todas mis ropas: y quedar
sin camisa en cueros como mi padre me pario. E yo vos lo
doy y sea todo vuestro: y si por ventura venciere yo a vos que}
[fol. 10v]
{CB1.
vos hagays esso mismo: y q<ue> vos me deys todos vuestros paños porque quedeys desnudo como el dia en q<ue> nacistes y co<n>
esta razo<n> plugo mucho al sabio judio: porq<ue> la pensaua amen-
guar y creyendo q<ue> la tenia vencida y respondio q<ue> le plazia: y
esto fue assi otorgado por entramas p<ar>tes en p<re>sencia del rey
y dela noble caualleria y sabios: y de toda la otra gente pidio
la do<n>zella al rey q<ue> passase por auto de notario porque ninguno no se pudiesse llamar a ynorancia y el sabio co<n>sintio en todo ello: porque se creya q<ue> la tenia vencida: y al rey plugo mucho dello: y mandolo assi guardar: fue el mismo fiador de todo ello para pagar ala parte que ganasse y hazer pagar ala
parte que perdiesse y hizo seguro real
% {RUB. Capitulo sexto delas preguntas que
hizo Abraham el trobador ala donzella y delas respuestas
que le dio.}
{=MIN=.}[129]
{IN2.} PRegunto el sabio ala donzella. Dime qual es la cosa
mas pesada de todo el mundo. Respondio la donzella
que era la deuda[130]: y dixo el Sabio que era la verdad: y pre-}

[129] Factotum strip, from left to right: castle (repeated from sig. A3 recto), scholar, young woman (repeated from sig. A3 recto), seated king (repeated from title page).

[fol. 11r]
{CB1.
guntole mas: que qual era la cosa mas aguda en todas l(sa)[as] cosas. Respondio la donzella que la lengua del hombre y dela muger.[131] Preguntole mas que qual era la cosa mas apressurada que saeta: y dixo la donzella que el pensamiento.[132] Preguntole mas q<ue> qual era la cosa mas apressurada y mas ardie<n>te y quemante que el fuego: y dixo que era el coraçon.[133] Preguntole mas que qual era la cosa mas dulce que la miel. Respondio la donzella que la gran bienquerencia que tenia el padre o la madre a sus hijos.[134] Preguntole mas que qual era la cosa

---

[130] A similar *quaestio* occurs in the 15th-century Castilian redaction of the *Yfante Epitus* (Egerton MS 939): "La cosa mas pesada del mundo es la debda" [Bizzari 114: 92].

[131] Various analogues exist. In *Bocados*, the following appears: "¿Quál es la cosa que es más aguda que espada? E dixo: La lengua del mal ome" [*Bocados*, 24]. A similar *quaestio* exchange occurs in the 15th-century Castilian readaction of the *Ynfante Epitus*: "La lengua del onbre es mas aguda que la navaja" [Suchier 1910, Spanish N #104]. In the *De vita*, two examples of this same *quaestio* appear: "'¿Que cosa es mas aguda que el cuchillo?' dixo 'La lengua del mal onbre'" [*De vita*, 21] and "'Que cosa es buena y mala en los onbres?' rrespondio 'La lengua'" [*De vita*, 51]. The Arabic versions attest to the following: "...that which is sharper than the sword is the tongue" [*Arabian Nights*, IV:193] and "...más cortante que la espada es la lengua" ["Una versión del cuento..." 362].

[132] The 15th-century Castilian redaction of *Yfante Epitus* offers the following variant: "El ojo es más apresurado que la saeta, que en abriéndole le pone en vn punto donde quiere" [Bizzari 114: 93].

[133] The 15th-century Castilian redaction of *Yfante Epitus* contains: "El coraçon del omne es más ardiente que el fuego, quando está ayrado e enbuelto en saña" [Bizzari 114: 95].

[134] This *quaestio* seems to derive from the Arabic: "Now that which is sweeter than honey is the love of pious children to their two parents" [*Arabian Nights*, IV:193] and "¿Qué es más dulce que la miel...? --Más dulce que la miel es el amor que tienen los padres a los hijos..." ["Una versión del cuento..." 362]. Egerton MS

mas amarga que la hiel. Respondio la donzella y dixo que
era el mal hijo: y la mala hija. Preguntole mas que qual era
la dolencia sin medicina que era incurable. Respondio la do<n>-
zella que era la mala hija loca y de poco seso y poca verguença. Preguntole mas que qual era la deuda que nunca se pa-
ga. Respondio la donzella que era la locura.[135] Preguntole
mas que qual era la cosa mas dura que azero. Respondio
que era la verdad.[136] Preguntole[137] mas que qual era la cosa mas
deleytosa para vna hora. Respondio la do<n>zella que a ella era
gran verguença responder a tal demanda por quanto soy do<n>-
zella virgen que nunca conosci varon: mas porq<ue> no penseys
q<ue> no se responder: digo q<ue> el deleyte de vna hora: es dormir y
complir hombre su voluntad con vna gentil donzella o muger que sea graciosa ala qual hombre ama y quiere mas que
a todas las cosas del mundo: y duerme co<n> ella desnudo segu-
ramente sin temor: porque aquella hora es muy encendido el
amor: especialmente si ha sido penado de amores por ella mucho tiempo: y nunca la ha hauido hasta aquella hora: enel
qual tiempo esta el hombre tan encendido: que comportaria
la muerte por cumplir aquel plazer. E preguntole mas que
qual era el deleyte de vn dia. Respondio la donzella y dixo
que era la ganancia que gana el hombre o la muger que ven-
de o compra mercaderias de cada dia: sabed que aquel}
[fol. 11v]
{CB1.
es gran deleyte: y gran alegria. Preguntole mas que qual
era deleyte de vna semana: ella dixo que el nouio con su esposa quando bien se aman.[138] Pregu<n>tole mas que qual era el de-

---

939 of the *quaestio* offers the variant: "La ganança es más dulce que la miel" (Bizzari, 114: 96).

[135] The Egerton MS 939 offers an interesting variant for this *quaestio*: "La locura es dolençia syn sanidat" [Bizzari, 114: 97].

[136] The Egerton MS 939 offers a variant for this *quaestio*: "La verdat es más fuerte que el azero" [Bizzari, 114: 99].

[137] The four questions that follow reflect the Arabic context of the Teodor materials. For the sources, consult the annotations to the *princeps*, footnotes 51-53.

leyte de vn mes: respondio la donzella q<ue> era qua<n>do ho<m>bre viene de luengo camino donde se ha mucho detenido: y viene co<n>
bien a su casa y prosperidad y ganancia delo que ha trabaja-
do: y halla sanos y alegres a su muger y hijos: y parientes: y
a todos los que bien quiere. Preguntole mas dime donzella
qual es vna aue que anda enlos montes enla qual ay ocho señales los quales tienen los grandes animales. Respondio la
donzella y dixo assi. Sabed q<ue> aquella aue que dezis es la lan-
gosta: la qual tiene los cuernos como cieruo: y el cuello de toro: y los pechos de cauallo: y el rostro de vaca: y las alas de
aguila: y la cola de biuora: y los pies de cigueña: y los ojos d<e>
vna bestia que ha nombre Marcel: la qual bestia es grande y
fiera y es lexos destas tierras.
% El sabio le pregunto q<ue> cosa es ho<m>bre. La donzella le respo<n>-
dio ymagen de nuestro señor dios. % El sabio le pregu<n>to: do<n>-
zella q<ue> cosa es la muger: la donzella le respo<n>dio arca de mucho bien y de mucho mal ymagen de hombre bestia q<ue> nunca
se harta. % El sabio le pregu<n>to donzella que cosa es sueño: la
donzella le respo<n>dio ymagen de muerto. % El sabio le pregu<n>-
to donzella qual fue el que murio y no nascio. La donzella le
respondio nuestro padre adam.
% El sabio le pregunto donzella qual es la cosa dela qual no
puede ser harto. La donzella le respondio de ganar riquezas. % El sabio le pregunto: donzella que cosa es hombre
mancebo. La donzella le respondio candela encendida que
luego se mata. % El sabio le pregunto donzella que cosa es
hombre viejo. La donzella le respondio mal desseado vestidura de dolores. % El sabio le pregunto: donzella
que es la cosa mas incierta. La donzella le respondio la vida}
[fol. 12r]
{CB1.
del ho<m>bre. % El sabio le pregunto: donzella qual es la cosa
mas cierta: la donzella le respo<n>dio la muerte delas pers(a)[o]nas.

---

[138] In the original Arabic tale, Tawaddud displayed a keen interest in aspects of Koranic law and the doctrines associated with Islam. The *quaestio* in the Arabic version reflects that social-cultural concern: "'And for a year?' 'Marriage with a virgin.' 'And for ever?' 'To talk with friends in this world and the pleasures of Paradise in the next' [*The Glory* 175]; "...el gozo de una semana es la desposada..."["Una versión del cuento..." 362].

% El sabio le pregunto por quantas cosas o maneras mienten los hombres: la donzella le respondio por tres maneras:
por deleyte de hablar o por dezir bien de quien bien quieren
o por dezir mal de quien mal quieren. % El sabio le pregu<n>to
donzella quien fue el que puso nombre a todas las cosas que
dios crio: la donzella le respondio nuestro padre Adam.
% El sabio le pregunto: qual es la cosa mas graue y peor de
saber. La donzella le respondio el coraçon del hombre y los
pensamientos que no ay persona enel mundo que los pueda
saber sino vn solo dios y aquellos a quien el hombre los quiere reuelar. % El sabio le pregunto donzella qual es la cosa
mas ligera del mundo: la donzella le respondio: el coraçon d<e>l
hombre y el pensamiento: que en vn punto lo pone do quiere
aunque sea al cabo del mundo.
% El sabio le pregunto: qual es la cosa que el ho<m>bre mas vee
y no puede llegar a ella ni la puede tocar: la donzella le respo<n>-
dio el sol la luna y las estrellas.
% El sabio le pregunto que haze el sol de noche: la donzella
le respondio horas ay q<ue> alu<m>bra o da lu<m>bre al purgatorio y horas ay q<ue> alumbra a todo el mundo y pone al poniente.
% El sabio le pregunto: donzella quien sostiene la tierra: la do<n>-
zella le respondio los quatro elementos fuego infernal los
abismos que son debaxo dela tierra.
% El sabio le pregu<n>to donzella quien sostiene los abismos q<ue>
son deyuso la tierra. La donzella le respondio el arbol que fue
plantado enel parayso que las rayzes del yuan enel infierno
ante de la passion de Jesu christo.
% El sabio le pregunto: donzella que cosa es la noche. La do<n>-
zella le respondio descanso delos trabajadores y encobrido
ra delos malhechores.}
[fol. 12v]
{CB1.
% El sabio le pregunto: donzella quales fuero<n> los q<ue> nasciero<n>
y no murieron ni moriran hasta el fin del mundo: la donzella le
respo<n>dio Helias y Enoch q<ue> fuero<n> lleuados en cuerpo y en a-
nima al parayso terrenal y esta<n> ay y estara<n> hasta q<ue> venga el an-
techristo: y ento<n>ces saldra<n> a pelear co<n> el. % El sabio le pregu<n>-
to: donzella qual fue el primero rey: la donzella le respondio
Nembrot. % El sabio le pregu<n>to donzella qual lfue la primera ciudad: la do<n>zella le respo<n>dio: la ciudad de Niniue.
% El sabio le pregu<n>to do<n>zella qual fue el que anduuo eneste
mundo en dos vientres: la donzella le respo<n>dio: Joanas pro-

pheta que anduuo enel vientre de su madre: y enel vientre de
la ballena tres dias y tres noches.
% El sabio le pregu<n>to donzella qual fueel primer conquista-
dor del mundo q<ue> en menos tiempo mas tierra ganasse.[139] La do<n>-
zella le respo<n>dio. Alexandre q<ue> en .xii. años gano y conquisto-
todo el mundo: y quando murio hauia .xxxxvi. años.
% El sabio le pregunto: qual fue el que eneste mundo mayor
sentencia dio: la do<n>zella le respo<n>dio: Pilato que mando matar a nuestro señor Jesu christo q<ue> es verdadero dios y verdadero ho<m>bre que sabia el bien que era sin culpa. % El sabio le
pregunto: donzella qual fue el mejor luchador que enel mundo ouo: la donzella le respondio: el patriarca Jacob q<ue> lucho
toda la noche con el angel. % El sabio le pregunto: donzella
qual fue la primera fusta que anduuo por la mar: la donzella
le respondio el arca de Noe. El sabio le pregu<n>to do<n>zella qual
es el hombre de mas complida bondad: la do<n>zella le respondio el que priua su yra y vence su voluntad.
% El sabio le pregunto: donzella qual es la cosa que endeuda al que no deue nada: la donzella le respondio el que descu-
bre su secreto a otro hombre o muger. % El sabio le pregu<n>to:
donzella qual fue el hombre mas rezio enel mundo: la donzella le respondio: en fuerça Sanson: mas Hector en armas.}
[fol. 13r]
{CB1.
% El sabio le pregunto: donzella por q<ue> p<er>sona fuero<n> mas muertes: la donzella le respo<n>dio por la reyna Elena sobre Troya.
% El sabio le p<re>gunto do<n>de fue mayor ayu<n>tamiento de gentes
enel mu<n>do: la do<n>zella le respo<n>dio sobre Troya q<ue> viniero<n> gentes de todo el mu<n>do vnos para destruyr: otros p<ar>a guarecer.
% El sabio le p<re>gunto donzella quales son las mejores cosas
quel hombre puede auer en si: la donzella le respondio la verdad y la verguença. % El sabio le pregunto donzella qual es
el mayor mal que los hombres codician: la donzella le respo<n>-
io la vejez. % El sabio le pregunto: donzella qual es la cosa mas aguda que la nauaja: dixo que la lengua dela muger
quando esta ayrada. El sabio le pregu<n>to: donzella qual es la
cosa mas ardiente q<ue> el fuego: la donzella le respondio el cora-

[139] This *quaestio*, missing from Castilian Versions A and B of the *Diálogo*, is present in the *princeps*.

çon del hombre quando esta ayrado.[140]
% El sabio le pregu<n>to: donzella qual es la cosa mas dulce q<ue> la miel: la donzella le respondio la ganancia.
% El sabio le pregunto: donzella qual es la dolencia sin sanidad: la donzella le respondio la locura. % El sabio le pregunto: donzella qual es la cosa mas rezia que azero: la donzella le respondio: la verdad. % El sabio le pregunto do<n>zella qual es mejor plazer delos plazeres: la donzella le dixo: el vencimiento de su enemigo. % El sabio le pregunto donzella quales son los peores y mas principales pecados: la donzella dixo el no creer enla santa fe catholica: y desesperar dela misericordia de dios. % El sabio le pregu<n>to quales son las cosas mas ciertas que lleuan el hombre a parayso: la donzella le respondio obra esperança y charidad.
% El sabio le pregunto donzella qual es la mejor cosa y peor del mu<n>do: la donzella le respondio: la palabra con esta se puede hazer mucho bien y mucho mal.
% El sabio le pregunto: donzella qual es el mejor dia.[141] La do<n>-zella le respondio el viernes por estas cinco razones. La pri-}
[fol. 13v]
{CB1.
mera porque enel dia sancto del viernes crio dios a nuestro padre Adan. La segunda porque enel dia sancto del viernes vino a tomar carne el hijo de dios en santa Maria: y nacio de ella verdadero dios y hombre sin simiente de varon y sin ningun corronpimie(a)[n]to. La .iii. porq<ue> enel dia sancto del viernes fue bautizado n<uest>ro señor Jesu christo delas manos de sanct Juan bautista. La .iiii. fue porque enel dia sancto del viernes fue crucificado nuestro señor Jesu christo: y tomo muerte y passion por saluar el humanal linage. La .v. porque enel dia sancto del viernes verna muestro señor Jesu christo a juzgar los muertos y los biuos: y alos buenos dara gloria: y alos males pena para siempre sin fin.

---

[140] The *quaestio*, missing from Version A and B of the *Diálogo*, occurs in the *princeps* (see page ????? above) and shares affinity with the text in Egerton MS 939: "El coraçón del omne es más ardiente que el fuego quando está ayrado e enbuelto en sanna" [Bizzari 114: 95].

[141] For information concerning this *quaestio*, see footnotes 80 and 81.

% El sabio le pregunto donzella que condicion tiene el hombre: la donzella le respo<n>dio: el hombre tiene en si todas las co<n>-
diciones y virtudes que tienen todas las aues y animales q<ue>
dios crio: que son estas que se pueden hallar.
% Es brauo como leon franco como gallo ardid[o] como hu-
ron alegre como ximio callado como pece suzio como puerco manso como oueja ligero como cieruo artero como raposo hermoso como pauon tragon como lobo casto como
abeja leal como cauallo perezoso como taxo escasso como
can couarde como liebre triste como araña p<ar>lero como tordo limpio como cisne necio como asno feo como erizo ayunador como topo: fornicador como chiche: falso como sierpe[142]
% {RUB. Capitulo octauo como se dio por ven-
cido el tercero sabio: el qual llamauan Abraham el trobador
y maestro en toddas otras ciencias.}
{IN3.} DIze la historia que aquel sabio tercero desque vido las
respuestas que la donzella Theodor le daua y todas
tan bien concertadas: y dando su conclusion por muy}
[fol. 14r]
{CB1.
{=MIN=.}[143]
acabada. y le hauia respondido muy agudame<n>te a todo qua<n>-
to le havia preguntado. E miro bien en si que reya que no hauia cosa enel mundo que le preguntasse que no diesse a todo
muy buena salida y conclusion. Leuantosse de donde estaua
assentado y hizo su reuerecia al señor rey y dozo a grandes
bozes: yo hos digo señor ciertamente que esta donzella sabe
mas que yo: y desde a qui hos digo que ella es bastante para
disputar con todo el mundo y quedar vencedora: y que vuestra alteza le deue dar señaladas mercedes y hazerle mucha
honra: y despues que el sabio houo acabado su razon leuantosse de alli: y luego la donzella Theodor se fue delante el rey
con muy gran verguença: y besole los pies y las manos y acatandole como a rey y señor dixo assi. Muy alto y muy poderoso señor: la vuestra muy alta señoria plega de mandar lue-

---

[142] This sequence, attested in the *princeps*, appears in *Las preguntas queel empera-dor Adriano hizo* (Burgos: Juan de Junta 1540) folios 10r-10v [Suchier 1910, 386].

[143] Factotum block repeated from sig. A4 verso.

go a este vuestro sabio q<ue> luego sin tardança se desnude a qui-
en presencia de vuestra alteza y de todos estos grandes señores y discretos varones todos sus paños y los me entregue
sin otra ninguna tardança: y sin poner enello escusacion ni lo<n>-
gueria: y vista por el rey la peticion q<ue> la buena y discreta don-}
[fol. 14v]
{CB1.
zella le dezia y conosciendo su alta señoria la razon y justicia
que para ello tenia segun el contrato que entre ellos hauia passado: delo qual el era fiador por ambas las partes: mando al
sabio por sentencia que luego enesse punto se desnudass(a)[e] todos sus paños: y los entregasse ala donzella.
% E viendo el sabio que el rey mandaua justicia y razon: luego enesse punto se assento a desnudar todos sus paños con
gran verguença y diolos ala donzella: y quedo desnudo sin ropa ninguna: por tal manera que no tenia en todo su cuerpo sino los paños con que cobria las partes vergonçosas. y qua<n>-
do la donzella le vido todo desnudo y que tenia los paños menores calçados y no otra cosa ninguna dixo le la donzella a
grandes bozes: porque el rey y toda la caualleria y discretos
hombres que alli estauan lo oyessen. Que luego se descalças
se los paños menores y ge los diesse y entregasse luego pues-
que assi estaua enla conueniencia: que el que perdiesse hauia
de quedar desnudo como la hora en que nascio. E pues que
el sabio assi lo hauia causado: y dixo ante el rey a altas bozes
quele diesse los paños menores pues que era todo suyo: y lo
hauia ganado segun a la conuiniencia. El rey mando luego
al sabio que se descalçasse y se los diesse ala donzella so pena
de su merced. Porque otro dia se auisasse como apostaua: y
el Sabio le respondio al Rey y ala donzella que no lo haria
aunque supiesse morir por ello: por quanto no podia hazer o
racion sin ellos segun lo que mandaua su ley. E dixo la donzella. Reuerendo maestro yo hos mostrare como hagays oracion sin ellos y alcanceys lo q<ue> justamente demandaredes a nuestro señor dios. Quanto mas que otros tenees en vuastra casa o los podeys mandar hazer: y respondio el sabio. Bien es
lo que dizes: mas porque son quitados donde soy auergon-
çado no los puedo mas calçar. Entonces le respondio la
Donzella. Maestro todo esto es alargar razones yo hos}
[fol. 15r]
{CB 1.
mostrare como los podreys alcançar y podras tornar a ha-

zer oracion a dios por tanto plega hos de me los dar: hinco
las rodillas ante ella y tomole las manos y besosselas: roga<n>-
dole ahincadamente que no le hiziesse tal verguença ante el
señor rey: y delante tan noble caualleria y discretos hombres
y que el le queria dar .x. mil doblas de buen oro bermejo: porque no le hiziesse descalçar sus paños menores: la donzella
houo piedad del pues queya se rescataua: y cumplio el ruego del sabio con que el ganasse licencia del rey. y entonces el
rey dio licencia ala donzella: y agradescioselo: y el rey mando
al sabio q<ue> luego enesse punto embiasse a su casa por las .x. mil
doblas y se las diesse ala donzella: el sabio lo hizo assi: y dio
se las luego: el rey dixo ala donzella que demandasse en merced todo quanto ella quisiesse que el se lo daria: y ella le beso
los pies y demandole en merced que la dexasse tornar con su
mercader y que la venda sea ninguna que de mi tiene hecha
vuestra alteza: porque el ha gastado por mi quanto tenia: y el
me puso a deprender todo esto que yo se: porende señor el des-
conoscimiento es malo: y el conoscimiento es bueno: delo q<ua>l
se yo enesto mas que vuestra alteza: porque esto no es nada
con lo que yo se: y podria bien hablar: y quando el rey esto o-
yo ala donzella pesole mucho por la merced que le dema<n>do
que el bien pensaua que ya era suya: y pues que ya lo hauia
mandado no se pudo desdezir: entonces el rey rogo ala donzella que pues tanto sabia que le rogaua q<ue> le soltasse ciertas
dudas que tenia: porque enello le haria gran plazer: entonces la donzella respondio que dixesse su alteza todo lo q<ue> man-
dasse que ella responderia.

% {RUB. Las demandas que el rey Almançor hizo
ala donzella Theodor.}[144]

% El rey le pregunto[145] donzella que virtud es tomar el hom-

---

[144] This *demanda* section is missing from the manuscript witnesses of the text and from the early imprints of Toledo 1500, Sevilla 1516-20, and Sevilla 1526-28. These responses focus on religious precepts and dogma. The addition of this material to the 1540 Zaragoza represents a third phase in the textual evolution of the Teodor material. The publisher provides useful precepts which reflects the moral and religious codes prevalent in Early Modern Castile. For this phenomenon, see the comments by Whinnom (170) and Nalle (92).

bre penitencia. La donzella le respondio perdonar los peca-}
[fol. 15v]
{CB1.
dos: y haze el hombre ser en gracia de dios: y abre las puer-
tas del parayso p<ar>a el a<n>i<m>a del pecador q<ue> antes estaua en pecado mortal: y enla yra de n<uest>ro señor dios. % El rey le p<re>gunto
donzella q<ue> virtudes tiene el ho<m>bre en oyr missa: la donzella le
respondio las virtudes q<ue> tiene la missa a aq<ue>llos que deuota-
mente la van a oyr son .viii. La primera q<ue> el que aq<ue>l dia oye-
ra missa no le faltara el mantenimiento necessario. La .ii. que
los pecados veniales le seran perdonados. La .iii. todo jura-
mento que aya hecho no siendo en daño de su proximo le sera
perdonado. La .iiii. q<ue> aquel dia q<ue> oyra missa y adorare el cuerpo de dios no perdera esse dia la vista delos ojos. La .v. q<ue>
aquel dia que oyere missa no morira de muerte supitaña. La
vi. si estuuiere descomulgado y muriere aquel dia q<ue> oyere missa: muere absuelto de descomunion. La .vii. que mientra[s] q<ue> estuuiere en missa no enuegece. La .viii. que quantos passos da
yendo y viniendo a oyr missa ala yglesia: tantos le sera<n> guar-
dados para poner delante de n<uest>ro señor dios el dia de su muerte y el dia del juyzio. % El rey le p<re>gunto do<n>zella qual fue
y ha de ser el peor dia q<ue> enel mu<n>do fuere: la donzella le respo<n>-
dio: el dia del juyzio q<ue> alli parescera n<uest>ro señor Jesu christo
muy ayrado co<n> las mismas llagas q<ue> rescibio enla santa passion: y alli recebiran los malos muy crueles penas y sentencias sin ninguna piedad: y seran lançados enel infierno a sufrir crueles penas y tormentos para siempre jamas sin fin.
% El rey le pregunto[146] donzella qual es el mejor estame<n>to en
q<ue> el hombre se pueda mejor saluar: la donzella le respondio
todos son buenos si guarda<n> cada vno en su regla lo que dios
les mando: porque en cada vno dellos se puede saluar el ho<m>-

---

[145] A possible source for these observations is *Las preguntas que el emperador Adriano hizo al infante Epitus* (Burgos: Juan de Junta, 1540), folio 12r [Suchier 1910, 389-90].

[146] The section, missing from the earlier printed editions, is attested in *Las preguntas que el emperador Adriano hizo al infante Epitus* (Burgos: Juan de Junta, 1540), folios 11v-12r [Suchier 1910, 388-89]. In the Burgos 1540, this sequence occurs before the section on "virtud". See footnote 124.

bre y: por el estado dell sacramento y del matrimonio se sostiene el mundo: ca sin el no hauria clerigos ni religiosos ni
reyes ni caualleros que sostienen el mundo y la santa fe cato-
[lica]. E por tanto es mejor el que puede hauer ayu<n>tamie<n>to con}
[fol. 16r]
{CB1.
muger sin pecado mortal por donde viene generacion enel
mundo que es muy sancta orden por estas cosas que aqui dire. Lo primero porque dios la establescio luego enel comienço del mundo. Lo segundo por la dignidad del lugar donde
fue establescido que es el parayso terrenal. Lo .iii. que houo
establescimiento nueuo. Lo .iiii. que Adan y Eua eran sin pecado qua<n>do el establescimiento fue hecho enellos. Lo .v. por
q<ue> esta orden saluo dios enel diluuio. Lo .vi. porq<ue> santa Maria quiso ser desta orde<n>. Lo .vii. porq<ue> nuestro señor Jesu xp<ist>o
co<n> la virgen santa Maria su madre quiso ser co<n>bidado enlas
bodas por nos monstrar el bien q<ue> es enel casamiento. Lo .viii.
porq<ue> es vno delos sacramentos dela yglesia. Lo .ix. por el fru-
to q<ue> del viene q<ue> son los hijos buenos: por estas cosas y por
otras muchas y muy santas y notables: y los q<ue> en esta orden
quisieren entrar entre las otras cosas deuen catar estas. La
primera q<ue> la muger q<ue> ouiere de tomar sea de hedad p<ar>a hauer
hijos: ca por esto la ordeno dios. Lo segundo q<ue> sea de buena
generacion hija de buen padre y de buena madre. Lo .iii. q<ue>
sea ella buena y de buena fama: cuerda y discreta: y sea sana
de sus mie<m>bros: despues si pudiere hauer riquezas sera bien:
empero las riquezas gananse y pierdense quando el ho<m>bre
no cuyda: a se de parar mientes que enel dote no se deue mi-
rar la quantidad: mas la calidad como fue ganado: o con q<ue>
artes o maneras porque ay dotes tan malamente ganados
y adqueridos: y mugeres tan malas y desonestas: que a sus
maridos hazen morir. Empero si desta qualidad no pudieres hallar toma lo mas que dello pudieres. La mas buena
y mejor hermosura para la muger es la bondad dela buena
muger: esta haze florescer y acrescentar la honra y la hazien-
da y estado de su marido. Si las otras cosas sobredichas ha-
llares enla muger no cures dela hermosura saluo por la bondad como dicho es.}
[fol. 16v]
{CB1.
% E quando el rey vido que tan sabiamente le hauia respondido dixole por cierto donzella tu eres merecedora de ser se-

ñora de todo mi reyno y no me pesa sino porque te he otorgado libertad y entonces le mando dar ala discreta do<n>zella diez mil doblas de oro: y mando asu camarero que se las diesse luego y mandola vestir toda muy bien d<e> brocado: y embio a ella y a su señor con muy grande honra para su tierra: y assi la discreta donzella dio cuenta de si: y saco a su señor de trabajo: y otras muchas cosas hizo y mostro por esperiencia q<ue> aqui no se ponen por lo qual dios sea loado para siempre jamas. Amen.

% Fue impresso el presente tratado enla insigne ciu-
dad de Çaragoça: por Juana Milian biuda de
Pedro Hardoyn. A quinze dias del mes de
Mayo: año de .M.D.xxxx.
{SYMB.}[147]
{MIN. IRIS IN CELO IRIS HALO}}

[147] Printer's Device, consisting of two arcs and suns.

GLOSSARY

acuçioso "listo, astuto" Today 'acucioso' means "diligent, hasty, eager," but its 13th century meaning was generally "astute, clever." Derived from late Latin ACUTIA "astuteness, cunning," < Latin ACUTU, plus adjectival suffix *-oso* (*DCECH* 1:44-45, *s.v.* ACUCIA).

ayna "de prisa, pronto" Derived from Latin AGINA "activity" and first documented in the *Cid* (*DCECH* 1:88-89, *s.v.* AÍNA). The meaning here is clearly "early," as it contrasts with 'tarde': Si fuere tal que viniere a la muger su talente tarde, e la del varon **ayna**..."

alcaçeria "bazar" Corominas & Pascual define 'alcaçería' as: "lonja a modo de bazar, donde tenían los mercaderes sus tiendas, del ár[abe] *qaisariya*." It is first documented in 1229. The diphthongized form 'alcaicería' does not appear until the later 16th century (*DCECH* 1:126, *s.v.* ALCAICERÍA).

amjnazillastes "heriste" As is clear from a comparison of the variants from the other witnesses to the text, the form meant here must be **amanzillastes** (cf. Ms. *g*) or **manzillastes** (cf. Ms. *h*). Modern 'amanzillar' derives from "mancilla", itself from Vulgar Latin MACELLA "stain." According to Corominas and Pascual, this latter term was "influido por el verbo *mancillar*, que en parte procede del lat. vg. *MACELLARE 'matar, sacrificar', derivado de MACELLUM 'matadero', voz de origen independiente; sin embargo, existe la posibilidad de que *mancilla* sea un mero postverbal de este *mancillar*, derivado en el sentido de 'herida', que habría evolucionado secundariamente hacia los de 'mancha moral' y 'lástima'" (*DCECH* 3:796-97, *s.v.* MANCILLA). It seems clear from the context here that our verb has the sense of 'to wound, afflict' ("mucho me **amjnazillastes** mi coraçón").

amos "ambos" Both 'amos' and 'ambos' existed in medieval Spanish; Corominas & Pascual characterize 'amos' as the more common form, and 'ambos' as a "dialectalismo leonés" (*DCECH* 1:238-39).

animalias "animales" Derived from the Latin plural ANIMALIA, with the plural marker *-s* added, this form is quite common in texts from the mid-13th century on (*Setenario*, *Calila*, *Conde Lucanor*, etc.) (*DCECH* 1:173-74, *s.v.* ALIMAÑA).

ascondido "escondido" Archaic form, < Latin ABSCONDERE. The earliest texts have 'asconder' (Cid); Berceo has both forms but Corominas & Pascual believe that 'esconder' is a modernization of the MSS or later editors; both forms appear in the *Libro de buen amor* (*DCECH* 2:704-5, *s.v.* ESCONDER). The prefix *as-* is unusual in Spanish, and was often replaced by the more common *es-* < EX-.

çelado "ocultado" See entry below for **reçelar**.

colora "cólera" Both variants appeared in 13th century texts; < CHOLERA (*DCECH* 2:136).

comidiendo "pensando" (infinitive: **comedir**) Found in the *Cid*; "del lat. COMMETIRI 'medir un conjunto de cosas, confrontar', de donde 'pensar' o 'moderar' (*DCECH* 4:17, *s.v.* MEDIR).

comigo "conmigo" Shows assimilation of /nm/ > /m/.

confaçion "complexión"? The meaning here ("dezitme de la confaçion del cuerpo o del omne") seems to be that of "constitution" or "complexion." Corominas & Pascual give the earliest appearance of 'confación' as 1490, as a variant of 'confección' (*DCECH* 3:299, *s.v.* AFECTO).

debda "deuda" Archaic form, retaining the /b/ from DEBITA.

destrauado "destrabado, desprendido" In this context ("el estómago **destrauado** de la vianda") it seems to mean "cleared, emptied" rather than "untangled, loosened."

dezilde "decidle" Shows metathesis of /dl/ > /ld/.

do "doy" There are at least three common theories that attempt to explain the addition of *-y* to the 1st person singular present tense of 'ser, ir, dar, estar.' It may be a reflex of IBI (cf. 'hay'); it may be due to anticipation of the semiconsonant in verb-subject order 'so yo' (> 'soy yo'); or it may be due to Leonese influence, wherein forms like 'sou,' 'dou,' 'vou' > 'soy,' 'doy,' 'voy' (for a fuller description of this phenomenon, see Lloyd).

federian "apestarían, hederían" Older form of 'heder' with initial /f-/ preserved. Derived from Latin FOETERE "to stink," and first documented in Berceo (*DCECH* 3:338, s.v. HEDER).

fuelgos "aliento, respiración"? The context here ("si non fuese por los bafos de la tierra, federian nuestros **fuelgos** contra el çielo e la tierra") seems to suggest a broader, more negative sense: perhaps "odors" or "humors"?

gelo "se lo" Regular development when dative and accusative pronouns were combined: ILLI + ILLU >elielo > ljelo > 'gelo.' Later > 'se lo' by analogy to reflexive pronoun 'se.'

luengo "largo" Derived from Latin LONGU "long," and widely used in Old Spanish; now archaic.

melezina "medicina" Latin MEDICINA gave 'medezina' in Old Spanish, but there are several common variants: 'medicina,' probably a learned form; 'medezina,' the expected result; and 'melezina,' with the change from /d/ > /l/ probably due to dissimilation from the first element of *z* /dz/.

mill "mil" "La forma *mill* es la empleada por los escribas del *Cid* y de J. Ruiz, y aun por autores mucho más tardíos ... pero Nebr[ija] ya sólo da *mil* en su diccionario, y en la gramática habla del «error de los que escriven *mill* con doblada *ll*» ... Esta reducción se debe a la repugnancia del castellano por la palatal *ll* en fin de sílaba; con arreglo a lo cual es de esperar que la palatal se mantuviera cuando *mill* antecedía a palabra de inicial vocálica ...; finalmente la forma *mil* se generalizó por analogía. (*DCECH* 4:75-76)

omnes "hombres" Latin HOMINES > 'omnes,' later 'hombres' after dissimilation /mn/ > /mr/, and subsequent epenthesis of /b/.

pedit "pedid" Shows devoicing of word-final /d/.

pagose dello "estaba contenta de ello" From Latin PACARE, "to pacify, placate," 'pagar' came to mean "to satisfy." In medieval Spanish this was its common meaning; in this construction, 'pagarse de' = "to content oneself with, to be satisfied with." Eventually the sense of "to satsfy" became associated with the satisfaction of a debt, and the verb came to have its current meaning of "to pay" (*DCECH* 4:337).

prieto "negro" In modern Spanish, it generally means "dense, compact," but 'prieto' was a very commonly used term for the color black in Old Spanish. Corominas & Pascual explain: "Es notable la ac[epción] 'moreno, 'negro', que han tomado el cast[ellano] ant[iguo] *prieto* y el port[ugués] *preto*: procede de la idea de 'denso, espeso' ... que hablando de niebla, polvo y análogos, equivale a 'oscuro' (*DCECH* 1:302-4, *s.v.* APRETAR).

reçelar "temer" First documented 1251, in *Calila*. It also appears in the *Primera crónica general*, *Zifar*, *Conde Lucanor* and Juan Ruiz. "A primera vista *recelar*, por su significado, parece derivado de CELAR I 'demostrar celo, tener celos', ... pero la *c* sorda del catalán y occitano ... demuestra que ha de venir de *celar* 'ocultar' (comp. cat., oc. *zel* 'celo', *gelós* 'celoso', *gelosia* 'celos'), con paso de *recelar-se de* 'ocultarse de alguien' a 'desconfiar de alguien' ...; la construcción original fué *recelarse de*, como escriben J. Manuel ... y J. Ruiz" (*DCECH* 2:18-19 *s.v.* CELAR)

sallir "salir" Corominas & Pascual cite forms of 'salir' with *ll*, which seems to represent the palatal lateral: "hay variante antigua *sallir*, corriente desde los orígenes hasta el S. XVI, y resultante por vía fonética de formas como *salió*, *saliera*, *saliendo*, etc." It may be problematic that most of the examples cited come from texts with strong dialectal character (*Santa María Egipciaca*, *Santa Oria*, *Fuero aragonés*, documents from Murcia, etc.) (*DCECH* 5:139-40, *s.v.* SALIR).

so See entry for **do** above.

sodes "sois" For a full description of the evolution of this form, see Penny (138, 161-62).

talente "deseo, líbido" All texts except MS *g* have **talente:** *g* has **talante.** This latter form, **talante,** is in fact the more usual medieval form. Both derive from Greek ταλαντον, possibly via TALENTUM, as does 'talento,' "talent." According to Corominas & Pascual, 'talento' was first documented in 1155 but was rare through the 16th century, while 'talante' was first documented in the 13th century (*DCECH* 5:386-88, *s.v.* TALENTO). Penny characterizes 'talento' as a Hellenism (212). Our form, **talente,** is somewhat unusual in its final vowel, possibly to distinguish it from 'talento,' "talent," but its meaning is clear in our text.

terniades "tendríais" Shows metathesis instead of epenthesis of /d/ in stem; *-ades* was the usual 2nd pl. ending (for a full explanation of the evolution of this ending, see Penny [138-39]).

vido "vio" This variant retained the intervocalic /d/; also found in Berceo, *Poema de Yuçuf*, and other early texts (*DCECH* 5:773-74, *s.v.* VER).

BIBLIOGRAPHY

Alfonso X. *Especulo de la leyes. Opúsculos legales del rey Don Alfonso el Sabio*. Ed. Real Academia de la Historial. 2 vols. Madrid: Real Academia de la Historia, 1936. [I.XII]

———. *General Estoria*. Ed. A.G. Solalinde. Madrid: Junta para Ampliación de Estudios e Investigaciones Científicas, 1930.

———. *Lapidario (Según el manuscrito escurialense H.I.15)*. Ed. Sagrario Rodríguez M. Montalvo. Madrid: Gredos, 1981.

———. *Siete Partidas. Opúsculos legales del rey Don Alfonso el Sabio*. Ed. Real Academia de la Historial. 2 vols. Madrid: Real Academia de la Historia, 1936. [I.XII]

Altercatio. Altercatio Hadrian Agusti et Epicteti Philosophi. Eds. Lloyd William Daly and Walter Suchier. Illinois Studies in Language and Literature, 24. Urbana: Univ. of Illinois, 1939.

Arabian Nights. The Book of the Thousand Nights and a Night. Trans. R. F. Burton. 12 vols. London: Nichols, 1897.

Aristotle. *On the Generation of Animals*. Trans. A.L. Peck. Cambridge, MA: Harvard Univ. Press, 1979.

Baranda, Nieves and Víctor Infantes, Eds. *Narrativa popular de la edad media: La Doncella Teodor, Flores y Blancaflor y París y Viana*. Madrid: Akal, 1995.

———. "Post Mettmann. Variantes textuales y transmisión editorial de la *Historia de la donzella Teodor*." *La corónica* 22 (1993-94): 61-88.

Berceo, Gonzalo de. *Los loores de Nuestra Señora*. Ed. Brian Dutton. London: Tamesis, 1975. Vol. 3 of *Obras completas*. 5 vols. 1967-81.

Bizzari, Hugo Oscar, ed. *Diálogo de Epicteto y el emperador Adriano (Derivaciones de un texto escolar en el siglo XIII)*. Frankfurt am Main: Vervuert, 1995.

———. "La labor crítica de Hermann Knust en la edición de textos medievales castellanos: Ante la crítica actual." *Incipit* 8 (1988): 81-97.

Blumenfeld-Kosinski, Renate. *Not of Woman Born: Representations of Caesarean Birth in Medieval and Renaissance Culturey*. Ithaca: Cornell University Press, 1990.

Bocados de oro: Kritische Ausgabe des altspanischen Textes. Ed Mechthild Crombach. Romanistisches Versuche und Vorarbetiten, 37. Romanisches Seminar der Universität Bonn: Bonn 1971.

Bremond, Claude and Bernard Dabord. "Tawaddud et Teodor: les enjeux ludiques du savoir." *L'enciclopedismo medievale*. Ed. Michelangelo Picone. Ravenna: Longo, 1994. 253-73.

Brotherston, Gordon. *Book of the Fourth World: Reading the Native Americas through their Literature*. Cambridge: Cambridge University Press, 1992.

Brown, Cynthia. *Poets, Patrons, and Printers: Crisis of Authority in Late Medieval France*. Ithaca: Cornell University Press, 1995.

Burlaeus, Gualterus. *De vita et moribus philosophorum*. Ed. Hermann Knust. Bibliothek des Litterarischer Vereins in Stuttgart, 177. Stuttgart: Litteratischer Verein, 1886.

Cadden, Joan. *Meanings of Sex Difference in the Middle Ages. Medicine, Science, and Culture*. Cambridge: Cambridge University Press, 1993.

Blecua, Juan Manuel Cacho and María Jesús Lacarra, Eds. *Calila e Dimna* Madrid: Castalia, 1987.

Chartier, Roger. *The Order of Books: Readers, Authors, and Libraries in Europe between the Fourteenth and Eighteenth Centuries*. Stanford: Stanford University Press, 1994.

Chejne, Anwar. *Muslim Spain: Its History and Culture.* Minneapolis: University of Minnesota Press, 1974.

Collectanea Bedae. PL 94, cols. 539-60.

Collectio Salernitana: ossia documenti inediti e trattati di medicina appartenenti all scuola medica salernitana. Ed. Salvatore de Renzi. 5 vols. Naples: Filstre-Sebezio, 1852-1859.

Compendio de la humana salud. Biblioteca Nacional I-51. Ed. María Teresa Herrera. Madison: Hispanic Seminary, 1987.

Constantinus Africanus. *Constantini Liber de Coitu: El tratado de andrología de Constantino el Africano.* Ed. Enrique Montero Cartelle. Santiago de Compostella: Universidad de Santiago de Compostella, 1983.

Corominas, Joan and José A. Pascual. *Diccionario crítico etimológico castellano e hispánico.* 6 vols. Madrid: Gredos, 1989.

Cross, James E. and Thomas D. Hill. *The Prose Solomon and Saturn and Adrian and Ritheus.* Toronto: University of Toronto Press, 1982.

Daniel, Norman. *The Arabs and Medieval Europe.* London: Longmans, 1970.

Darbord, Bernard. "La tradición del saber en la *Doncella Teodor.*" *Medioevo y Literatura: Actas del V Congreso de la Asociación Hispánica de Literatura Medieval (Granada, 27 septiembre - 1 octubre 1993).* Ed. Juan de Peredes. 4 vols. Granada: Universidad de Granada, 1995. 1:13-30.

de Aviñón, Juan. *Sevillana Medicina (Burgos, 1545).* Ed. Eric Naylor. Madison: Hispanic Seminary, 1987.

de Córdoba, Fray Martín. *Jardín de nobles donzellas.* Ed. Harriet Goldberg. North Carolina Studies in the Romance Languages and Literatures, 137. Chapel Hill: University of North Carolina, 1974.

de Gordonio, Bernardo. *Lilio de medicina.* Ed. Brian Dutton and María Nieves Sánchez. Madrid: Arcos/Libros, 1993.

de Ketham, Johannes. *Compendio de la salud humana.* Ed. María Teresa Herrera Hernández. Fundación Juan March, Serie Universitaria 53. Madrid: Fundación Juan March, 1978.

Delbrugge, Laura. "A Critical Edition of Andrés de Li's *Reportorio de los tiempos* (1495)." Diss. The Pennsylvania State University, 1996.

Deyermond, Alan D. *La Edad Media.* Trans. Luis Alonso López. Historia de la literatura española 1. Barcelona: Ariel, 1980.

Dozy, R. y C. Pellat. *Le Calendrier de Cordoue.* Leiden: Brill, 1961.

Dutton, Brian. *Catálogo índice de la poesía cancioneril del siglo XV.* Bibliographic Series 3. Madison: Hispanic Seminary of Medieval Studies, 1982.

Eamon, William. *Science and the Secrets of Nature: Books of Secrets in Medieval and Early Modern Culture.* Princeton: Princeton University Press, 1994.

Eugenio, Damiana L. "'Awit' and "Corrido": A Study of Fifty Philippine Metrical Romances." Diss. University of California, Los Angeles, 1965.

Ferrante, Joan. *To the Glory of her Sex: Women's Roles in the Composition of Medieval Texts.* Bloomington: Indiana University Press, 1997.

French, Roger. "Astrology in Medical Practice." *Practical Medicine from Salerno to the Black Death.* Ed. Luis García-Ballester *et al.* Cambridge: University of Cambridge Press, 1994. 30-59.

Gabrieli, Francesco. "Islam in the Mediterranean World." *Cambridge History of Islam.* Eds. P.M. Holt, Ann K. S. Lambton, and Bernard Lewis. Cambridge: Cambridge University Press, 1970. 63-104

————. "The Transmission of Learning and Literary Influences to Western Europe." *Cambridge History of Islam.* Eds. P.M. Holt, Ann K. S. Lambton, and Bernard Lewis. Cambridge: Cambridge University Press, 1970. II: 851-889.

García-Ballester, Luis. "Changes in the *Regimina sanitatis*: The Role of the Jewish Physicians." *Health, Disease and Healing in Medieval Culture.* Ed. Sheila Campbell, Bert Hall, and David Klausner. New York: St. Martin's Press, 1992. 119-31.

Gerresch, Claudine. "Un récit des Mille et une Nuits: Tawaddud." *Bulletin de l'Institut Fondamental D'Afrique Noire. Série B, Sciences Humaines* 35 (1973): 57-175.

Gil, José S. *La escuela de traductores de Toledo y los colaboradores judíos.* Toledo: Instituto Provincial, 1985.

Gil-Sotres, Pedro. "Derivation and Revulsion: The Theory and Practice of Medieval Phlebotomy." *Practical Medicine from Salerno to the Black Death.* Ed. Luis García-Ballester *et al.* Cambridge: University of Cambridge Press, 1994. 110-55.

Glosa castellana al Regimiento de príncipes de Egidio Romano. Ed. Juan Beneyto Pérez. Madrid: Instituto de Estudios Políticos, 1947. 3 Vols.

Goldberg, Harriet. "Women Riddlers in Hispanic Folklore and Literature." *Hispanic Review* 59 (1991): 57-75.

Grotzfeld, Heinz, and Sophia Grotzfeld. *Die Erzählungen aus 'Tausendundeiner Nach.* Darmstadt: Wissenschaftliche Buchgesellschaft, 1984.

Haro Cortés, Marta. *Los compendios de castigos del siglo XIII: Técnicas narrativas y contenido ético.* Valencia: Universitat de València, 1995.

Harthan, John. *The Books of Hours.* New York: Crowell, 1977.

Haskins, Charles H. *Studies in Medieval Sciences.* Cambridge, Mass: Harvard University Press, 1924.

Herlihy, David. *Opera muliebria: Women and Work in Medieval Europe.* Philadelphia: Temple University Press, 1990.

Hourani, George F. "The Medieval Translations from Arabic to Latin Made in Spain." *The Muslim World* 62 (1970): 97-114.

Ibn Habib. *Mujtasar fi l-tibb (Compendio de medicina)*. Eds. Camilo Álvarez de Morales & Fernando Girón Irueste. Fuentes Arábico-hispanas, 2. Madrid: CSIC, 1992.

Irwin, Robert. *The Arabian Nights: A Companion*. London: Penguin Press, 1994.

Isidore of Seville. *Etymologiarum sive originum Libri XX*. Ed. W.M Lindsay. 2 vols. Oxford: Oxford Univ. Press, 1911.

Isidore. *De ecclesiasticis officiis*. PL 83, cols. 757-826.

Jacobus de Voragine. *The Golden Legend: Readings on the Saints*. Trans. William Granger Ryan. 2 vols. Princeton: Princeton University Press, 1993.

Jacquart, Danielle, and Claude Thomasset. *Sexuality and Medicine in the Middle Ages*. Princeton: Princeton University Press, 1988.

Kalinke, Marianne E. *Bridal-Quest Romance in Medieval Iceland*. Islandica 46. Ithaca: Cornell University Press, 1990.

Keil, Gundolf. "Das *Regimen duodecim mensium* der 'Düdescher Aristedie' und das *Regimen sanitatis Coppernici*." *Niederdeutsches Jahrbuch* 81(1958): 33-48.

————. "Eine lateinische Fassung von Meister Alexanders Monatsregeln." In *Medizin im mittelalterlichen Abendland*. Darmstadt: Wissenschaftliche Buchgesellschaft, 1982. 228-59.

Kemble, John M. *The Dialogue of Salomen and Saturn with an Historical Introduction*. London: Taylor, 1848.

Ketham, Johannes de. *Compendio de la humana salud*. Ed. María Teresa Herrera. Madrid: Arco, 1990.

Knust, Hermann. *Mittheilungen aus dem Eskurial*. Bibliothek des Litterarischen Vereins in Stuttgart, CXLI. Tübingen: Litterarischen Verein in Stuttgart, 1879.

Kritzech, James. *Peter the Venerable and Islam*. Princeton: Princeton University Press, 1964.

Lawn, Brian. *The Salernitan Questions. An Introduction to the History of Medieval and Renaissance Problem Literature.* Oxford: Clarendon Press, 1963.

Lemay, Richard. "The True Place of Astrology in Medieval Science and Philosophy: Towards a Definition." *Astrology, Science, and Society: Historical Essays.* Ed. Patrick Curry. Woodbridge, Suffolk: Boydell Press, 1987. 57-73.

Li, Andrés de. *Reportorio de los tiempos.* Burgos, Fadrique de Basilea, May 21st, 1493, New York, The Hispanic Society of America.

Li, Andrés de. *Reportorio de los tiempos.* Zaragoza, Paulus Hurus, 1495, Madrid, Biblioteca Nacional, I/2470[2].

Libro de Alexandre. Ed. Jesús Cañas. Madrid: Cátedra, 1988.

Libro de Apolonio. Ed. Carmen Monedero. Madrid: Castalia, 1987.

Libro de Paladio-Obra de agricultura. Ed.Thomas Capuano. Madison: Hispanic Seminary, 1990.

Libro del cuidado de la salud durante las estaciones del año o "Libro de higiene" de Muhammad B. 'Abdallah B. Al-Jatib. Ed. María de la Concepción Vázquez de Benito. Salamanca: Ediciones Universidad de Salamanca, 1984.

Lindberg, David C. "The Transmission of Greek and Arabic Learning to the West." *Science in the Middle Ages.* Ed. David C. Lindberg. Chicago: University of Chicago Press, 1978. 52-90.

Lloyd, Paul. *From Latin to Spanish.* Philadelphia: American Philosophical Society, 1987.

López Piñero, José María. *Ciencia y técnica en la sociedad española de los siglos XVI y XVII.* Barcelona: Labor, 1979.

Lowe, E. A. *The Bobbio Missal.* 3 Vols. London: Harrison, 1920.

MacKay, Angus. *Spain in the Middle Ages: From Frontier to Empire, 1000-1500.* New York: St. Martins Press, 1977.

Márquez Villanueva, Francisco. *El concepto cultural alfonsí.* Madrid: Editorial MAPFRE, 1994.

Martínez Gázquez, José y Julio Samsó. "Una nueva traducción latina del Calendario de Córdoba." *Textos y estudios sobre astronomía española del s. XIII.* Ed. Juan Vernet. Barcelona: Universidad de Barcelona, 1982. 9-78.

Martínez Gázquez, José, and Luis García Ballester. "Las *Epistulae de flebotomia* y los *Calendaria* en el galenismo práctico de los siglos XIII y XIV en la corona de Aragón." *Galeno: Obra, pensamiento e influencia.* Ed. J. A. López Férez. Madrid: Universidad Nacional de Educación a Distancia, 1991. 281-89.

McBain, William, Ed. *"De Sainte Katherine": An Anonymous Picard Version of the Life of St. Catherine of Alexandria.*. Fairfax, Va.: George Mason University Press, 1987.

Menéndez Pelayo, Marcelino. "La Doncella Teodor (Un cuento de las *Mil y Una Noches,* un libro de cordel y una comedia de Lope de Vega)." *Homenaje a D. Francisco Codera en su jubuliación del profesorado.* Zaragoza: Mariano Escar, 1904. 483-511.

Menocal, María Rosa. *The Arabic Role in Medieval Literary History.* Philadephia: University of Pennsylvania Press, 1987.

Metlitzki, Dorothee. *The Matter of Araby in Medieval England.* New Haven: Yale University Press, 1977.

Mettmann, Walter, Ed. *La historia de la doncella Teodor: Ein spanische Volksbuch arabischen Ursprung.* Akademie der Wissenschaften und der Literatur, Mainz. Abhandlungen der Geistes- und Sozialwissenchschaftlichen Klasse, Jahrgang, 1962, nr. 3. Wiesbaden: Akademie der Wissenschaften und der Literatur, 1962.

Migne, Jacques Paul. *Patrologiae cursus completus [series latina].* 221 vols. Paris: Migne, 1844-82.

Mignolo, Walter D. *The Darker Side of the Renaissance: Literacy, Territoriality and Colonization.* Ann Arbor: The University of Michigan Press, 1995.

Morrás, María. "'Tractado de Segundo filósofo que fue en Athenas': Otro manuscrito inédito." *Bulletin of Hispanic Studies* 67 (1990): 279-84.

Nalle, Sara T. "Literacy and Culture in Early Modern Castile." *Past and Present* 125 (1989): 65-96.

Nevanlinna, Saara and Irma Taavitsainen, Eds. *St. Katherine of Alexandria: The Late Middle English Prose Legend in Southwell Minster Ms 7.* Cambridge: D.S. Brewer, 1993.

Norton, F.J. *A Descriptive Catalogue of Printing in Spain and Portugal 1501-1520.* Cambridge: Cambridge University Press, 1978.

O'Callaghan, Joseph. *History of Medieval Spain.* Ithaca: Cornell University Press, 1975.

Palladius Publius Rutilius Taurus Aemilianus. *Opvs agricvltvrae.* Ed. Robert Rodgers. Leipzig: Teubner, 1975.

Parker, Margaret R. *The Story of a Story Across Cultures: The Case of the Doncella Teodor.* London: Tamesis, 1996.

Penny, Ralph. *A History of the Spanish Language.* Cambridge: Cambridge University Press, 1991.

Poridat de las poridades. Ed. Lloyd Kasten. Madrid: Hispanic Seminary, 1957.

Primera crónica general de España. Ed. R. Menéndez Pidal. Madrid: Gredos, 1956.

Pseudo-Albertus Magnus. *Women's Secrets: A Translation of Pseudo-Albertus Magnus's De Secretis Mulierum with Commentaries.* Trans. Helen Rodnite Lemay. Albany: State University of New York Press, 1992.

Rabanus Maurus. *Comment. in Genesim.* PL 107.

Renart, Jean. *Galeran de Bretagne.* Ed. Lucien Foulet. Paris: Champion, 1925.

Riha, Ortrum. *Meister Alexanders Monatsregeln. Untersuchungen zu einem spätmittelalterlichem Regimen duodecim mensium mit kritische Textausgabe.* Würzburg: Bohler, 1985.

Rodinson, Maxime. "The Western Image and Western Studies of Islam." *The Legacy of Islam.* Eds. Joseph Schacht and C. E. Bosworth. Oxford: Clarendon Press, 1974. 9-62

Rodnite Lemay, Helen. "William of Saliceto on Human Sexuality." *Viator* 12 (1981): 165-181.

Ruiz, Juan. *Libro de buen amor.* Ed. G.B. Gybbon-Monypenny. Madrid: Castalia, 1989.

Said, Edward W. *Orientalism.* New York: Pantheon, 1978.

Secundus the Silent Philosopher: The Greek Life of Secundus. Ed. Ben Edwin Perry. Philological Monographs, 22. Ithaca: American Philological Association, 1964.

Severin, Dorothy Sherman. "'El ynfante Epitus': The Earliest Complete Castilian Version of the Dialogue of 'Epictetus and the Emperor Hadrian'." *Bulletin of Hispanic Studies* 62 (1985): 25-30.

Simón Díaz, José. "La literatura medieval castellana y sus ediciones españolas de 1501 a 1560." *El libro antiguo español: Actas del primer Coloquio Internacional (Madrid, 18 al 20 de diciembre de 1986).* Eds. María Luisa López-Vidriero and Pedro M. Cátedra. Salamanca: Ediciones de la Universidad de Salamanca, 1988. 371-396.

Siraisi, Nancy G. "How to write a Latin Book on Surgery: Organizing Principles and Authorial Devices in Guglielmo da Saliceto and Dino del Garbo." *Practical Medicine from Salerno to the Black Death.* Ed. Luis García-Ballester *et al.* Cambridge: Cambridge University Press, 1994. 88-109.

Solterer, Helen. *The Master and Minerva: Disputing Women in French Medieval Culture.* Berkeley: University of California Press, 1995.

Southern, R. W. *Western Views of Islam in the Middle Ages.* Cambridge, Mass.: Harvard University Press, 1962.

Speculum al foder (Cod. Bibl. Nac. de Madrid, n_ 3356). Ed. Teresa Vicens. Barcelona: Calamus, 1978.

Suchier, Walter. *L'Enfant sage (Das Gespräch des Kaisers Hadrian mit dem klugen Kinde Epitus).* Gesellschaft für romanische Literatur, 24. Dresden: Max Niemeyer, 1910.

Suchier, Walther. *Das mittellateinische Gespräch Adrian und Epictetus nebst verwandten Texten (Joca Monachorum).* Tübingen: Niemeyer, 1955.

Taylor, Barry. "Old Spanish Wisdom Texts: Some Relationships." *La corónica* 14 (1985): 71-85.

The Arabian Nights. Trans. Husain Haddawy. New York: Norton, 1990.

The Glory of the Perfumed Garden: The Missing Flowers. London: Neville Spearman, 1975.

The Prose Salernitan Questions. Ed. Brian Lawn. Auctores Britannici Medii Aevi, 5. London: The British Academy, 1979.

The Wyse Chylde and the Emperor Adrian. Ed. J.O. Halliwell. London: Whittingham and Wilkins, 1860.

Tratado del ynfante Dorothy Sherman Severin. "'El ynfante Epitus': The Earliest Complete Castilian Version of the Dialogue of 'Epictetus and the Emperor Hadrian'." *BHS* 62(1985): 25-30.

Valero Cuadra, Pino. "El mito literario medieval de la mujer sabia: La doncella Teodor." *Las sabias mujeres: educación, saber y autoría (siglos III-XVII).* Ed. María del Mar Graña Cid. Madrid: Asociación Al-Mudayna, 1994. 147-54.

———. *La Doncella Teodor: Un cuento hispanoárabe.* Alicante: Instituto de Cultura "Juan Gil-Albert," 1996.

Vázquez Ruiz, José. "Una nueva versión árabe del cuento de la Doncella Teodor." *Miscelánea de estudios árabes y herbaicos.* Granada: Universidad de Granada, 1952. 149-53.

———. "Una versión en árabe granadino del "Cuento de la Doncella Teodor". *Prohemio* 2 (1971): 331-65.

Vescovini, Graziella Federici. "Peter of Abano and Astrology." *Astrology, Science, and Society: Historical Essays.* Ed. Patrick Curry. Woodbridge, Suffolk: Boydell Press, 1987. 19-39.

Walzer, Richard. "Arabic Transmission of Greek Thought to Medieval Europe." *Bulletin of the Johns Rylands Library* 29 (1945-46): 160-83;

Webster, James Carson. *The Labors of the Month in Antique and Medieval Art to the End of the Twelfth Century.* Evanston: Northwestern University Press, 1938.

Wesselski, Albert. "Die gelehrten Sklavinnen der Islams und ihre byzantischen Vorbilder." *Archiv Orientální* 9(1937): 353-378.

Whinnom, Keith. "The Problem of the 'Best-Seller' in Spanish Golden-Age Literature." *Medieval and Renaissance Spanish Literature: Selected Essays.* Eds. Alan Deyermond, W. F. Hunter, and Joseph T. Snow. Exeter: University of Exeter Press, 1994. 159-75.

Wölfflin-Tröll, E. "Joca monachorum: ein Beitrag zur mittalterlichen Rathselliteratur." *Monatsberichte der Preuss. Akademie der Wissenschaften, aus dem Jahre 1872.* (Berlin, 1872). 106-115.